Ritwik Ghatak

Five Plays

Ritwik Ghatak

Five Plays

Translated from the Bengali original by

Amrita Nilanjana

Foreword by

Samik Bandyopadhyay

THORNBIRD

NIYOGI BOOKS

Published by
NIYOGI BOOKS
Block D, Building No. 77,
Okhla Industrial Area, Phase-I,
New Delhi-110 020, INDIA
Tel: 91-11-26816301, 26818960
Email: niyogibooks@gmail.com
Website: www.niyogibooksindia.com

Editor: Srotoswini Majumdar
Design: Shraboni Roy

ISBN: 978-93-86906-11-3
Publication: 2018
Reprint: 2025

Printed at Niyogi Offset Pvt. Ltd., New Delhi, India

Contents

Foreword 7

⁂

Charter 13

⁂

Communication 93

⁂

Agony 207

⁂

Ablaze 245

⁂

That Woman 281

Foreword

With his five surviving playscripts and still abiding memories of his directorial work and performances in theatre, Ritwik Ghatak remains a marginal presence in Bengali theatre, in no way comparable to his formidable—and controversial—iconic status in Indian cinema. With his first serious engagement with theatre, in his participation as an actor in Sombhu Mitra's revival of the IPTA classic *Nabanna* for his new theatre group, yet to be named Bohurupee, in 1948, Ghatak inherited the theatrical tradition of the new Indian realism initiated and defined by Bijan Bhattacharya (1915–68) in the seminal 1944 production of *Nabanna*, that Bhattacharya directed jointly with Sombhu Mitra for IPTA from his own text, and in subsequent works like *Mora Chand* (1946), *Jeeyankanya* (1947), *Kalanka* (1951), *Gotrantar* (1956–57), *Debigarjan* (1966) and *Garbhabati Janani* (1969). Offering his evaluation of the Bengali theatre scene in 1966, Ghatak wrote: 'Nobody seems to take the right perspective and recognize that what we really lack is the drama. The one or two playwrights, who retain the vision of truth as it grows out of emotional intensity and the sense of commitment that it brings along with it, are being deliberately stifled, and being told from all around, you are insignificant, you are nothing! Bijan Bhattacharya is one such figure. Right now it is only in his plays that I see the mark of genius, and the daring to reach beyond realism.'[1]

In yet another piece, Ghatak wrote: 'Bijan Bhattacharya was the first to show us how to register in theatre one's commitment to the people, how to achieve collectivity in performance, and how to create on stage the seamless totality of a slice of reality. We, who were trying at the time, will never forget those days. It was a massive turbulence that ran like an electric shock through the whole of Bengal from one end to another . . . I haven't read all his works since then or seen them staged, since over the years I have gradually moved away from theatre. But what I know is that he has never stopped in his tracks. All that he has had for his capital is a pristine honesty. And with that honesty for his approach, whenever a problem stares him in the face, he immerses himself in it to the very depths. It would be a travesty of truth to claim that he succeeds every time. But I have not seen anyone else in Bengal serving theatre through a lifetime with such a clear mind. He is not concerned about reputation. It is not in his nature to seek to set up a school with a label to it. In other words, this gentleman hasn't learnt to cheat.'[2]

Nabanna, and the film *Chhinnamul* (1951), directed by Nimai Ghosh, in which he acted, were the immediate models for Ghatak's first forays into playwriting and direction. Both centered on displacement and migration, the former located against the Bengal Famine of 1943-44, the latter documenting the Partition of 1947 and its aftermath. *Dalil* (translated as *Charter* in the present collection) that Ghatak wrote and directed for the IPTA (now in its second phase, after it had come out of the ban of 1948–50, and had lost a large section of its founding generation) in 1953, bringing him national recognition at the national congress of the IPTA in Bombay, focused more on the Partition and he divides and enduring fissures and agonies that it left behind in its wake. The same theme seems to be carried into a later phase in historical time, with the communal cleavage and the violence it generates continuing in both the fragments of the 'partitioned' territory, in *Sanko* (translated in the present collection as *Communications*).

Dalil has obvious reverberations of both *Nabanna* and *Chhinnamul*, and what I call the 'new realism' associated with

Bhattacharya (as a matter of fact, the core of the *Chhinnamul* cast were actors trained by Bhattacharya for his stage production of *Nabanna*). Bhattacharya, unlike his co-director Sombhu Mitra in *Nabanna*, did not come to theatre along the colonial Bengali theatre route, a theatre dominated by over theatrical histrionics, projections of star / 'heroic' performers at the cost of psychological realism or physical / spatial objectivity, and sentimental flights. Moved by the horror of the Famine and the migrants from the starving villages dying on the streets of Kolkata, Bhattacharya in his plays sought to capture the authentic reality of Bengal in its villages or tribal margins, as he saw it (as a roving Communist journalist) crumbling, disintegrating, and losing its rich verbal idiom and the genetic physicality of its lifestyle, both its voice and body, under the onslaught and with the inroads of a fast expanding, brutally exploitative urban economy. Both Sova Sen and Tripti Mitra, the lead actresses of *Nabanna*, in their conversations with me, recalled the care, sensitivity and concern for authentic detail with which Bhattacharya had trained them in the dialectal speech, and taught them how to make their bodies—their actorial physicality—tune themselves to the rhythm of the speech. Ghatak had a taste of this when working with Bhattacharya on the stage in the second *Nabanna*. The direct charge of this experience and the powerfully committed collectivity of the new generation of IPTA activist-actors (with Sova Sen from the original *Nabanna* serving as a continuity with the tradition) gave *Dalil* a scale that Ghatak would not touch again in his later work in theatre as playwright and director.

Creatively, Ghatak was already moving away into cinema, when he was writing his first plays, and was moving away from the breeding / burgeoning space of theatric creativity, the actors' ensemble. Cut off from that space and with the long gaps between his work in cinema and his short flirtations with theatre, his theatre imagination suffered. As a matter of fact, later in life, whenever he returned to theatre, he brought to it the burden and pain of his frustrations in his cinematic career, his sense of unrealized potentials and the constrictions that cribbed and confined him in the film 'industry', and his desperation and rage burst forth in plays like *Jwalanta* (translated as *Ablaze* in the present collection) that had lost performativity altogether. And then there was of course the inadequately recorded and documented phase of his creativity in the spell he spent in the mental asylum.

In his films, the more earthy immediacy and reality of the Partition and the migration that followed, in *Dalil* or *Sanko*, gave way to a more mythical evocation of that slice of history, now engrafted in a state of mind that had turned it all into a continuing sense of homelessness, restlessness, and nostalgia for the lost home, sometimes even a quest for it, as at the close of *Subarnarekha*; the rugged realism breaking into great moments of poetry in speech and an almost dancing body, so characteristic of Bijan Bhattacharya's theatre, transmuted into a cinematic expressionism far away from theatre.

Samik Bandyopadhyay

1. Translated from 'Natak O Bartaman Kaal' ['Plays and the Present Times'], reprinted in *Natyakatha*, special issue on Ritwik Ghatak in Theatre, ed. Saumitra Kumar Chatterjee, March 2004.

2. Translated from 'Bijan Bhattacharya: Jeebaner Sutradhar' ['Bijan Bhattacharya: Pathbreaker in Life'], first published in *Natyadarpan*, May 1975, reproduced in *Natyakatha*, March 2004.

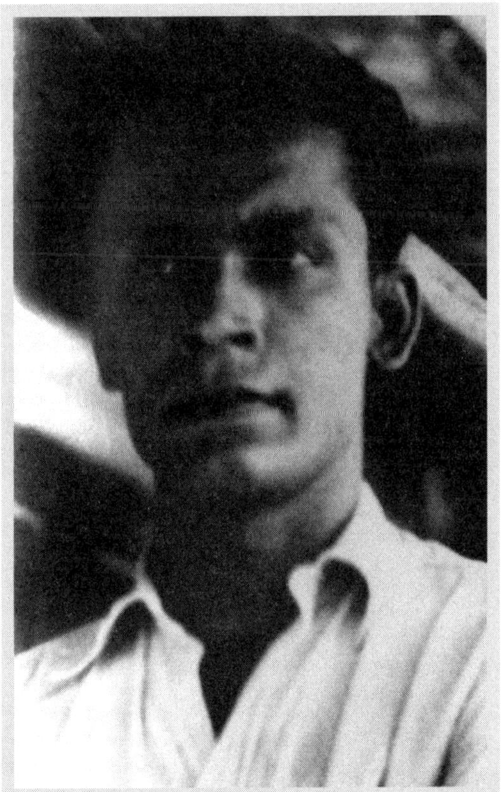

Charter

1

Translator's Note

This play depicts the situation that arose before and immediately after Partition. The play begins with a vignette featuring a Hindu family's daily life in undivided Bengal. This play, originally named *Dalil* by the author, has many characters, with each having his or her say in the story in equal measure. There is no protagonist of the piece as such. However, the script uses dialects that were translated into English after deep research. Some Bangla words, however, have been left untouched to keep the flow of dialogues smooth.

FIRST WAVE: First Part

[*Deep into the stage is an embankment. It is not difficult to make out that behind the embankment is the river Padma, as brown and blue sails are seen crossing the stretch. The sound of oars slicing the waters can be heard. The night sky is slate blue. To the left of the stage is a thatched-roof earthen hut, a part of which is visible. Its door and the dawa (An elevated seating area in the front of a hut), are jutting into the stage. A fence made of bamboo strips runs up to the embankment. Behind the fencing is fishing net. Carrying a lantern, a married woman of 25 or 26 years of age appears from the right side of the stage—walks across, opens the door and enters the hut. She had stopped for a few moments when she reached the centre of the stage. The tune of a sad song emerges from the other side of the embankment, disturbing the still of the night. The woman shakes her head and resumes her walk. A part of the head of the man, who is singing the song, can be seen on the other side of the embankment. He keeps on singing...*]

Gopal: *Hamar jan-er gang re, hamar shonar gang re,*
Hamar Padma gang.
Tumi-i hamar mon bhulale, tumi-i hamar pran.
- Ho amar gang.
Jey tane-te bhashao tumi hamar bhyatal nao,
Shey batash-e tumi hamar badam bhorya dao,
Gahin rat-e jey dheu-te poran-kotha kao,
Tarai hamar pran karache, dichey akul tan,
- Ho amar gang.

(The river belongs to my heart, my golden river, my Padma river. You have stolen my heart, you are my soul. The way you make my boat sail, the way you fill up the sail of my boat with wind, the way you pour your heart out to me in the dark night have robbed my heart.)

[*The manner in which he drags the tunes reflects a unique loneliness, something which casts a spell on the entire scene. The married woman comes out, sits on the dawa and listens to the song. The woman stands up once the song fades.*]

Swanro: *Thakurpo* (Used by a married woman when referring to the younger brother of her husband), the songs that you string together make my heart grieve.

[*Gopal spoke to Swarno from where he was sitting.*]

Gopal: [*From where he was sitting.*] Did you say something, *Bouthan* (The wife of the elder brother)?

Swarno: I am curious to know what keeps you so engrossed at the end of the year?

Gopal: I don't feel like going anywhere today. This edge of the river has caught my fancy.

Swarno: That's why you sit there to write songs of the heart.

Gopal: What did you say?

Swarno: I said, don't vanish. You have to take me to the *Gombhira's Asor* (folk theatre featuring Lord Shiva and stories associated with him). Don't go anywhere.

[*A 22-year-old boy appears with the fishing net.*]

Gopal: Where can I go? Give me the discs. Let me tie them to the net, sitting here.

[*Swarno fetches him the iron discs in a small container. Gopal spreads the net and hums a tune.*]

Gopal: The house is so quiet today.

Swarno: Everybody has gone to that fritters' shop at the september fair. Baba is also there. They should be back anytime soon.

Gopal: Alright. But where is Haruchandra?

Swarno: I don't know where he went with Padmamani. He was here just a while ago.

Gopal: Padma has taken him along with her. Now I get it. Some girl this Padma is! Day or night, companion or no companion, she is moving around in the jungles and the woods. She is having a good time. But she is not being able to set her mind on studies in spite of my best efforts.

[*Swarna goes inside the house. Gopal keeps on mumbling with his head bowed.*]

Gopal: You know Bouthan, she could have been somebody had she pursued education. She is sharp but I have no idea what goes on in her mind all day long. I find it strange.

[*He raises his faces but sees no one around. He smiles and hums a tune. From the other side of the embankment appears a girl of 14 wearing a yellow saree with red hoops. She is also wearing a nose ring. Her hair is unkempt. A lotus with its stem hangs from the ponytail on her head. In her hand is a length of rope that is tied to one of the two ankles of a boy, who is about 10. Boy wears a very satisfied look on his face with a dash of wisdom. Even though he feels ill at ease whenever the rope tightens, he doesn't break his short-stepped walk. He is carrying a locally made flute in his hand. The girl comes and scouts her surroundings with her bright eyes. Then she uses her eyes to draw the boy's notice to Gopal. Without batting an eyelid, the boy walks up to Gopal and blows the flute into his ears. Choking on his breath, Gopal drops everything and springs in fright. He stumbles as his feet and get entangled in the net. Swarno comes running saying, 'what happened?' Padma covers her face with her hands and rolls in the centre of the stage in delight. She is laughing out loud. Haru is dragging the rope towards the house.*]

Swarno: What is this?

Gopal: Why did you blow it so hard?

Haru: Pishi asked me to do so.

Swarno: She is so devilish!

Gopal: Just wait!

[*He flings the net away. Padma jumps onto the rear of the dawa. She is trying to run away but Swarno holds her by the ear and brings her down.*]

Swarno: There is no end to her pranks even after she returns from dancing around in the neighbourhood during the peak of the afternoon. I see, my Padma has a lotus in her hair! It seems you won't understand until I use strong medicine for you.

[*Swarno slaps Padma and tells Padma to go inside.*]

Swarno: Go, go inside!

[*Swarno pushes her away. Padma stands on the dawa with her head bowed and appearing recalcitrant. Swarno looks at Gopal and her face breaks into a smile.*]

Gopal: Padma, come here. [*Padma steps forward*] Where did you go?

Padma: I went to the jungle of Bhimsen.

Swarno: O! Does it hurt?

[*Swarno places a hand on Padma's shoulders. Padma nods.*]

Swarno: Why are you like this? Now go. I will take you today to the Gombhira's Asor.

[*Padma's face lights up.*]

Padma: Today's act is 'Mantri Mission'. When shall we go, Bouthan?

Swarno: Don't be impatient. We will go.

Gopal: Hey Padi, come to me.

[*Padma walks up to him.*]

Gopal: Sit down. How are you?

Padma: I see! Friendly banter!

Gopal: How can I do that!

Haru: Ma, untie the rope. It's begun to hurt.

Swarno: Come to me, you stupid boy.

[*She sits next to Haru and unties the rope from his ankle. Padma makes eye contact with Haru and sends him a signal. Haru ties the other end of the rope to Swarno's ankle.*]

Swarno: Now go to the room. It's time for lunch.

[*Haru gets up and tries to walk away holding the rope in his hand. The tug almost made Swarno fall.*]

Swarno: O My God!

[*Blowing the flute, Haru jumps around. Padma, laughing out loud, leans on Swarno. Swarno slaps her gently.*]

Swarno: You are so impish!

Gopal: Let it be, Bouthan.

Swarno: She has gone down the embankment. Padma, come inside the house. Don't go now. I can't take it anymore. I feel like crying.

[*As Padma walks down the slope of the embankment, Haren Pandit can be seen walking briskly from the other side. He is a fidgety and busy man of 30. Padma and Haren collide. Padma says 'Oh' and runs straight into the house. Swarno pulls the tail of her saree across her head. Haren picks up the books that fell on the ground.*]

Gopal: How come you are here now, Haren Pandit?

Haren: I don't have much time in hand. I have to walk a long distance to be at the town.

Gopal: Why are you going to town in the night?

Haren: Don't extend the conversation, or else I will get late. I have to go to Nimchand's Kayan's office.

Gopal: Nimchand Kayan's office!

Haren: Don't you know? The news about Partition will be broadcast on the radio tonight.

Gopal: On radio?

Haren: Our leaders feel that Chanakya's slokas indeed contain wisdom—having half is wise.

Gopal: What does that mean?

Haren: It means that my primary school has to shut down its shutters. I worked so hard to get a teacher's degree and set up a school in this village. All that effort will be washed away. It seems I will now have to leave for India—lock, stock and barrel.

Gopal: But why?

Haren: That's because Pakistan will come into being. Of course, my plans would depend on whether this district ultimately goes to Pakistan after partition. I heard Nimchand was pouring in a great deal of money to prevent this district from becoming a part of Pakistan. But you know, bribing the English is a different proposition altogether. They will accept money but may not do your work in the end. But Nimachand is not the one who will give up. He built a rice mill last year and a movie theatre. Don't you think he is going to fight till the end to make this happen?

Gopal: Do we also have to fight once Pakistan becomes a reality?

Haren: Of course! Pakistan would be a country of the Muslims. Why would they tolerate Hindus?

Gopal: So what? Kalim is a Muslim and so is Feroza Nani. Even some of my neighbours are.

Haren: They are a minority community among Muslims and prefer to coexist peacefully with Hindus. But do you remember Noakhali? Muslims from the other parts of the Indian landmass will arrive. I am really concerned. Partition will be announced today. Hey!

Gopal: What happened?

Haren: I am already late. Bye bye.

Gopal: You are a crazy man. Wait a while.

Haren: Look here, I am usually a very tame person. I have much work to do tonight. If I hear news about anything untoward, I will inform you on my way back. Bye bye.

[*He leaves.*]

Swarno: Thakurpo... Where are you, Gopal?

Gopal: Yes?

[*Padma was peeping out of the house. She now comes and sits to the right and plucks the petals of the lotus she is wearing on in her ponytail.*]

Swarno: Kalim used to talk about Pakistan—does that mean migrating to another country?

Haru: Uncle, I have heard of Pakistan. Some person playing the role of an Englishman in that Gombhira's Asor had mentioned Pakistan.

Gopal: Bouthan, if we have to migrate to another country, what kind of a situation that would be?

Swarno: These are all rumours.

Gopal: Of course! But are they really so? I don't know.

Gopal: I find it amusing to imagine that within a second, we may have to leave for another country, bidding goodbye to the land and this environment that were so dearly ours for ages.

Swarno: All these are rumours.

Gopal: No Bouthan. The riots in Kolkata are not rumours. The happenings in Noakhali are not rumours. What that is emerging is making me scared.

Swarno: There is no sign of anyone else returning home. You people sit down for dinner.

Gopal: [*smiles.*] That's better. Let's go and watch the Gombhira's Asor after dinner.

[*Gopal wraps his arms around Padma and Haru. Padma pinches him and Gopal moves away. Haru blows into the flute twice. Annoyed,*

Swarno snatches the flute from him. Haru makes faces at her from a distance. Then he breaks into a run as he is chased by Swarno. Padma quietly sidesteps Swarno and enters the house. Swarno follows them. Gopal pauses for a while before entering the house. The stage is empty. From the left, Kalim and Kiru Sheikh enter. They are carrying a pole each on their shoulders, with earthen pots hanging from either ends. Kiru Sheikh is an aged Muslim.]

Kalim: [*Puts down the pole on the floor.*] Sheikh, my home is next to this house.

Kiru: Alright, you go. I will use the water of the river to wash up. What would you get for Iftar?

Kalim: *Mian* (A title used by the Muslims to refer to another man in general), you have come to my humble abode. I will get whatever is available in my house.

Kiru: Go then and don't be late. Hope you remember that we have to be at the League office!

Kalim: Yes, to get news about Pakistan.

Kiru: We have to galvanise the National Guards now. You have to teach them the use of lathi.

Kalim: That I will! How about teaching them the use of stiletto? The eye becomes sharp if you do that.

Kiru: Do whatever you wish to but you have to assume the responsibilities this time.

Kalim: Why don't you do something? Do you know Mahinder, the son of Khetu Ghosh? He is a lathi user.

Kiru: I know him.

Kalim: This house is theirs. He is my bosom friend and very useful. He is an expert with the stiletto. Why don't you entrust him with that responsibility?

Kiru: What are you saying? They are Hindus and he is so rustic! Besides, are they going to stay back when Pakistan happens?

Kalim: Where will they go then? This is not Muslim Guard. It is going to be the Pakistan National Guard.

Kiru: They have their Hindustan. All Hindus will have to leave after Pakistan comes into being. Pakistan will be only for Muslims.

Kalim: Wait. Let me get a grip on this issue. It's alright that we are asking for Pakistan. That's because the landlords and the hoarders are all Hindus. But there are many Hindus, too, who struggle to make their both ends meet.

Kiru: Pakistan is a country for Muslims. They are all infidels!

Kalim: Infidels! Mahinder's mother is no more, but I remember being brought up by her since my childhood. Feroza Nani and his Mother were my world. Infidel! [*Smiles.*] What you are saying is unbelievable. People like Mahinder will stay but despot Hindus will have to leave and Muslims will get land for farming. Are you the ruler of Pakistan that you are decreeing the banishment of Hindus from this land? I can't make head or tail of your words.

Kiru: Why do you find it strange? Mohammed Ali Jinnah said Hindus would have to leave Pakistan.

Kalim: He never said that.

[*Feroza comes. She is about sixty-five.*]

Feroza:	You mad ox, I have been hollering for you for long. Why are you still outside?
Kalim:	Grandma, Kiru Sheikh says people like Mahinder have to leave after Pakistan is created.
Feroza:	Let Pakistan be created first! Forget these ifs and buts now.
Kalim:	I am told the new borders will be demarcated today.
Feroza:	No problem. Listen, did you take the small *dinghy* (a small boat) to the river today?
Kalim:	No, but I know who did.
Feroza:	Who?
Kalim:	I won't slander.
Feroza:	At least tell me who that person was? Gopal? Mahinder?
Kalim:	Yes.
Feroza:	But why has he left that dinghy broken?
Kalim:	Don't know why he went to the town market to wink at whom!
Feroza:	Let that rascal come!
Kalim:	Don't tell him anything, please.
Feroza:	Why? You think I am going to beat him up? I am overwhelmed by your show of sympathy for him. Let me tell you, I love him more than you do.
Kalim:	I know that. Maybe, I don't know that. I know you have an emotional attachment for that boy. Hey, Mian, where are you off to?
Kiru:	I have to go to the Muslim League office. You join me after your meal.
Kalim:	I am not going there. Do the Iftar with us.
Kiru:	Why wouldn't you come along?

Kalim: Why should I? I am not for joining those who are planning to drive my countrymen out of this land.

Kiru: I don't eat at unholy Iftars.

Feroza: We are slaughtering the lamb the Islamic way. Eat something now.

[*Kalim and Kiru are walking together. Mahinder comes with a hand drum hanging from his neck. He is drumming it loudly and accompanying it with oral beats. Behind him are the old man, Khetu, and Debendir—both carrying some merchandise.*]

Mahinder: Kur-kur—kur-kur-kur...dang dang dang! Hey Kalim!

Kalim: What, my dear friend?

Khetu: Debendir, tell him.

Debendir: What do I tell him?

Khetu: Speak up those unbelievable words. I set up a shop on an empty field but I still have to pay taxes. The authorities have summoned me.

Feroza: This is so strange! If you set up a shop on an open field during the fair, you have to pay taxes? I have never heard anything like this before!

Mahinder: But it's happening. Debendir, go tell them that it is not possible for us to pay two rupees in taxes.

Debendir: Do you think they would reduce the taxes if we convey the message to them so lightly?

Khetu: Look here, I cannot compromise my pride to beg. I don't have wealth. Nobody in this world values hard work. But I have held on to my self-esteem. I won't be a human the day I lose it. Sorry, I can't beg.

Debendir: This seems to be a family of hotheads! By the way Debendir, it's settled that you and I would be sharecroppers on your land. Let's see how the sugarcane field behaves. I am now going to talk to the collector about the taxes.

[*He leaves.*]

Kalim: Uncle, what are you carrying in your hands?

Khetu: Don't tell me! I went to the fair to buy fertilizer for my crop and some seeds for growing eggplants on the roof. But when I saw those toys, I remembered the children and couldn't resist myself.

[*He walks into his house.*]

Mahinder: *Loya gacher soya begun tumi te!*
Pantabhat-e peyanj tumi te, tumi hamar nayonmoni,
Ghat-e naitey giey kolshi fellya bap-er bari kane gelal

(You are my eggplant, you are my onion in overnight rice, you are the apple of my eye. Why did you drop the water container and leave for your parents' home?)

Kalim: Who said she has left for her parents' place? She is sitting here, lighting up the entire house.

Feroza: Mahinder is in mood today.

Mahinder: I am in good mood today. It will rain soon Kalim, I will set out with your finishing net. Let's go out tonight.

Feroza: Are you sailing tonight?

Mahinder: The fun is, tonight it's going to rain soon and then the Hilsas will break surface. Have you ever tried to sail the Padma in the night when it is raining? Ah! I am going to sail up to the Mahananda.

Kalim: And we have the folk theatre today!

Mahinder: Folk theatre?

[*Mahinder sings in tune.*]

> *Shaheb Rajar Bate, swadesh ta re kate,*
> *Hamra akhon Swaraj holam*
> *Desher joto netar, cholchaturir kothai*
> *Akhon mora shagore bhashlam*

(I am a bit confused. First the strikethroughs, and then I realise that the song in the original Bangla script doesn't appear here. I can't figure out why it has been repeated here. The song, in fact, appears a little later in the translated script that you and I are reading now.)

[*Gopal and Swarno walk up to the dawa.*]

Swarno: Gopal, tell your elder brother that the rice is getting cold.

Gopal: Leave it! Don't pamper him so much.

Swarno: We will be late for the folk theatre.

Mahinder: Why you troubling me? Let me spend some easy time with them.

Kalim: I am also supposed to be at the play.

Feroza: Mahinder, I need to talk to you.

Mahinder: Why?

Feroza: You have caused damage to the bow of my small dinghy!

Mahinder: Grandma, it just happened all of a sudden!

Feroza: Then you pay up for the damage all of a sudden so that I can fix it.

Mahinder: Come on! Money doesn't grow on trees.

Feroza: Do you think boats grow on trees?

Mahinder: Do whatever you want.

Kalim: I will erase you from the face of the earth!

Mahinder: Come on then, come on then!

Kalim: Tonight is the night for a bloodbath!

[*Both of them engage in a sham encounter. Feroza stands in the middle and watches the fun. Meanwhile, Khetu enters quarrelling illegibly with Padma and Haru. Kalim emits a war cry.*]

Khetu: Hey, Mahinder!

Mahinder: What did I do? It was Kalim who...

Kalim: Kaka, you saw with your own eyes. It was Mahinder.

Khetu: Shut up!

Mahinder: Actually, the root cause of all trouble is that old woman. See, she is laughing now.

Swarno: Nobody seems to be interested in everything but eating. Gopal, tell them that I won't be able to do it.

[*Padma points Haru to the country drum. Haru steps forward.*]

Haru: Baba, whom have you got that drum for?

Mahinder: I brought it because I am going to play it everyday. I will play the first night's beats of sacrifice near your mother's head.

Haru: Won't you give it to me?

Mahinder: Why should I give it to you? I got this drum with much difficulty. Do you want to listen to the drum beats? Want to dance along with Lord Shiva?

[*He begins to play the drum. Sings in tune.*]

Shaheb rajar bat-e, swadesh to re kate
Hamra akhon swaraj holam,
Desher joto neta-r, cholchaturi kothai,
Akhon mora sagar-e bhashlam

(The decree of the English king slices up my country, setting us up in our own land. We are at sea due to pretensions of our leaders.)

[*He holds Haru by the hand and dances around. Haru pulls Gopal towards him. Padma begins to clap.*]

Kalim: O Lord Shiva!

[*He joins the jig, taking Feroza along.*]

Kalim: Come on, Nani.

[*Khetu tries to scold them but begins to laugh out. Feroza joins the party.*]

Swarno: O my, my, look at them!

Mahinder: Why don't you join us, too?

Swarno: Ah!

[*The dancing begins to intensify. Haren walks down swiftly from the embankment.*]

Haren: Dance, Lord Shiva, Dance. First class! So holy and honest!

Gopal: Hey Pandit, what happened?

[*Haren turns.*]

Haren: There's no time. It is already late.

Mahinder: You rascal, do you want to dance?

Haren: No. I met Kayan's clerk on the way.

Gopal: O.

Haren: He said a lot many things. The news has been broadcast on either sides of the river. Kayan has gone into his shell. Our country is now called Pakistan.

Kalim: Pakistan!

Kiru: Pakistan!

Mahinder: Pakistan!

Haren: Yes, Pakistan. This district has gone to Pakistan. From that corner onwards, it is Hindustan, the Indian nation.

Gopal: Has this demarcation been already set in motion?

Kiru: What a momentous occasion! Hail Allah!

Kalim: *Allah ho Akbar!*

Kiru: Kalim, come quickly to the League office.

[*Kiru dashed off. Placing the pole back on his shoulder.*]

Kalim: Nani, serve me a meal now. *Allah ho Akbar!*

[*Kalimpulls at a morose Feroza.*]

Kalim: Don't be late. Let's go quickly.

[*Outside, in many voices Allah ho Akbar! Feroza and Kalim leave.*]

Haren: This is the story. Pakistan is here to stay.

Mahinder: The beats have suddenly lost rhythm. Swarno, serve dinner to us.

[*He takes Haru with him as he leaves.*]

Haren: I know I am not supposed to say this, but my heart shrinks. Change is imminent.

Gopal: Change!

Haren: Yes, intense change. Change is rushing at us like a group of bandits. I am leaving for West Bengal tomorrow. I don't have time.

[*Haren leaves. Padma enters the house. Khetu and Swarno flank the stage. Gopal climbs the embankment and a faint sound escaped his mouth. Gopal appears jolted. Swarno and Khetu stare at him.*]

Gopal: Oh! Beyond that darkness lies hidden Hindusthan!

Swarno: Now is the time to keep cool.

Khetu: How disturbing!

[*Gopal climbs down.*]

Gopal: But we don't need to spend time worrying. That would throw everything into complete disarray.

Khetu: Disarray?

Gopal: Yes.

[*Gopal makes them leave for the play. From the other side of Padma, the noise of thunder comes in. It was just a streak of lightning tearing the clouds. Thereafter, Gopal, with his head bowed, enters the house. The waters of the Padma begin to coil in exuberant bursts. The stage is dark. From far away can be heard 'Allah ho Akbar'. Gradually, the sound comes close before fading. The stage wakes up in lights.*]

FIRST WAVE: Second Part

[*It's the same scene. The sky is illuminated by the dying sun of the afternoon. To a corner of the house, Khetu, leaning his head on a pillar made from bamboo, watches the sky with melancholy. In the other corner, Swarno, her head covered by the tail of her saree, is cutting vegetables and keeping them on a brass plate. Outside the house, Mahinder is saying something aloud. He is asking Haru: 'Grab it. Come here. You are no good.' A little later, he keeps an almost-broken-tin trunk on the dawa. Fanning himself with gamchha (a countrymade cotton towel), he speaks to Swarno.*]

Mahinder: Didn't I tell you half an hour ago to fetch me the key to the trunk?

[*Khetu is taken aback.*]

Khetu: Why should we leave this place? Explain this to me, why should we leave?

Mahinder: Why should we leave? Well, what I heard was frightful.

Khetu: You are saying the same thing since yesterday. What is it?

Mahinder: The severed head of a cow was found at the temple of *Nandalal Jeur* (Lord Krishna). The ornaments that were on the idol are missing. The men from the cities are going back.

Khetu: How are we connected with the city folk?

[*Haru brings a rope.*]

Haru: Baba, I could get only this much.

Mahinder: Alright.

[*Mahinder tells Khetu...*]

Mahinder: Engaging you in a conversation is not up my street.

[*Mahinder walks towards the house.*]

Khetu: Oh, God! What's happening to the people of this country? Everybody is leaving this serene country.

[*Mahinder comes out of the house.*]

Mahinder: That's why I say, Rupaikandi has turned barren over the past four months. Were you able to be at any Durga Puja this time? The idols were being guarded by members of the National Guard.

Khetu: Where has the peace of this country gone? Suddenly they caused a vertical split in a big family. I don't understand the reason behind this unrest.

Mahinder: You will. Can't you see the pogrom of doom coming our way? Look at Bihar and Punjab. People there have virtually nothing to eat. We must walk with those well-placed people of the town to safety.

Khetu: What about the things we have here? Things that we have now?

[*Haru calls out.*]

Haru: How long am I going to hold this rope?

[*Mahinder walks away.*]

Khetu: *Bouma* (Used by the father-in-law and the mother-in-law when referring to the wife of their son)!

Swarno: Yes?

Khetu: What happens to humans when they are seized with fear? The brain refuses to function.

[*Padma walks in with a Cape Jasmine sapling, followed by Feroza.*]

Padma: Baba, see what I have got!

Khetu: Wow! That's a Cape Jasmine! Where did you get it from?

Padma: I got it from the jungles behind Nani's house. I found this sapling as I was looking for Paniculata. I was so taken over! I will plant this sapling in our garden. Let me find the spot where I can plant it.

[*Padma leaves.*]

Khetu: Be careful! I have prepared the eastern corner of the garden for farming potatoes.

[*Mahinder comes.*]

Mahinder: It's a dog's life in Pakistan. We are living like slaves of the Muslims.

Feroza: Are you a servant of the entire Muslim race?

Mahinder: What? *Bou* (Wife or bride), where is the key?

Swarno: Let Gopal come first.

Mahinder: What has Gopal got to do with the key?

Swarno: We will all sit down, discuss and come to a decision.

Mahinder: Forget it. You want to discuss with Gopal? He is an idiot.

Feroza: Mahinder is always following the same track.

Swarno: Nani!

Feroza: What?

Swarno: Normal life has been thrown completely out of gear. Everybody is trying to leave the country out of fear.

Feroza: That's what I am witnessing. As it is, there was no end to our own problems and now, out of the blue, a fresh hassle. You know, Khetu, my mind is telling me that some people somewhere along the line have split the country and trying to trigger an exodus to pursue their own ends.

[*Mahinder returns with a bundle.*]

Mahinder: We have to leave the utensils behind. We will not take them with us.

Feroza: Hello Mahinder, all your feelings and love for your country have vanished in a moment?

Mahinder: Keep quiet. I have seen enough sympathy.

Khetu: Mahinder, what are you saying to chachi?

Mahinder: Keep your sympathy with yourself Echhak Mian of Charchilmari was trying to drive fear in us yesterday. He was saying, 'Riots have again broken out in Kolkata. Unless all of you put pressure on your leaders to help stop the riots, it would be difficult for me to save your lives!' O my very dear saviour! I felt like slapping him with all my might. Echak wants to save Mahinder, the lathi expert!

Khetu: Think before you say such things.

Mahinder: I already have. On the one hand, they take away our home and land, give threats of life often and belittle us; on the other hand, they pretend to sympathise with us, cry for us. Nani, I have read into the psyche of your people. Now, spare me. Understood?

[*Mahinder was gesticulating agitatedly in front of Feroza. He stops as Swarno comes close.*]

Swarno: What are you saying? What are you?

Mahinder: Why are you standing there? Go and gather the clothes.

[*He leaves.*]

Swarno: Nani, please forgive us.

Feroza: [*From near the door.*] No, it's alright. Whatever he has said is not wrong. He has spoken the truth.

Swarno: He is so petrified since yesterday!

Feroza: Do you assume that I do not realise what's going on in his mind? Are you taking the steamer today?

Swarno: Where? Let's hear what Gopal has to say after he returns. Besides, my husband has a habit of packing things everyday.

Feroza: I am going now. Before you leave, ask Gopal to see me once. And you, too.

Swarno: Are you upset with us?

Feroza: No, I am not. It's just that I got a jolt because I am hearing these things for the first time in my life. Bou, I don't blame Mahinder. This is like a trap. The one who is snared cannot escape! But when would I get to see Padma and Haru again? They are in my heart.

[*Feroza leaves. Swarno, too, departs carrying the sliced vegetables. Mahinder looks at the old man from the door.*]

Khetu: What a beautiful country! What a beautiful and serene country!

Padma: Baba what's all this?

Mahinder: What happened?

Padma: Somebody has taken away the ribbed gourds from where they were growing in the garden. Nothing is left.

Khetu: Probably a stray goat.

Mahinder: Yes, a stray goat has left your head tonsured!

Padma: I shall build a fence around them.

Mahinder: Where are you going?

Padma: To the garden.

Mahinder: Go inside and start packing.

Padma: Why?

Mahinder: We crossing to the other side of the river today.

Padma: The other side?

Mahinder: Yes, to the other side. If you are always roaming in the jungles, how would you keep touch with what's happening around us? Now go.

[*Padma goes to the dawa. Baba I am not saying this in annoyance, but the neighbourhood at the edge of the river has been vacated.*]

Khetu: Where are the Roys and the Mandals?

Mahinder: Didn't you notice Haren pandit? He cleared out of this place just after Pakistan was created. Now look at the town.

Khetu: Why should I look at the town? Why must we compete with the town's well-placed people?

Mahinder: You have to if you don't want to stay without food. Who is going to feed you? These well-placed people were our strength. If they go away without us, we will be in peril.

[*Khetu sits with his head bowed.*]

Mahinder: The government of Hindustan has made arrangements for people like us. Something or the other will work out. We will not get this opportunity again. I will be back soon from Mandal's place.

There's very little time. The steamer will leave in the evening.

[*Mahinder leaves. Swarno comes and sits.*]

Padma: Yes.

Khetu: Yes?

Padma: Kolkata is a huge city, isn't it?

Khetu: Maybe.

Padma: What's the city like?

Swarno: Padma!

Padma: Bouthan!

Swarno: Go from here now.

Padma: Haru says Kolkata is a great city but not so sparsely populated. It is very crowded.

Swarno: Yes. Go inside.

Khetu: The stretch along the river is empty. So are the fields and the garden.

[*He stands up.*]

Swarno: Where are you going?

Khetu: I will sit in the garden because I won't be able to see it again.

[*Khetu leaves.*]

Swarno: Please wait, Baba. I will place a *piri* (A square or rectangular wooden plan used for sitting on the floor) for you.

[*She takes the piri from the dawa. Gopal arrives.*]

Gopal: [*Gopal sings.*]

Ei desh chairya jaba cholya bulyachile tumi,
Shei jawa gele botey kaitya Bharatbhumi.

Gopal: Padma, I wrote this song a while ago. I have rhymed it well, don't you think so?

Padma: I have just come inside.

[*Gopal points to books.*]

Gopal: I have got two books for you. I will make you study.

Padma: How can I do that? We are taking the steamer from the town today.

Gopal: The moment something untoward happens, people lose rationality. In fact the military captain at the border got Haran Mandal. What's that?

[*Gopal says with surprise. Swarno returns from the garden.*]

Gopal: Bouthan, what's all this?

Swarno: That's your elder brother's. We are taking the steamer today.

Gopal: Come on! He keeps changing his mind every now and then. Where is he?

Swarno: He has gone to the town.

[*Kalim comes.*]

Kalim: Gopal, call Mahinder.

Gopal: Hey, where were you in the afternoon?

Kalim: Call Mahinder.

Gopal: But he is not at home.

Kalim: Not at home?

Gopal: Why, what happened?

Kalim: Nani came to your place. She returned home and locked herself up. When she came out of the room, I asked her where she was going. Looking despondent, she went out without replying. That's why I am here to ask about her.

Gopal: Bouthan, Bouthan.

[*Khetu comes.*]

Khetu: Tell him, Bouma. Mahinder says Muslims are our enemy.

[*Kalim smiles.*]

Kalim: He is mad. Even Nani. Has she gone mad after fighting with Mahinder?

Gopal: Madness!

Khetu: He says happiness awaits us on the other side of the river. He says we will get land to secure a home.

Gopal: That's the basic problem. The newspapers send us teasing invites to entice people. Heaven on earth is to the west.

Khetu: I find such tranquility in this garden. It is so peaceful! Ah!

[*Khetu leaves.*]

Gopal: Kalimuiddi Mian, how have you been keeping of late?

[*Padma goes inside.*]

Kalim: What can I say about myself? You say how I am.

Gopal: We? You are the masters. The day belongs to you.

Kalim: And the night to you? You are the guests of the night.

[*Haru arrives.*]

Haru: Baba says we are going to Hindusthan today.

Kalim: All the way to Hindusthan?

Haru: Yes. We will cross the river.

Kalim: You will ride my shoulders straight to Kolkata.

[*Kalim holds Haru fondly and makes him sit on the dawa.*]

Gopal: Now that the Emperor has wished so, let's go.

Kalim: Who is going to look after me, now that I am left behind?

Gopal: How can we think about our immediate neighbours when so many guests are arriving from Punjab and Bihar?

Kalim: Look at me. Let me see beneath your tunic and put my head in.

[*Gopal hums a tune.*]

Kalim: There's nothing. It's empty.

[*Mahinder looks at them with his eyes wide open. Then holds Haru by the hand.*]

Mahinder: Haru, come inside.

Kalim: Would he lose his religion if he stays here?

Gopal: Dada, are we leaving?

Mahinder: Not today.

Gopal: You say that everyday. What have you said to Nani?

Mahinder: I didn't commit any crime. I told her that which is true.

Gopal: Maybe you have not committed any crime, but you might have insulted her!

Mahinder: What? Are you going to talk to me like that? Look—

Kalim: Gopal, stop! We are the enemy, isn't it?

Mahinder: I don't have the courage to say that. After all we are in Pakistan.

Kalim: Had it been Hindusthan, would you have said Muslims are the enemy?

Mahinder: No point talking about it.

Kalim: You are a top-notch rascal! I Am so moved by your concerns!

Gopal: We are not sure if we are leaving. I don't know why we are packing.

Mahinder: What do you mean? I will go. You can stay back.

Gopal: What did you say?

Mahinder: Amazing!

Kalim: Sheer madness! Gopal, I will return to take you to Jainuddin's place.

[*He leaves.*]

Gopal: Think again, Dada.

Mahinder: There's nothing to think about. See it, look into it. I find much relief when I am away from home. But no longer do I hope for peace.

[*Khetu comes.*]

Baba, Haran Mandal has been held by a military Captain at the border.

Khetu: What?

Gopal: I know about it. During some discussions, he had said the two countries were bound to be one. That led to the problem.

Mahinder: That's not a crime. It was only an old man talking.

Khetu: When was he apprehended?

Mahinder: In the afternoon. The situation is so tense that you cannot even make any noise. This is an enemy state, an enemy state!

[*Swarno comes.*]

Mahinder: Bou, they will take your ornaments away at the border. You and Padma should conceal under your clothes those ornaments that were given to you at the time of our marriage.

Khetu: But Mahinder...

Mahinder: What?

Khetu: I won't leave. I am not afraid to die.

Mahinder: Oh! You don't care for us.

Gopal: Dada!

Mahinder: You know it too well that we won't leave without you. You have grown old and you will remain selfish all your life.

Khetu: I don't understand you.

Mahinder: Consider us, too. Think about Padma and Haru. Stop thinking about only yourself.

Khetu: You could say that to me?

[*Padma comes.*]

Mahinder: Yes, I did.

Gopal: Dada!

Swarno: Baba!

Khetu: Wait Bouma. Let me hear him out.

Mahinder: Almost the entire village is empty. In order not to reach further pain to him, I keep thinking that I won't tell the old man about the present situation anymore than I already have.

Khetu: Alright. Take me wherever you want to. Take me.

Gopal: Come on, Baba!

Khetu: Even if it's hell, I will go with you. Let's go.

[*Gopal takes an excited Khetu into the room.*]

Gopal: Baba, don't go off the handle. Cool down.

Mahinder: I am going to settle this matter today, once and for all.

[*Says sharply from the other side of the stage.*]

Swarno: Do you love to live with ill will?

Mahinder: It's a curse! Yes!

Swarno: Where will you go?

Mahinder: To the other side of the river with the town people.

Swarno: And then?

Mahinder: After that, either to Murshidabad, or to Kolkata.

Swarno: Where would you stay there?

Mahinder: The government has made arrangements. Besides, our Hindu brothers will help us. There's nothing much to worry.

Swarno: And what would you do for sustenance?

Mahinder: Why are you probing? Why?

Swarno: Stay quiet. Is this your assurance?

Mahinder: The people of the village left on lesser assurances.

Swarno: Don't you have any sense or wisdom? Kill me. Throttle me to death with your foot.

Mahinder: Hey Haru's ma! Are you not in your senses?

Padma: Bouthan, come away.

Swarno: I can't believe that a son could be so ruthless with his father!

Padma: Dada!

Mahinder: Yes?

Padma: Once you leave, all doors back to this place will be closed. Doesn't that thought bite you? You don't know anybody whom you can call your own on the other side.

Mahinder: You? You are saying this?

Gopal: Dada, give it a second thought. You are our elder brother.

Mahinder: You mean to say I will stay back because nobody wants to leave? Make them realize that if something happens—

Gopal: Do you think we are going to stay here if something happens?

Mahinder: Make sure that nobody comes after me with baring their fangs and claws. Tell them clearly.

Gopal: Where are you going?

Mahinder: I have to inform those townspeople of the change of our plans. Nani is too angry today, isn't she?

Gopal: She is hurt.

Mahinder: I am leaving now. Hey!

[*Debendir arrives.*]

Debendir: That gentleman from Birkutsa wants us to take our luggage to the pier. The steamer will leave in the evening.

Mahinder: Why?

Debendir: He went through the almanac and found the evening hours to be a safe time for leaving. Have you heard about Haran Mandal?

Mahinder: Yes, but—

Debendir: After hearing about Haran, everybody in that neighbourhood wants to leave. It would be difficult to accommodate everyone on the boat.

Mahinder: We have decided not to leave.

Debendir: What are you saying?

Mahinder: Yes. My father doesn't want us to leave.

[*Khetu appears at the door.*]

Khetu: I am not against leaving. Debendir, you go. I am sending the luggage.

[*Debendir leaves.*]

Mahinder: Now what, Baba?

Khetu: I wish you understood!

Gopal: Do you really want to go?

Khetu: I will. Gopal, go and have our luggage ready.

Mahinder: Everything is ready. Gopal, I am taking the trunk. You bring the rest.

[*Enthusiastically, Mahinder leaves. Gopal picks up a bundle.*]

Gopal: Baba, this is nothing but your anger.

Khetu: No, Gopal. Let's go. What's the harm in seeing a new country?

[*Kalim comes.*]

Kalim: Which country, Uncle? Gopal, let's go to Jainuddin's abode.

Gopal: [*Hides the bundle. Then he speaks with a faint smile—*] Kalim, we are leaving.

Kalim: So much time we spent together, so much good time we had together. Everything comes to an end?

Gopal: Time to leave, Kalim.

Gopal: Padma, take Haru with you and show Karim what we are not taking with us. They will be in his custody. Bouthan, bring the padlocks. We need to lock up all doors and boxes.

Kalim: Are you really going to leave all these behind as memories?

[*Gopal drops the bundle.*]

Gopal: Bouthan, I am going near the river for a while.

[*Gopal starts to walk.*]

Kalim: Uncle, don't worry. I will take care of your home. I will sail along the steamer on a boat for a certain distance. No idea when I would meet all of you again. Bouthan, hope you would not dismiss me from memory. Please remember me. Dear Padma, on the sides of my pond, the Kalmi herb will grow even in this monsoon, but you won't be there to pluck them. But I know uncle, we will meet one day. This is inevitable. Let me have your address after you reach that country. Uncle, Bouthan, Padma—Goodbye.

[*Kalim walks away at a fast pace. Gopal stands still on the embankment and watches the river. Swarno walks up to the front of the stage where Khetu is standing.*]

Swarno: Where are we going!

Khetu: Bouma, Bouma... I chanted Lord Hari's name for my mother in this house. She is here until now. She passed away a long time ago. How many have died and how many footprints mark this place! Ohl Ma!

[*He goes away mumbling. The stage darkens. The last rays of the Sun turn the skies red. Gopal moves from the place where he was standing. He comes down singing, 'Hamar shonar gang re'. The lyrics jumble up and only the melody can be heard. Swarno moves to the left of the stage and Padma to the rear. Haru arrives. Tiptoeing into the stage, he stands behind Padma. Feroza runs in haplessly from atop the embankment. Haru says something on the lighter vein. Padma turns around, surprised. She tries to slap Haru. But she wraps her arms around him and begins to cry profusely. Feroza and Swarno were staring at each other without moving. They hug each other as they hear Padma cry.*]

Swarno: Oh! Ma!

Padma: Oh! Ma! Everything is like a stone. Everyone is a stone.

[*Feroza runs her hand on Swarno's head. Padma and Haru keep holding each other. The song can't be heard anymore. Darkness descends on the stage. A lonely sail is seen crossing the embankment slowly, from the left to the right. From far away, comes a call — Badr-Badr...Badr-Badr.*]

— Curtains —

SECOND WAVE

[*The scene shifts to the Sealdah Station in Kolkata. A baffle wall can be seen at the back of the stage and a pillar to the left as well. The sound of trains arriving and departing, and locomotive whistles, can be heard in the background. The noise that emanates reflects that it is a crowded place. Many people are lying on beds, laid out on platforms and around the station. Trunks and bundles of clothes and other belongings are strewn all over the place. Khetu, wrapped in a shawl, is sitting at one side. Swarno is dozing off the back. Debendir is sitting opposite Khetu. Khetu hums.*]

Khetu: In what colour have you made this home, I am trapped in this world...

Debendir: Kaka, for how long do you think this situation will prevail?

Khetu: Until I climb my funeral pyre.

Debendir: Worse days seem to be ahead. The volunteers are not going to distribute milk from today. What will be our fate then?

Khetu: We can no longer set up a home in this fake world. I am baffled after seeing the situation we are in. I have become mute.

Debendir: Where are you going?

Khetu: To the washing area. We still don't have to buy water. But I guess that will change soon in this country.

[*He leaves.*]

Debendir: Bouthan!

Swarno: Yes?

Debendir: Where is Padma?

Swarno: She is sitting outside and reading a book.

Debendir: That girl is changing ever since we arrived here.

Swarno: It seems something particular keeps striking her mind. She is always pensive and buying books.

Debendir: It was a mistake on part of Gopal to introduce her to books. Otherwise...

Swarno: I am not feeling good about anything these days. I have quarrelled as much as I did ever since we landed here. This noise and the crowds are killing me.

Debendir: Let me take you into confidence. I bumped into that clerk who was working at Birkutsa yesterday. I told him something.

Swarno: What?

Debendir: Please keep this from Gopal. He says that the well-placed people from the town, with whom we had migrated, have found jobs in Kolkata but we are still languishing. I think the clerk is going talk to them today. I may get a piece of land. But I have to go to Ranaghat with them. I must leave now.

Swarno: Listen, we have nothing to eat today. Could you please take this to that gold merchant at the Baithakhana market?

[*She takes off her gold bangle.*]

Debendir: Again? What else is left, Bouthan?

Swarno: Don't talk. Just take it and go. They will be sad if they see me do this.

[*Debendir leaves. Khetu comes.*]

Khetu: Get up, Mahinder. Our train is about to come.

[*Mahinder turn his side and continues to stay on his bed.*]

Swarno: It's late morning.

[*She prepares to leave.*]

Khetu: Bouma, prepare the hookah. Let me smoke it with heart's content.

Swarno: It's already late. If I don't go now, I won't find the washing area free.

Khetu: Alright. Go and fetch water. People are becoming strange, huhl And look at the sky! When will it ever smile? It has become an eyesore now.

[*Accidentally, one person steps on Mahinder.*]

Mahinder: Hey!

Man: Sorry, I accidentally stepped on you.

Mahinder: Can't you seen that someone is lying here?

Man: You are all sleeping on a passage that is a thoroughfare. What can I do?

Mahinder: Give us a place to sleep. Give. We are not sleeping here because we like to do so.

Khetu: Let him go. Don't get into an altercation in the morning and spoil your mood.

[*The man walks away. Gopal gets up.*]

Mahinder: Alright. Haru, don't be lazy. You should go and wash up now.

Haru: Baba, isn't the rally being taken out today? Aren't we joining it?

Mahinder: Why do you want to know about it so early in the day? Come.

[*Mahinder takes Haru along with him.*]

Khetu: Gopal, give me a *bidi* (Tobacco rolled in Tendu leaves and is meant for smoking).

Gopal: Yes.

Khetu: The sky here is smokey.

Gopal: This is the city of Kolkata!

Khetu: Kolkata!

Gopal: Why, what happened?

Khetu: I have had enough of Kolkata; of the Hindustan and Hindu brethren.

Gopal: Watch carefully.

Khetu: Don't waste time. Go to the washing area.

[*Gopal smiles and walks away. Padma comes with a book in her hand.*]

Khetu: Is your morning walk over?

Padma: Baba, I saw many people gather outside. Are they going to meet government representatives?

Khetu: Yes.

Padma: We are here because of the government. Pakistan has come into being because of the government.

Khetu: Yes.

Padma: In that case, it is the responsibility of the government to take care of us.

Khetu: True.

Padma: They are going to convey this message to the government.

Khetu: Yes.

Padma: Let me go and see what's happening.

[*Khetu tugs Padma by the tail of her saree. Padma looks at him in surprise.*]

Khetu: I have not liked this country.

[*Padma smiles.*]

Padma: Are you remembering the garden back home?

Khetu: No. Even the air of this place protests when I try to breathe in. Do you remember Bhimsen's jungle near the Padma river? Do you remember the slope along the embankment and my sugarcane field next to it?

Padma: Why?

Khetu: I felt free in that environment.

Padma: But I have begun to like Kolkata. It is a great city—the cars, the lights, the music! Where do so many people come from? They are literally rubbing shoulders as they walk. I want to laugh when I look at this city.

Khetu: Why so?

Padma: I feel amused for no reason. I can't figure out where all these people rush to everyday. The pace of city life amazes me. It seems a big game is on! I mean, I cannot explain to you, Baba.

[*Swarno comes.*]

Swarno: Fetch a bucket of water.

Padma: Give me the bucket. You returned with an empty bucket?

Swarno: Either I am getting out of this everyday rigmarole, or I am going to hang myself to death.

Padma: Why, what happened?

Swarno: Hundreds of people are at the washing area. You just cannot wash up or collect water. Those terrible men keep ogling. I wish I could hold them by the hair and rub their faces on the ground.

Padma: I am going.

[*Padma leaves.*]

[*Swarno prepares the earthen oven. Opens a box, applies the vermilion powder on her head and combs her hair. Khetu notices.*]

Khetu: Are you also joining that rally of beggars? Keep walking with them. Those who brought us along have settled down, whereas out duty is to walk in rallies.

Swarno: The aunt and her family from Faridpur will also be in the rally.

Khetu: Go, go. All of you go dancing to the rally. Go.

[*Debendir rushes in.*]

Debendir: Bouthan! Kaka!

Khetu: What?

Swarno: You?

Debendir: On my way back from Baithakkhana market, I stopped to watch the gathering crowds. Just when I was planning to visit our townspeople, I saw our 'Pagla' with another man in the crowd. I was so surprised to see him.

[*Haren pandit appears. He is being followed by an old man with unruly hair. The name of that man is Arjun Malakar. He is gripping something in his fist.*]

Haren: Isn't this our Khetu?

Khetu: Who are you?

Haren: I am your Haren Pandit, from Panchabati.

Debendir: I see that Pagla is wolfing around.

Swarno: Debendir, I will face problems if the work is not done.

Debendir: That work has been done. Here, take it. Those rascals are marked cheats. I am going now to see the townspeople. It would be dark when I return. Pandit, see you later.

[*Debendir leaves.*]

Haren: All of you are here. Good—

Arjun: I gave my address—

Haren: Go, go, go. Go now. There's no time.

[*Mahinder leaves, taking Haru along with him.*]

Haren: Hello, Mahinder! Good to see that all of you are here. So the Sealdah shed is now your home. Good.

Khetu: Weren't you teaching back home?

Haren: We have set up a colony in Jadavpur. I have also opened a small school. Some people from the north of our erstwhile country have settled their homes in Jadavpur. I do have some students. The school only has primary classes. But I have plans to—

Mahinder: Where are you going now?

Haren: I am going to join the rally of all the refugees today. Pandit Nehru is in Kolkata now. We will present him a memorandum at the Governor's House. We are planning to draw his notice to the real situation. I just led a team of my students to join the rally. But I have talking about myself. How are you all doing?

Mahinder: We are in a pitiable condition as we spend our days and nights without a break on this platform.

Haren: That's true. Isn't he your son? He has lost weight considerably.

Khetu: The situation has become unbearable. Since you are from our village, I am telling you. Our savings are now severely depleted. I don't know what's going to happen next.

Haren: The next step is efforts. That's the reason why we are submitting a memorandum today.

Arjun: Sir.

Haren: What a pest! Why do every hassle has to come up now and here? I have no time.

Mahinder: Who is that man?

Haren: Who knows? He has been sticking to me from that gate. What's this? This place is so crowded. But the police have lined up outside.

Mahinder: The policemen are there since the morning.

Haren: I hope you are also joining the rally.

Mahinder: We have plans to go.

Haren: I am also going to the rally. But why are these policemen toting batons?

Khetu: That's why I feel there's no point in being part of that agitation.

[*Gopal comes.*]

Gopal: Demanding food means agitation?

Khetu: Shut up! You are always saying something or the other.

[*Outside, a loudspeaker announces: 'Friends, come and line up for the rally'.*]

Haren: No more, no more—I mean...

[*He stops in the middle of his speech. Gopal takes Haru by the hand and leaves. Swarno follows them.*]

Haren: Old man, why are you continuing to stay here?

Khetu: That's because I have no place to go.

Haren: All of you are struggling. Why don't you do something? Why don't you come with me?

Mahinder: Where?

Haren: Our colony is full. But there are some barracks next to us. Let me take you there. Once you settle there, we can try and find work for you. That barrack is not a good place to stay in, but it is better than your life on this platform.

Mahinder: You really mean it?

Haren: I don't have much time, but you can give it a thought. If you decide, you can come with me.

Mahinder: Pandit, you will be our saviour then.

[*Outside, a commotion breaks out.*]

Haren. Trouble! But we can still go.

Mahinder: Hey! We will go with you.

Haren: Yes, come with me. This is some problem. Even if you don't come with me, the students remain.

[*Haren and Mahinder leave together. Padma comes. Takes a look at the outside and says—*]

Padma: This rally will take so many roads, so many new roads. Baba, I am leaving now for the rally.

Khetu: Go and spare me.

Padma: Why are you getting annoyed? So nice to see so many people together!

[*She leaves.*]

Khetu: Hey, listen.

[*As Arjun was coming, Gopal and Haru were walking in. They collide. The piece of paper Arjun is carrying drops to the ground. He jumps at the paper and recovers it.*]

Gopal: Sorry. Did you get hurt?

Arjun: No.

Khetu: Why have you come back?

Gopal: I am expecting chaos outside.

Khetu: So?

Gopal: I am leaving Haru with you.

Haru: No—

Gopal: Shut up!

Haru: Kaka, let me come. Dadu, please tell him.

Gopal: If you keep quiet, I will take you to the museum tomorrow.

Haru: I don't want to go the museum. I don't like to be alone all the time.

Khetu: If you leave him in my custody, he will make my life miserable.

Gopal: I will send for Bouthan. They need not go out in this chaotic situation.

Khetu: What a relief that would be if everyone perishes in this chaos.

Gopal: If they don't stay alive, who would you depend on?

Arjun: What dependence!

Gopal: What?

[*Arjun smiles.*]

Arjun: I belong to Nakalya in Pabna. My name is Arjun Malakar.

Gopal: Is it?

Arjun: I just wanted to let you know.

Gopal: Alright. I am wiser now.

[*Arjun smiles.*]

Khetu: So what do you do here?

Arjun: That's why I am asking why I am here. I arrived today.

Gopal: O! Are you carrying a hexed treasure trove in your hand?

Arjun: This one? This one is—can you show me the direction to the King's court?

Khetu: What is he saying?

Gopal: King...

Arjun: Yes, the King, the King of Hindusthan.

Gopal: Hindusthan doesn't have a King.

Arjun: Who else is there if there is no King?

Khetu: Are you a lunatic?

Gopal: A government is in place and the government has a Prime Minister.

Arjun: Isn't there an apex leader?

Gopal: I told you. He is the Prime Minister.

Arjun: Who is that?

Gopal: Pandit Nehru is the Prime Minister.

Arjun: What am I going to do then? I had some question for the King.

Khetu: Gopal, can't you make out? Go and do your work. He has a problem upstairs.

Arjun: What did you say his name was? Pandit or something?

[*The loudspeaker is blaring: 'Friends, who are still not here, come and join us. We are about to start.' Gopal wants to leave for the Rally but Arjun stops him.*]

Arjun: Before you leave, tell me his name.

Gopal: Pandit Nehru. He is the supreme authority of this country.

Arjun: Do you think I can meet him?

Gopal: Why don't you try to meet him instead of pestering us? By the way, why do you want to meet him?

Arjun: I have to show him that piece of paper.

Gopal: What's that?

[*Arjun smiles.*]

Arjun: Want to see? Well, it's a legal document. I left my home. They insisted that I leave with them. That old man said I could submit the document later and things would fall in place. He had said the Hindu Government had made extensive arrangements for our convenience.

[*Gopal laughs out loud. Haru joins him. The man tries to laugh twice like a fool and stops. Khetu is taken aback.*]

Khetu: Are you carrying documents related to your house?

Gopal: Something wrong inside his head.

[*Gopal Points to his own head.*]

Gopal: Somebody must have switched him on. When you begin to believe in rumours—

Arjun: I will meet that Pandit and tell him about everybody's misery. I have seen it with my own eyes. They have no food to eat and no bed to sleep. I will tell him that it is him who has to make arrangements for these unfortunate people. There are so many guests that he has.

[*Outside, the loudspeaker screamed: 'Friends...'. Gopal suddenly leaves. Arjun was looking foolish.*]

Arjun: Ha!

[*Haru begins to laugh as Arjun steps towards him.*]

Haru: You really have a very jovial kid here.

Khetu: Have you brought a fool-proof document?

[*Arjun walks upto Khetu.*]

Arjun: I had a house, a contiguous piece of land and a paddy field. I say since I have grown old, what's the harm in coming to this place to see new developments.

Khetu: Home. I also had a home near the banks of the Padma river. I used to grow vegetables on the adjacent land. When I left, the garden had just begun to blossom. I am sure the pumpkins have begun to ripen. But who cares! Everything must be gone by now.

Arjun: I also had a garden. But I wasn't growing eggplants. Do you know what I was nurturing in my garden? Flowers. I was growing flowers and more flowers. It is now the winter. The flowers have grown to be as big as my palm. There were so many different kinds of flowers.

[*Khetu gets up.*]

Khetu: The sky here is so slate-grey.

Arjun: You got it right! I didn't notice it before.

[*Arjun tries to take a look at the sky. Outside, a commotion breaks out. Two men, rubbing their eyes, run across the stage. A curious Arjun follows them. They exit. The loudspeaker says: 'Friends, line up on the station premises. We will start again.' A tense Swarno rushes in.*]

Swarno: Baba, I cannot find Haru anywhere. Haru—

[*Now she notices Haru. She begins to shake as she holds Haru in her lap. Outside, the noise dissipates. Mahinder comes.*]

Mahinder: They used some smoke that caused our eyes to burn tearfully. Pandit wonders what a reception this is in our town country. Baba, I will go with Pandit to take a look at the place where we are going to stay. It seems, finally, there is a way out of this squalor.

[*Gopal arrives. From inside, a few more arrive.*]

Gopal: They used a baton to open a wound on the head of a boy. Are they humans?

[*Mahinder is about to leave but Swarno stops her.*]

Swarno: They can open fire.

Mahinder: Good. Now let me go.

Swarno: If something happens to you?

Mahinder: If something happens to me, you won't have to sell your ornaments to buy food. You won't have to spend nights among the fifty-thousand people who have taken refuge inside the Sealdah Station. You won't have to ward off cold with a torn bedsheet and die of cholera.

Swarno: Why are you saying such things?

Mahinder: Let's go.

[*Gopal is looking at the scenario outside. Arjun tries to peep over his shoulders. Gopal turns to find him right behind him.*]

Gopal: Hello Sir! Do you have the guts to go out?

Arjun: Yes. That Pandit.

Gopal: Come, I will take you along with me. Do you notice those raised guns?

Arjun: Yes.

Gopal: Did you also notice that the injured man was being taken away in an ambulance?

Arjun: Yes.

Gopal: That's what is happening.

Arjun: Why? They said we will get all facilities once we come here. Even the newspapers said so.

Gopal: They keep talking.

Arjun: What happens to my land, my garden, my home?

Gopal: You will never get them back.

Arjun: Then, why did they say so? Why?

[*He sits down.*]

Gopal: You and I are goners. It seems only death awaits us.

[*Reports of gunfire can be heard outside.*]

Mahinder: Firing!

Gopal: Dada!

Mahinder: Gopal!

[*They rush out. Swarno sits with Haru on her lap. Khetu goes near Arjun, who appears overwhelmed with the turn of events.*]

Khetu: Even if you beg, you won't get alms. I am not going to seek aid from the people who have sliced up this country. I just learned about statehood.

[*Arjun lifts his face. He cries out 'Home'. Groaning, he tears up the document in tiny bits. The he covers his face. Khetu gets up.*]

Khetu: I feel as if I should jump into this chaos like a warrior and, and...

[*Coughing violently, Khetu steps back. Haren runs to him. He looks at the ground after locking eyes with Khetu.*]

Haren: Khetu, I have failed. I have failed. I was paralysed by fear. Can you tell me why I couldn't march ahead? What has happened to me?

Arjun: [*A completely changed person.*] Who is the enemy? Who? I will catch him one day. I will be able to mark him out one day. The day I do that, I would break into a war cry and tear off their windpipes.

[*Arjun runs out like a possessed man. The loudspeaker says: 'Brothers, the blood shed by the martyrs will strengthen our resolve. We will march ahead. There will be no compromise.' All of a sudden, a very loud report of gunfire erupts. And then, silence. Khetu was looking from the side of the pillar. He wobble back. Swarno, who was sitting quietly, is jolted by the way Khetu steps back.*]

Swarno: What happened to you? O God! Baba!

Khetu: Arjun Malakar!

[*Gopal comes in, pulling Padma by the hand. Her clothes are almost falling off her. Outside, the loudspeaker continues to exhort the people. Padma uses Khetu as a shield and calls out with fear—*]

Padma: Baba.

Khetu: Who?

[*Padma snugs up to him. She is trembling. Khetu raises Padma's face.*]

Padma: What did I see! He fell after being shot, as if he was a doll. His limbs were flailing and blood came out from the wound in bursts. It was all over. I am so scared, Baba. What have I witness in Kolkata! This Kolkata.

[*Khetu stares at her without blinking. Padma grabs Khetu tightly, as if in fear. Everybody else looks at the area outside the station.*]

— Curtains —

Change of scenario

THIRD WAVE: First Part

[*A refugee colony near Kolkata. A worn-out, dilapidated barrack. A door is to the right and a window on the other side. Debendir is perched on a high area of the barrack. He leaves his seat to go near the door but returns to the spot where he was sitting. He looks restive. Padma comes in from one side of the stage with a new flower pot and saplings wrapped in a paper. She puts them down carefully and digs into a basket to test soil, mixed with fertilizer. Debendir gets up and walks up to her.*]

Debendir: Padma!

Padma: What, Debendir Da? What are you doing here?

Debendir: There's nobody home except Kaka. But he is sleeping.

Padma: Yes, everybody has gone out.

Debendir: What's that?

Padma: I bought a flower pot. I got a Cape Jasmine sapling.

Debendir: Good. I wanted to tell you something?

Padma: What?

Debendir: I heard last night that land is being doled out in Orissa. Any idea where Orissa is?

Padma: Towards the south.

Debendir: I will leave for Orissa then. I am getting asphyxiated here.

Padma: Who said land is being doled out?

Debendir: Who cares! I will go anyway. It's been long I have not tilled land.

Padma: When will you leave?

Debendir: I will leave this evening. If I can get some acres of fertile land—ah! I am leaving for Orissa.

Padma: You will come back.

Debendir: Why?

Padma: Nobody is going to offer you a fertile land on the platter. You will not get such land anywhere.

Debendir: I have to get land. I feel dead and gone without owning any land. Life seems so incomplete. Tell Gopal that I will get all of you over there after two months. All you have to do is to wait for some more time.

Padma: [*Laughs.*] Alright.

Debendir: Don't laugh. The days of struggle are over. I understand that land in Orissa is usually fertile. Not much effort is required to have a good harvest.

Padma: *O amar gang, hamar Padma gang re, hamar*
shonar gang re, hamar jan-er gang re

(O my river, my Padma river, my golden river, the river in my heart.)

Haru: *Pishi* (Father's sister, both younger and elder), Pishi, listen please. [*Padma goes near Haru.*] Where's Ma?

Padma: She is out looking for work. The babus of Tollygunge said they needed a maid. She's gone there.

Haru: Would you do something, Pishi?

Padma: Tell me.

Haru: You are so nice. Can you get me ten annas from under Ma's bed?

Padma: Ten annas? What are you going to do with that money?

Haru: Rehana and we all are going.

Padma: To the movies?

Haru: Tell me, how often have I been to a movie theatre in the past two years? Please, please get me that money. The movie has a nice song—Ho La La! Ho La! La!

Padma: What if you come home late?

Haru: I will say I was with Haren Pandit, or whatever. I am getting late.

[*Khetu comes out from the room. His eyes are shut, as if he is a sleep-walker. He says—*]

Khetu: Padma!

[*Haru's back is facing Khetu.*]

Haru: Who?

Khetu: Is that Haru? Come here.

[*Unwillingly, Haru walks up to Khetu. Khetu lifts him into his lap. Padma, comes and stands behind. Padma leans on his back.*]

Padma: Why did you stop singing?

Padma: Haru was calling me.

Khetu: Haru has grown up. Now is the time for him to look for work.

Haru: Panchu Da said he would employ me at his tea stall. I have to make tea and serve.

Khetu: The Earth keeps rotating, no matter you are awake or asleep. But, listen, haven't I heard Gopal sing that song once?

Padma: Yes, when we were at Rupaikandi. He doesn't sing anymore. That song is really so full of melodies.

Khetu: Something happened to me while you were singing that song.

Padma: What?

Khetu: That song woke me up. It seemed I was having a dream in an awakened state.

Padma: Dream?

Khetu: A very strange dream. It seemed I was back at Rupaikandi after ages. I tied my boat to the pier at Buro Shibtola. I climbed the embankment and crossed the road. The road seemed to be short in length. Sand was blowing into the room through the west window from the banks of the Padma. A layer of sand was covering the floor, the shelves. Sand was everywhere. When this was happening, a song wafted in from the riverside. We used to fix sails on our dinghies before going out for fishing. I saw my mother on the sails. The song exuded great encrgy and the rhythm of the oars was deep and firm. My heart still does not accept a country split into two.

[*Haru comes near Padma and gently gives her a push. Irritated, Padma pushes him away.*]

Padma: Go and take it yourself. Nobody is in the room.

Khetu: What?

Padma: Nothing. Go on.

[*Harun goes into the room.*]

Khetu: The dream ended there.

[*He gets up.*]

Khetu: The atmosphere in this country is not good. They say we are refugees. Tell me, can you call a human being refugee? I lived for nothing but self-esteem.

Even that has deserted me. Now I feel as if I am a thief and hiding from society. Why? What have we done to deserve this fate?

[*Haru comes running in.*]

Haru: Pishi, there's no money. Give me some.

Padma: How do I know? Let your mother come.

Haru: I don't care. I am getting late. Will you give me the money or not?

Khetu: What money?

Haru: You don't have any money with you?! Give, Pishi.

Padma: I am telling you the truth. Why are you behaving in that manner?

Haru: Everybody has left for the movie theatre. Now give me money, or else I will lose control.

Khetu: Haru—

Haru: Give, Pishi, otherwise I will break your flower pot.

Padma: Haru, I bought the flower pot this morning. Hey! Hey! What are you doing?

[*Padma falls silent because Haru has already thrown the flower pot onto the floor, breaking it in many pieces. The sapling lay twisted. Haru looks at them for a moment and then runs out of the room. Khetu get up.*]

Khetu: Die, die! Perish! All demons, a bunch of demons!

[*In spite of being sad, Padma laughs out.*]

Padma: I know how much I struggled to buy that flower pot.

[*Khetu comes near Padma and places a hand on her head.*]

Khetu: Come. Let's run away.

Padma: Where?

Khetu: To the other side, to our country.

[*Padma looks at him and smiles. Swarno comes wearing a partially torn saree.*]

Swarno: Padma!

Padma: Bouthan!

Swarno: I saw Haru crying near the gate. He ran away the moment I called him. What happened?

Padma: He broke my new flower pot.

Swarno: Just for that you hit a small boy like him?

Padma: No, I didn't.

Swarno: If you haven't, then why is he crying? Does he love to cry or what?

Khetu: Bouma, Padma is telling the truth.

Swarno: Ask your father not to intervene in these matters.

Khetu: Why Bouma? What difference does it make if I intervene?

Swarno: Padma, tell your father that he should control his tongue especially when his daughter-in-law's ornaments are being sold to make two ends meet in this family.

Khetu: Alright. I am going now.

[*Khetu goes into the room. Padma assists him.*]

Padma: What happened to your work?

Swarno: It won't happen. I cannot lose my modesty and honour.

Padma: Tell me, what?

Swarno: Don't look so surprised. I could have easily got that job if I had chosen to surrender.

Padma: Oh! Bouthan!

Swarno: You won't understand. You would have to lose your honour and modesty and you would lose it when all the *Ghoti*s (The original inhabitants of West

Bengal) and *Bangal*s (Bengalis who originated from Bangladesh or East Bengal) have lost everything, when honour would be sold for a dime. This is your problem.

Padma: Bouthan, you are becoming strange these days.

Swarno: You are saying all this now? You have no idea what's coming our way.

Padma: Bouthan, you have gone mad. You are talking insane.

[*Swarno begins to cry.*]

Swarno: Padma, you tell me what do I do and where do I go? Not another ornament is left on me to sell. Yesterday—

Padma: Yesterday—

Swarno: Yesterday, a deep gorge—

Padma: Relax! Don't be so tense. There has to be a way out.

[*Haren and Gopal arrive.*]

Haren: You have to erase that word from your lexicon.

Gopal: No.

Haren: That Kalim and his ilk have become prominent people. Everyone is now an important guest of the Arab State. Even culture, sense and sensibilities have been forcibly divided. So, at least for me, you have to erase the word kidding.

Gopal: No, no. I don't accept.

Haren: What you can't accept?

Gopal: Humans haven't changed yet. In Pakistan, Kalim has remained Kalim.

Padma: What are you talking about?

Gopal: Look here Padma, I have written to Kalim about our home we have left behind in Pakistan. For news about this place, I thought I would talk about Pandit. Instead of doing that—

Haren: You tell me Padma, we can pour our heart out to those who are our own, but to someone who is not in that circle—

Gopal: For Kalim?

Haren: Sure.

Gopal: I don't agree.

Padma: Have you written?

Gopal: You want to listen?

Haren: Sure, sure. Bouthan is present here. Listen to it later. I have told you many times, Gopal, to publish a book of songs at two annas each. You will earn decent money. But you won't listen to me.

Gopal: No need to listen.

Haren: Why?

Gopal: You don't make money by selling songs. It feels as if I am begging in the city.

Haren: Padma, see, the farmer is sulking.

Padma: Yes, I can see that, but the letter?

Gopal: Listen.

Haren: Bouma, that work we talked about—

Padma: Leave her alone.

Gopal: Here it is—What can I say about the situation here! Too much struggle and too much pain continue to afflict the people. However, in spite of these trying times, Haren Pandit's paunch hasn't slumped even a bit. To this date, he continues to act pricey by saying, 'I have no time'. The students' community here.

Haren: Too much of— I mean, this is meaningless, Gopal.

Gopal: Huh! Pandit—Look, who's is here! [*Debu Bose comes.*] Bouthan, send that short stool. That babu from the newspaper has come.

Debu: Not babu from the newspaper. Debu Bose.

Haren: Sit down, sit down. We are all on the floor and you are sitting on a mat. Why?

Debu: I don't mind if I am given one.

Gopal: Let me say now, Babu. Why did you bluff that day?

Debu: Bluff?

Gopal: You had said that you were representing a newspaper.

Debu: Yes, I did.

Gopal: But I went through your newspaper for a few days. There has been no coverage.

Debu: I am collecting information. After that I will examine all information and write my report. If not so, why would I then waste my time by coming to places such as these to watch the misery of people? What can I do? I need to earn, too.

Haren: Unless you control your tongue, you would not be able to earn.

Debu: I cannot lie. I really do not have any connection with so much misery.

Gopal: Understood. So what brings you here today?

Debu: The reason is the same. I am gathering experience. Later, I would use the information to write a big piece.

Swarno: Babu—

Debu: Yes?

Swarno: You will earn some money by writing.

Debu: I expect to.

Swarno: I can tell you many stories.

Debu: Good.

Swarno: Then pay me something.

Gopal: Bouthan!

Padma: Again, Bouthan?

Swarno: Why? He wants to gather experience. He doesn't know that we have no money to buy food for tomorrow. Not a morsel of rice is available in this home today. All ornaments and utensils have been sold. What is left arc some torn sheets.

Gopal: Stay quietl Stay quiet!

Swarno: The whole world is empty and the room is silent.

Padma: Too much worry doesn't shine any light. Let's go inside.

[*She pulls Swarno away. Khetu was coming. He makes way for Swarno and then comes in.*]

Haren: Anyway, I don't have much time. Now tell me, what were you saying about the meeting?

Debu: I will tell you. But where's your elder brother?

Haren: Well, he is not a complete human being.

Gopal: My brother has gone out.

Debu: Where?

Gopal: Somewhere.

Khetu: Why don't you tell him? He got information in the morning that workers were striking at mill in Dumdum. The owner now wants take truckloads of labourers from here to keep the mill going. Each labourer will get one-and-half rupee everyday.

Haren: It was not like this during my time. But I realized following clashes between the homeless and the workers. I also saw the game-plan that is used in the case of farmers. I realized how vile it is to use the want of the homeless people as a tool. But the way they glared at me—

Debu: Struggling families—

Haren: But does that mitigate struggle? It's only for three days. After that, these very workers will kick people like Mahinder out.

Gopal: I cannot tolerate this any longer. I keep remembering those days when Kalim was there, Nani was there, the Rupaikandi village was there.

Haren: Gopal, stop the harangue. [*Addressing Debu.*] Now tell us about the meeting.

Debu: You all know about the Eviction Bill. That agitation is—

Haren: It is very important to see the end of it. We became guests of this country after being prompted by the leaders. But they didn't give us a place to stay. Somehow, we built a society of our own. We made keen efforts to make barren, abandoned and condemned land habitable. Now they want a slice of that, too. This is betrayal upon betrayal. One must rise against this malaise.

Gopal: So why don't you rise?

Haren: There are many like me—almost everyone is. That's why they burn from inside.

Debu: Anyway, there a meeting to be held at the Maidan. A rally will start from here—

Khetu: Rally?

Debu: Yes. Gopal, if you can make everyone agree to join the rally—

Khetu: No, Babu. We are not interested in rallies.

Haren: See, it has started from inside the house.

Khetu: Stop there! I know the meaning of rallies. They molly coddle us so much when they want to take us out of our homes to join rallies. And when the meeting is over, none of these leaders can be seen anywhere. The other day, we were abandoned in front of some park. We didn't know the area and it was dark. What a disaster that was! No, these rallies are useless.

Gopal: But useful rallies will happen only if we keep on trying. They will emerge from our hard work.

Khetu: I don't know which way they would come, but our days are being spent expecting those useful rallies. Their colour is different. The day that happens, our pride will return; we will do something that day. I haven't forgotten Arjun Malakar.

[*Mahinder comes in panting.*]

Khetu: Mahinder!

Haren: Hey!

Debu: Hello!

Haren: You are speechless.

Gopal: Once you are shamed, you become speechless.

Mahinder: What does that mean?

Mahinder: You figure that out.

Haren: What's the matter, Mahinder?

Mahinder: I have walked all the way from Sealdah. I had no money. Besides, I lost my way. I had to walk in the sun the entire afternoon.

Haren: What about your work?

Mahinder: Work?

Haren: The work at the mill.

[*Swarno comes.*]

Mahinder: Today is the twenty-fourth day of the strike. The hutments where the workers say appear empty. I could see that their children were famished and the workers in a state of despair. I saw all that when our truck passed through their hutments.

Gopal: Then?

Mahinder: After that, I noticed their eyes. There was fire in them. It seemed bright rays were coming out of their eyes. Have you ever seen the face of an expert stiletto fighter after he receives a fatal blow, especially when he takes one final aim?

Haren: What about your work?

Mahinder: I got off the truck at the gate of the mill and returned. I desperately need money, but I cannot be a puny outsider in a battle of men. I couldn't condescend to that level.

Haren: This is what I was—

Mahinder: Bou, Bou, lay out the bed. I will wash up and go to sleep.

Swarno: We have to sell that bed tomorrow to eat.

Mahinder: We will think about tomorrow on the morrow. Let me sleep today.

[*He and Swarno exit.*]

Haren: The more I see all this, the deeper is the thought that keeps striking me these days.

Gopal: What?

Haren: I have little time. I need to go back and convince the students of the need for them joining the rally.

Gopal: Say it before you leave.

Haren: Life on this planet finds many ways to survive in their struggle against the vagaries of nature. We sharpen our fangs and claws, increase our breed, and adapt our bodies to changes. Humans do that, too. But humans are cursed. So the armour would have to be worn on the mind, and not on the body. Otherwise, you would be washed away in these trying times.

Gopal: You always throw puzzles at me.

Haren: It's alright brother. I have no time.

[*He prepares to leave.*]

Gopal: Wait. [*Holds his hand.*] I have no puzzles to offer. I talk straight. I need to arrange food for my family. You said you would help me publish books of songs. You make arrangements. I will sell.

Haren: Then come with me. [*Addresses Debu Bose.*] See you, Debu Babu. Come on, let's go. But you have to do something.

Gopal: What?

Haren: You have to erase that word from your lexicon.

Gopal: O My God!

Khetu: Tell me.

Gopal: I am writing to Kalim about selling our land and house. I am also sending him our address.

Khetu: Selling?

Gopal: We came to this conclusion after discussing with brother.

Khetu: You have come to a conclusion, but have I taken any decision?

Gopal: There you go again! What's the point in keeping that land and the house at this juncture? Think about it. We have property there and here we are starving to death. Does this make sense? Instead, we can use the sales proceeds to do something here. Once we hear from Kalim, either me or brother will go with the relevant documents to settle the matter.

Khetu: You know, you still have an address? But if you lose it, you will become like wild foliage in divided Bangla. You will have no address in this world.

Gopal: We will establish an address here. Padma, tell brother that I have written to Kalim. I am sure he would reply in a few days.

Khetu: That land and that house are mine.

Gopal: See Baba, I am no longer bound by patience and tolerance. If you create problems in this matter.

Padma: Dada, you send that letter. I will try and convince Baba.

Khetu: I will not be convinced. I have nothing but that house.

Gopal: You want to die of starvation here while your house hundreds of miles away keeps rotting.

Khetu: Do you think anybody will survive here? Everybody will perish.

Haren: Kaka, what you made just now is a stand-alone comment.

Gopal: Stop. My father has gone insane. Nobody here can think with a steady mind. I will send that letter.

Khetu: No.

Gopal: Come what may, I will send this letter.

Khetu: No, Gopal.

Gopal: Let's go, Pandit.

Khetu: I had started my fife on a harmonious note. Should it end like this?

Gopal: Come on, Pandit. Let's go.

[*They leave.*]

Khetu: Is this fair, Padma?

[*Padma turns Khetu around and takes him into the room. When she returns, she finds Debu leaving a one rupee note behind.*]

Padma: Babu—

[*Debu was startled.*]

Debu: Yes, I mean—

Padma: What are you doing?

Debu: I am very poor, yet—

Padma: What?

Debu: Your Bouthan was saying that there is a cost to gathering experience. That's why I am leaving this rupee here.

[*He prepares to leave but Padma calls him back.*]

Padma: Babu—

Debu: You see, I have no intentions of being a part of your misery. I don't like to do that.

[*After Debu Bose exits, Padma looks at the broken flower pot. Haru returns. Padma puts an arm around him. Haru says 'Pishi' and begins to cry. Padma cuddles him.*]

— Curtains —

THIRD WAVE: Second Part

[*The same colony house. The door in the middle is open. Haru is lying on a blanket. Swarno is sitting next to him, looking stunned. Padma and Debu come in from outside. Her saree is sopping wet and torn. Padma wraps the saree tightly around herself.*]

Debu: Oh! Look at that slush and rain outside! And then there's a strong wind blowing, that, too, in the winter.

Padma: Babu, I did not notice a drop of tear in the eyes of Mandal's wife.

Debu: You are again thinking about that?

Padma: I cannot forget, babu. She saw her son die in front of her eyes. But how could so easily tell people to dump that body in the jungle just because she didn't have money to cremate him? Do you know what happens in that jungle?

Debu: What?

Padma: Jackals come in the night. Yesterday, jackals tore away the head of Janardan Mali's son.

Debu: What does that mean?

Padma: His son had died. Everyday, about a dozen children die here. It's an epidemic. This place is like hell.

Debu: Don't talk rubbish. The inoculation squad has arrived. After checking that barrack, it will come here. You have to escort them around and show them every room. Gather those who live on the other side in the centre of the field. We have to save the only water tank that this colony has.

Padma: My life seems to be like algae of the Padma during the monsoon.

Debu: Why are you talking nonsense?

Padma: I simply cannot forget, Babu. Being a mother, how could Mandal's wife not cry when her child died? Have our hearts become completely decayed?

Debu: Sit down. You must have looked after them all through the night?

Padma: Yes.

Debu: You should get some sleep after telling all of them about the water tank. The tank has to be taken back to its place in the evening. So we have to be ready for that.

Padma: Ready!

Debu: Yes. There is no other way. Such is the situation here. If the squad takes the tank away, wouldn't this colony be wiped out in three days?

Padma: You think so?

Debu: Yes. I feel frightened in the night. Nobody can be heard crying. Everybody is waiting for the next person to die. I can't take it.

Debu: You see, I had witnessed such a scenario when the big riots had broken out in Kolkata earlier. Death has become a normal way of life here. To be born and to survive are now strange phenomenal.

Padma: Birth!

[*Gopal enters.*]

Gopal: Babu, you?

Debu: Yes.

Gopal: Babu, I keep thinking these days that the Muslims were definitely bad people.

Debu: What do you mean?

Gopal: Kalim was our neighbor in Rupaikandi. I had left my house in his protective custody. I have written many letters to him, but there has been no reply. I think he has changed. It's a case of out of sight, out of mind. Muslims.

Debu: It's just that your letter have not been replied to?

Gopal: I had thought of travelling to Rupaikandi. But I heard the Ansars have moved to Karali. They are creating unrest over Bangla language. It serves them right. They are now going to have an internecine trouble. But, mark my words, they will blame it on Hindus.

Debu: You have no idea how many Muslim boys have perished in this chaos. There have been many strikes in many cities.

Gopal: I don't know, Babu. What purpose would it serve me to know about distant lands when I couldn't settle a home on my own soil?

Debu: Padma, ask the people living in homes along that row to see me. If we lose the water tank...

Gopal: That issue of the tank to be uprooted?

Padma: Alright, Babul.

[*Padma exits.*]

Debu: Yes. We must make an effort.

Gopal: I am not in it.

Debu: Why?

Gopal: What purpose would it serve? We won't find peace.

Debu: But whoever in the colony I speak to about this matter is becoming desperate.

Gopal: I don't believe it. But I am not joining you. Why should I? Such a big grinding machine and we, a handful of humans, are fighting for breath.

Debu: What has happened to you?

Gopal: What do we eat, Babu, what do we eat? Cash is not being doled out. We don't get ration. Besides, there is nothing more to sell. Even the beds have been sold. We just have one blanket in the house.

[*Khetu comes from the left and tries to pass then unobtrusively. Gopal notices him.*]

Gopal: Where arc you off to?

Khetu: I am going to Mandal's house. The weather is inclement today.

Gopal: No, you shall not go.

Khetu: Why?

Gopal: I know where you go.

Khetu: What do you know?

Gopal: Kangalicharan saw you last evening near the lake.

Khetu: Who says?

Gopal: You conceal your face in the darkness of the evening.

Khetu: Give me food then. I have not eaten since yesterday. Have you given me a penny?

Gopal: You—

Khetu: One year ends and another begins, the Sun rises and sinks, but we stay paralysed. I will beg. I will steal.

Gopal: Don't shout. You have lost your self-esteem too.

Khetu: Shut up. Neither the home across the river belongs to Muslims' country, nor the one this side is ours. One who doesn't have a home doesn't have pride.

Gopal: You have gone mad.

Khetu: Yes, I have. We are the weed of a divided Bengal, going around in circles. Haru vomited today.

Gopal: Haru!

Khetu: He fell ill after a runny stomach. We came here to find a home. We got divided into two sides. But there is no home on either sides.

[*Khetu tells.*]

Gopal: Haru! You are not going out now.

Khetu: Don't stop me.

[*He goes away. Gopal stares after him. Debu places an arm on his shoulder. Gopal steps away.*]

Gopal: Babu, we are the dead! We are the dead!

Debu: I heard someone was ill.

[*Goes to Swarno. Swarno was sitting with her face between her knees. She looks up. Debu also walks up to them.*]

Gopal: Why haven't you told us about Haru?

[*Swarno doesn't reply.*]

Debu: His bed is spoiled. We have to burn the blanket.

Gopal: Let's go and get those doctors.

Debu: Let's go.

[*They leave. Swarno tries to listen to something. She then gets up, fetches a glass of water and disappears. A tipsy Mahinder pushes aside a drenched Haren Pandit and enters.*]

Mahinder: *Amar Padma gang re.* Pandit!

Haren: Yes? Mahinder: I am going to sing the song of Lord Shiva. [*Using tune.*] *Saheb rajar hathe...* Wait, let me find the hand-drum. Had Kalim been here, we would have hit it off. I am high-strung today.

Haren: No.

[*Mahinder was moving towards the room. Turns back and returns to Pandit.*]

Mahinder: No showing of mood?

Haren: No. No Lord Shiva. I have work to do.

Mahinder: Sit. [*He sits too.*] Why so many people are gathering outside?

Haren: Haven't you heard that a protest rally is being taken out today? This is a rally to bring about change.

Mahinder: No, I haven't. I drank toddy today. After going without food for two days, I found work as a porter. Then I drank toddy.

Haren: I have no objections if you drink toddy. But you spare me.

Mahinder: Why?

Haren: We are staying without food. The small school has closed down. I will settle everything and get out of this place.

Mahinder: Won't you return home today?

Haren: Home? That home no longer exists. Of course, if I go to the rally. Trouble is bound to erupt today.

[*Suddenly begins to cry.*]

Mahinder: My home that I had so carefully set up is lying devastated today. Ohl How terrible I am! I drank toddy after earning some money! Bou...

[*Swarno eagerly listens to him call out for her, but doesn't reply.*]

Haren: I am sure something is going to happen today. You let me go.

Mahinder: Padma asked me to think. Do we really need to think? Life is a thought. The whole world is a thought.

Haren: I shall be leaving now, alright? [*He turns and gets up.*] We shall talk later. Let me come back, OK?

[*Haren halts near the gate in fear. Mahinder stands in front of him and says—*]

Mahinder: Wait! You are not sensitive to music.

Haren: I mean—

[*Turns around.*]

Mahinder: You can go now. On a rainy day like this, I will sing alone.

[*Haren quickly walks away.*]

Swarno: Haru!

[*Swarno screams. Mahinder is startled.*]

Mahinder: Who?

Swarno: Why isn't he drinking water? Why isn't he making any sound? Is he unconscious! Haru! Haru!

[*The glass falls from her hand.*]

Mahinder: What's this? Don't cry. Crying is an ominous sign. Don't cry.

[*Gopal arrives.*]

Gopal: Come, Babu, into this room.

[*Swarno quickly takes the blanket away and walks to the left of the stage. The doctor arrives followed by Debu. The doctor takes off his raincoat and hands it to Debu. He brings out the stethoscope and walks into the room. The Doctor comes out.*]

Doctor: Hmm.

Debu: [*Eagerly.*] What?

Doctor: One more! He is now beyond us. Burn the bed.

Gopal: Does that mean that...?

Mahinder: Doctor! Doctor, I am sure life is still in him. Please examine properly.

[*Swarno takes a step back. Mahinder grabs the doctor's feet.*]

Doctor: Ah I make way.

Mahinder: That boy has gone to sleep, but life is still inside him.

Debu: Doctor, why don't you look again since they are urging you to do so?

Doctor: Nothing doing. I have become so used to these that nothing moves me anymore. I shall go home now. Let me go.

[*The Doctor moves to a side.*]

Doctor: Spread the room with bleaching powder and burn the bed.

Mahinder: Does this mean that Haru will never return?

[*He moves towards the room. Gopal blocks his path.*]

Gopal: Dada, get a grip on yourself.

Debu: Go near the body and you die too! Gopal, we will have to removed the bed.

Mahinder: Are you taking them away?

Debu: They need to be incinerated.

Mahinder: So much of bedding?

Debu: Repeat use of this bed will spread the disease.

Mahinder: I could have washed it. I had paid a pocket to buy them.

Debu: That's not possible.

Mahinder: I could have sold them.

Debu: Don't talk rubbish.

Gopal: Dada!

Mahinder: No. Something is happening inside me.

[*He moves away. Debu pushes him aside and removes the bed.*]

Doctor: Wasn't anyone nursing the boy? The clothes of the person who was attending on him require to be disinfected.

[*A jolted Gopal look around. He notices Swarno in a corner. Goes near her. Swarno is wiping her nose. Debu comes out of the room. Before exiting, he stops, turns, comes to Mahinder.*]

Debu: Mahinder, let's go outside. We have some work. Come doctor, you are going home. I have to now make all arrangements.

[*The doctor, Debu and Mahinder leave. Swarno was walking towards the centre of the stage. Gopal stops her.*]

Gopal: Bouthan, how can you—

Swarno: They snatch, but why don't they give?

Gopal: Are you a human?

[*Swarno lifts the blanket.*]

Swarno: He's not there anymore. This winter will take away, snatch away. [*She was collapsing, but Gopal holds her.*] They have taken everything that I had but have not given me anything in return. Why?

Gopal: Bouthan!

[*Swarno collapses to the floor. Gopal takes her out of the stage from the left-hand side. Then he returns. He covers his face with his hands and begins to cry. He sits on the dawa. Khetu enters. Dries his wet hair and smokes a bidi. Gopal walks up to him.*]

Gopal: Baba! Did you get some money?

Khetu: Yes. Seeing an old man, they drop some money for me out of sympathy. I got three-and-half annas. I used two paise on bidi and four on puffed rice. Two annas are left. That's why I tell you Gopal, if Bouma and Haru begin to handle the pan together on the roads, there will be more.

Gopal: Give me the two annas. I have to buy medicines.

Khetu: No. Why should I give you my money, my hard-earned money? Anyway, a large crowd has gathered outside. But I am not joining them. It makes no sense.

[*Mahinder comes.*]

Mahinder: They took my Haru with them.

[*Gopal sits down.*]

Khetu: [*Anxiously looks at the room.*] Mahinder, what rubbish are you talking about? I don't like it at all!

[*Mahinder comes to the front of the stage.*]

Mahinder: Whatever was left in the family has been shattered.

[*He sits down.*]

[*A commotion breaks out in the colony. A lot of voices are shouting. The sound of the storm rises. They all look outside with an element of fear in their eyes. Padma rushes in.*]

Padma: Bhai. Bhai letter!

[*She raises her hand high to display the letter.*]

Gopal: Letter!

Padma: Letter! A letter from Pakistan!

[*She tears open the envelope.*]

Padma: A long letter! Read it, Bhai.

[*Gopal takes it.*]

Gopal: Letter!

Padma: The people have gathered outside. There's not much time. Read it quickly.

[*Gopal Stands up and begins to read.*]

Mahinder: Who has written it?

Gopal: Kalimuddi. Kalimuddi Sheikh!...

'Uncle Khetu,
I am replying to your letter after a long time. By the will of Khuda, we are carrying on. I have not been able to sell your house so far. We are witnessing a lot of trouble here. People are opposing the move to do away with the Bangla language. Feroza Nani and other women have dropped their burkhas and hit the streets. They are telling the men that there is no sin in their joining the rallies. They have petitioned the Marhums at the new Karbala in Dhaka. The Madrassa and the three Maktabs in Kajla have closed down. Strikes and protests have become an everyday affair in the town. We are being harassed. Look-outs have been issued. Kiru Sheikh is on the lam. Chacha, the fight for life, language and land has become Bangla's crusade. That's all the news I have about this place.—'

[*Chaotic noises can be heard outside. They look—Mahinder and Gopal are next to each other, on the other side is Padma. Khetu keeps sitting. Gopal resumes reading. Khetu gets up.*]

Khetu: What?

Gopal: —*Bangla re katicho kintu dile-re katibare paro nai.* Write dates in the letters. Thakuma said, she would have her Nati married. Nati?—

Padma: Kalim Dada!

Gopal: Would have her Nati married. The bride will be Lachiman, the daughter of Soleman Khalifa of Kajla. Let us know how all of you are. We will gain new strength from this struggle. I will pray to Allah for all of us. We will win the battle for the Bangla language.

[*The letter slips out of Gopal's hand. Khetu bends down slowly to pick it up. Haren looks away to the exterior of the house.*]

Haren: The rally will start from midnight. They are all... [*He turns and looks at them anxiously. From outside, a noise floats in.*] Why are your eyes fiery?

Khetu: [*Holds the letter close to his chest.*] *Bangla re katicho kintu dile-re katibare paro nai.*

[*The noise outside rises to a crescendo and keeps crashing like waves on the stage.*]

Communication

2

Translator's Note

The play, *Sanko* is one of the longest by Ritwik Ghatak. It was decidedly an onerous task to encapsulate events that took place simultaneously in two Bengals, West Bengal and East Bengal (erstwhile East Pakistan). The events unfold in the aftermath of the Partition of the Indian subcontinent. Colloquial conversation and Bangla dialects used in the erstwhile East Pakistan mark the entire play. Even though Bangladesh, as a country, was not born when this play was written, the word 'Bangladesh' appears in the course of the play on several occasions. In this case, Bangladesh refers to both West Bengal and East Bengal.

There are words in Bangla that cannot be transliterated into English. I have retained the following words: *Dhrupad* (a vocal genre in Hindustani classical music, said to be the oldest, still in use), *Khayal* (a modern genre of classical singing in the northern part of India, as also in Pakistan), *Jamai Babu* (Jamai is for son-in-law and babu is a suffix used as a mark of respect), *Bade Mian* & *Chote Mian* (the big brother and the kid brother, respectively), *Lungi* (a sarong-like cloth worn both in India and Bangladesh by men), *Khuda* (Allah), *Iftar* (the meal eaten by Muslims after sunset during the Ramadan fast period), *Piri* (a square or rectangular wooden plank used on the floor for sitting with legs folded), *Kaviraj* (a traditional practitioner of herbal healing), *Bhai* (a brother and has been used in the script as a suffix to a name, such as *Shankarbhai*), *Da* (a suffix to a name used by Bengalis for anyone who is like an elder brother), *Tanpura* (a four-stringed lute used as accompaniment in Indian music for a drone effect), and *Mahinder* (a pauper who works for food and accommodation in homes in Bangladesh). There are folksongs in the script that couldn't be translated verbatim. Therefore, I have retained them in their original forms with short synopses in English.

FIRST WAVE: First Scene

[*It is the drawing room of a house situated inside a lane in a middle-class Kolkata neighbourhood. To the left of the stage is a simple wooden bed. Behind the bed is a window. There's a door in the middle of the room. The window and the door are shut. To the right is a wooden clothes-rack. A few big trunks are placed atop each other near the rack. A tanpura is hanging from a firm hook on the wall. Books are strewn on a table. Some unfolded clothes are on the rack. Wrapping himself with a shawl, a young man of twenty-five enters the stage from the left of that dark room. He yawns and then spiritedly sings out: 'Utho, jago, mohan pyare'. As the volume of the song rises, screams can be suddenly heard at a distance, as if someone is wounded. The scream that started all of a sudden fades out into a groan. Outside, footsteps can be heard. The young man, curious, opens the door. A thick slice of bright sunlight falls on him. A section of the lane can be seen in that light. A letterbox hangs from the door. Some men, armed with hatchets and other weapons, can be seen running across the lane in front of the door. The young man takes a step down from the door and pulls a person by the hand.*]

Young man: Dasrath!

Dasrath: Let me go. I am going to bathe Goddess Kali with blood today!

Young man: What happened?

Dasrath: Hey, Bhimey, riots have broken out. I have two Muslims cornered. Let me go friend.

[*He dashes away. An elderly, plump man with a shawl around him, who was walking slowly, stops in his tracks.*]

Elderly man: Riots! Riots have broken out in Howrah since last night. Park Circus and this area have been affected since this morning, and it's mayhem in Dhaka. Two Pathans were hiding in our lane. I heard they are armed with sharp daggers. That's why the neighbourhood boys are after them.

Young man: Have they been caught?

Elderlyman: One of them has been caught. The other one is injured and is hiding somewhere.

[*The sound of a truck moving can be heard and then the report of gunfire.*]

Elderly man: God help us!

[*He walks away. The young man shuts the door with a loud bang. He turns around and calls out to someone called 'Sagar' repeatedly while he walks into the house hurriedly. The wind blowing from outside leaves the door slightly ajar. Shots are being fired outside. Then an eerie silence prevails. All of a sudden, it seems somebody is clawing on the window and even banging on the door. The window didn't open but the door did with a noise. Standing unsteadily in the frame of the door is a man wearing pyjamas. Blood oozing from one side of his head has turned his face ghastly. He is not a Pathan. He is a very ordinary young Bengali boy. He enters the room quickly and bolts the door from inside. Tired and running short of breath, he scouts the place. For a moment, he almost collapses to the ground. With fear in his eyes, he tries to gauge the insides of the house from where voices can be heard. Quickly, he reaches behind the boxes that are kept to the right of the room and next to the clothes-stand, and crouches under the clothes hanging from that stand. Then our young man enters the room along with another young man in his vest.*]

Young man: Yes Sagar, Mr Choudhury said two Pathans were hiding in the slums near us.

Sagar: Shankar, do you know what keeps crossing my mind?

Shankar: What?

Sagar: I keep thinking about Dhaka. My brother-in-law came from Dhaka earlier this week. He told me yesterday that he would go back to Dhaka today. He was insisting that I go with him.

Shankar: Although you keep on talking about Bangladesh, you have never been to a village. Besides, you love folk songs so much. Go to Dhaka with Khitish Babu.

Sagar: I don't think my brother-in-law can make it to Dhaka in view of the riots breaking out there. It is unfortunate that my sister Mili and her child are in Dhaka while he is here. I feel sad for my sister.

Shankar: I don't understand why the riots of 1946 would have to emerge in the January of 1950 in Kolkata. Besides, it is really not fair on part of Khitish Babu. This gentleman is not prepared to quit Pakistan.

[*He moves towards the door.*]

Sagar: Where are you going?

Shankar: I am going to Harrison Road to see Khitish Babu.

Sagar: Do you have to get out of the house now?

Shankar: That man must be as despondent as you are. The idea is to bring him here and cheer him up a bit.

Sagar: Look here, shot were fired just a while ago.

Shankar: Not to worry brother. You be happy. 'It's alright' is the only slogan these days.

[*He pulls at the door but is surprised to find it bolted from inside.*]

Shankar: How come?

Sagar: How come what?

Shankar: No. I guess it's alright.

Sagar: Are you shouting slogans?

Shankar: [*Smiles.*] That expression came out spontaneously. In fact, nothing is amiss.

Shankar: Nothing but amnesia. I clearly remember that I had not bolted the door when I went inside the house just a while ago.

Sagar: And now?

Shankar: [*Unbolts the door.*] It is bolted. I thought the bolt was missing, but it is there now.

Sagar: So you remember now?

Shankar: I forced the recall using logic. Since there is a bolt and I was the only one near the door at that point of time, it had to be me who bolted it. Anyway, stay happy brother. I am leaving now.

[*Shankar steps out of the house. Sagar was about to shut the door when Dasrath, wiping his hatchet with a country-made towel, rushes into the room.*]

Dasrath: Sagar Da, put away this hatchet somewhere.

Sagar: What's all this?

Dasrath: The police are after us. As I was finishing one Muslim in the hydrant that is next to Brindavan's shop, I heard the sound of the police car.

[*Choudhury, who was passing the house at that time, got startled and looked at them. Then he enters the room.*]

Choudhury: Dasrath, I was looking for you. What's the scene?

Dasrath: What?

Choudhury: Have the red turbans left?

Dasrath: Yes, they have. But they can come back anytime soon to launch search operations. They have the body.

Choudhury: That means the work has been done.

Dasrath: You bet! Hide this hatchet in your house.

Choudhury: But why?

Dasrath: I am a marked man since the riots of '46. This hatchet is your property because you had bought it.

Choudhury: God save me! Come on, you wanted a hatchet and I bought one for you. There ended my involvement. You own that hatchet now. What use a hatchet has for a lower-division clerk like me!

Dasrath: Your creed is so evil.

Choudhury: Sagar, listen to him now. God save us!

Dasrath: It's not fair that as we will kill by using weapons you have bought, you will return home peacefully to have a merry time. You know Sagar Da, these rats have the backing of the neighbourhood goons. People like these are dangerous!

Choudhury: Mind your language, Dasrath! After all, I am a friend of your elder brother.

Dasrath: I see that you are showing off. After giving me that hatchet in 1946, you had said who else will defend the neighbourhood but the local boys? The riots ended. I had no mind to pursue education following those disturbances. I was not even able to lead a normal life. Facing penury, I met him one day to ask for the price of a pint. You know Sagar Da, what this man had said to me that day? He said, 'you are a hooligan.' And today, I run errands for people who make promises. I know your kind, Choudhury Da, I know your kind.

Choudhury: Is this the way one speaks rubbish? Believe me, I have made Kali Saha to keep his shop still open—only for you.

Dasrath: Why didn't you say that before?

Choudhury: You guys started off the day with those two Pathans.

Dasrath: Choudhury Da, shall I say something?

Choudhury: Yes.

Dasrath: Not two but one. He looked more as a docile Bengali than a Pathan.

Choudhury: Whatever the case may be, you are saying there was one Pathan and not two?

Dasrath: There were two of them. We both saw them from a distance. But as I started converging on them, I found one of them vanishing in the thin air of these lanes. We will go out and find him after the police completes the search operation.

Choudhury: You mean to say he is hiding somewhere in these lanes? God save us!

Dasrath: That's alright. Let's now go and have that foreign liquor. After that, we can launch our own heady search for the other one.

Choudhury: Dasrath, there's blood on your clothes!

Dasrath: Yes. He was bleeding like a soda fountain. Tell me Sagar Da, how much blood a human body can contain?

Choudhury: We will discuss that later. You go and change your clothes. Leave the hatchet here. Sagar, is there a place where we can hide this hatchet?

Sagar: Give it to me.

[*He takes the hatchet and goes inside the house.*]

Dasrath: Sagar Da appears so quiet today. He seems to be engrossed in thoughts.

Choudhury: How does that matter to you? Neither I nor you are into the business of thoughts. He is involved in music and is a man of different tastes.

Dasrath: Is that the reason why he looks a bit off today? By the way, I, too, used to play flute once. I remember playing a great Khambaj piece on the flute.

Choudhury: You better leave now. The police are likely to arrive any moment.

Dasrath: Yes. I need to change.

Choudhury: We will stay in this room.

[*Dasrath leaves. As Choudhury gets up to shut the door after Dasrath, the sound of a speeding motorbike can be heard. Choudhury tries to listen carefully. The sound fades. Probably, the noise was being made by a random truck on the road. Choudhury turns back from the door and stands in the centre of the room. The clothes hanging from the wooden hangers of the stand were moving just a while ago, but not anymore. Choudhury stares into the blank walls of the room, appearing somewhat morose. It seems as if he is looking at something afar. Suddenly, he runs his fingers through the chords of a Tanpura that was in the room. A deep and solemn sound engulfs the room. Sagar enters.*]

Sagar: Choudhury Da!

Choudhury: [*Returns from his thoughts.*] By the way [*he turns around.*] Sagar, did you see that? Dasrath will keep drinking everyday, as long as these riots continue. But brother, I can't afford his liquor every time he wants to drink. I think the neighbours should also contribute.

Sagar: Money!

Choudhury: Correct. It's not my sole responsibility. We have to keep these hooligans happy.

Sagar: Why?

Choudhury: You surprise me. Who will protect us when the Muslims attack? You and I can't do such filthy work.

Sagar: You know, Choudhury Da, my mind was caving in when I saw blood on his clothes, the blood of a fellow human being. I felt worse when he asked how much blood circulates in a human body. The thought must have struck him when the man was sprouting blood while being killed. I hope I don't have to kill anyone ever.

Choudhury: That's the reason why we need to pay them. Muslims are like serpents. They are not exactly human beings. Can you imagine the situation Dhaka is facing now? Your younger sister is also in Dhaka, which is in the grip of a killing-spree. If we don't look after these hooligans here, we will get butchered the same way as in Dhaka. Aren't you going to say anything?

Sagar: How much?

Choudhury: What?

Sagar: How much should I pay?

Choudhury: [*Sheepishly.*] Give ten rupees for the time being.

[*Sagar walks up to the clothes-stand and looks inside the pocket of a shirt. It contained no money. Then he searches the pockets of another shirt and returns with money.*]

Sagar: Take it. [*As Choudhury prepares to leave, Sagar calls out to him.*] Wait. I will come with you. I don't feel like staying alone in this room.

Choudhury: Are you afraid to be alone after hearing about the missing Muslim?

Sagar: No. I feel sad after seeing so much blood. On top of it, I am thinking about my younger sister in Dhaka.

Choudhury: Let's go then. A walk outside will help.

[*Sagar returns to the clothes-stand again. He picked up the shirt from which he had fished out the money. He holds it in his hand and comes back to the centre of the room. Meanwhile, Choudhury steps off the door and into the lane to keep a watch on the road. Sagar can't believe his eyes as he begins to put on the shirt—there's blood on it.*]

Choudhury: [*From outside the door.*] Have you put on a shirt?

Sagar: [*Startled, covers the portion that has blood marks.*] Yes, yes. [*He steps ahead.*] Choudhury Da, you go.

Choudhury: What about you?

Sagar: You go. I am not in the mood to go out anymore.

Choudhury: God save us! I will come back after doing the rounds of the neighbourhood.

[*Choudhury leaves. Sagar stretches his neck out of the door to scout the area. Then he shuts the door. His countenance is calm. Slowly, he looks into the room and disappears inside the house. The stage is empty. The clothes on the stand move a little. Sagar comes back with the hatchet in his hand. He sits on a chair in the middle of the room and keeps the hatchet on a round table. He keeps his arms on his lap.*]

Sagar: [*Speaking calmly.*] Come out from behind the clothes-stand!

[*The clothes suddenly move again. Then silence follows.*]

Sagar: I know you are hiding there. You had bolted the door after entering the room.

[*There was no reply. Sagar leaves the chair, picks up the hatchet and steps ahead.*]

Sagar: I know your exact position. I can see your feet.

[*The feet disappear swiftly.*]

Sagar: The hatchet I hold in my hand has claimed the life of your friend. If I strike you with this... Shall I?

[*A trembling voice from behind the clothes-stand says 'No'.*]

Sagar: Then drop all your weapons.

[*The voice says: 'No weapons'.*]

Sagar: No weapons?

[*Once again the voice says, 'No'.*]

Sagar: Hmm. [*Mulls and then suddenly picks up the hatchet.*] I am going to strike you with this hatchet if you don't come out.

[*As Sagar steps towards the clothes-stand, the boy rushes out. His face, smeared with blood, was looking ghastly. Seeing him in that condition, Sagar shrieks and steps back. Sagar hasn't noticed that the hatchet has slipped out of his hand. From a distance, they look at each other in complete silence. Then, both of them plunge at the hatchet at the same time, pouncing like tigers. Sagar gets the hatchet. The Muslim boy screams and runs towards the door. Sagar turns back. With his back to the door, the Muslim boy looks at Sagar with terror-stricken eyes. Every movement made by Sagar's hands seems to be startling the Muslim boy, as if he is being struck by electricity surges. Sagar lifts the hatchet and the boy recoils. He is sweating and his lips are trembling. He tries to say something, but only a half-mute sound escapes his mouth. Sagar brings the hatchet down slowly and drops it near his feet. The boy keeps looking at Sagar innocently. Sagar runs his fingers through his hair and returns to the chair. A glimmer of mortal hope lights up the face of the Muslim boy. He tries with all his might to grab the hatchet, but fails. Completely exhausted, the boy grazes his back on the door and slowly drops himself into a squat on the floor. Sagar wears a soft smile on his face. The boy, wiping his face, is surprised to see Sagar smile. He smiles back at Sagar.*]

Sagar: Would you have some water? Shall I get some water?

The boy: [*Looks at his hands.*] No.

[*They keep looking at each other fondly.*]

Second Scene

[*The same day, a few hours later. A tired Sagar is lying on his side on the bed. The boy has changed into a fresh, white dhoti. He has a bandage around his head. The boy is picking up his soiled clothes from the floor.*]

Sagar: Keep those clothes on the table.

The boy: [*Keeps the clothes on the table.*] Are we not going to the other room?

Sagar: The interiors of that room can be seen from Choudhury's house. Besides, the windows of that room don't have shutters...What's your name?

The boy: Mohsin. Mohammad Mohsin. When is your friend returning?

Sagar: Friend?

Mohsin: I am talking about Shankar.

Sagar: Shankar is a cousin from my mother's side. Anyway, were you not aware that this neighbourhood is a predominantly Hindu area? Or, did you not have any information about riots breaking out?

Mohsin: I had no information at all. Neither was I aware of this being a Hindu area, nor of the riots. I landed in Kolkata this morning.

Sagar: Who was the other boy?

Mohsin: Him? He was my friend. We both went to the Dhaka University.

Sagar: Why have you come to Kolkata?

Mohsin: I had missed the All-India Music Conference. But I came to know that all the masters are in

Kolkata now. I thought I would try my luck at some of the known musical gatherings here.

Sagar: Music?

Mohsin: Yes. Rashid had a fantastic voice. Her mother will be completely devastated when she gets to hear the news of her son's death.

Sagar: Is your mother still alive?

Mohsin: Yes. I also have my father and a sister. My father is the headmaster of a village school. Do you sing as well? [*He goes near the tanpura and strums it.*] You might know my father. He used to play alongside sitarist Bhagwan in Dhaka. His name is Taslim Mia Pakhwaji.

Sagar: Yes, I have heard of him. Does he still play?

Mohsin: No. He is too old. He stays in his village these days and spends time researching history. The focus of his research is Bengalis and the Bangla language. Your name is Sagar, right? So strange!

Sagar: You mean the name?

Mohsin: No. I am talking about a coincidence. I had met another Sagar in 1946 in somewhat similar Situations in Kolkata itself. Sagar is not a common name. Isn't it?

Sagar: Do you sing?

Mohsin: A little.

Sagar: Khayal?

Mohsin: Khayal and Dhrupad as well. I took lessons in Dhrupad at the school of Banke Maharaj.

Sagar: Dasrath and the other goons will start searching the neighbourhood anytime soon. What are you going to do?

Mohsin: I have you.

Sagar: That's what I was thinking. You live in a village, right?

Mohsin: My parents live in a village. It is not exactly a village. You can call it a small, district town, muffaswal. We spend our holidays with our parents.

Sagar: We?

Mohsin: Me and my sister. She goes to a college in Dhaka.

Sagar: Bangladesh is a beautiful place, isn't it?

Mohsin: Yes. It is very beautiful.

Sagar: you stay in a village…you know I have never been to a real Bangladesh village.

Mohsin: You would have been happy if you would have seen it.

Sagar: Every time I think of Bangladesh, I begin to imagine its many hues. But all that is only imagination. I have never travelled outside Kolkata in any way. That's probably why I become so restless when I think of Bangladesh.

Mohsin: Maybe.

Sagar: Do you know the folksongs of the villages? Or have you not ever tried to sing them?

Mohsin: It is impossible not to sing them. The melodies of the songs of Bangladesh are so diverse and varied! One has no idea about the kind of melodies and harmonies that sweep our rivers, croplands and tree-lines. I just couldn't sing them all!

Sagar: [*Brings the tanpura.*] Sing a song, please.

Mohsin: Here?

Sagar: Why not?

Mohsin: You know, I don't have a practiced voice. It's still raw.

Sagar: Never mind. I am with you.

Mohsin: Yes. I know you are with me. Just see whether you like this song or not. I am not very conversant with this song though. One day, I was on a boat, crossing the Meghna to reach Bhairavbazar. The Meghna was restless and wavy that night. In the dark, I could see the waves crowned by white froth. The boat was swaying. The journey became monotonous at one point since we were sailing for a long period of time without a break. All of a sudden, the stretched melody of a song began to reach me from a distance. The melody of that voice seemed to be sweeping across rivers to fill up the empty skies. That song was from a bygone era written by a bard. Since I was not able to understand the whole song, I filled up the gaps myself. For ages, songs like these have woven together in colourful patterns the aspirations of my countrymen. The song sung by an unknown boatman was in perfect harmony with the state of my mind that night on the Meghna. Sitting here, I cannot properly express those feelings. Never mind, you can strum up a tune. I will sing.

[*Pacing around as he speaks, Mohsin comes to the middle of the room and stands there with his back to Sagar. He looks for a tune. Sagar begins to caress the strings of the tanpura. Mohsin finds the tune, turns around and starts to sing—*]

Mohsin: *Naiya bhai! Sujon naiya re!*
[Ami] dariyar kul pailam na.
Kalo megh shanjh korache, agey jani na.
Kul khunji te byakul hoichi, hodish bujhi na.

Kunchbaran konyakhan tar meghboron kesh,
Dudhboron kontha lo tor noyonlobhon besh,
[Mone-r] Agol khuila pagol hoichi, nagal paichi na.
Aj gogon-e diyae gherey, dik korey andhar.
Dil-er majhe dukhho bhore, chaipa ashey bhar,
[Amar] Chokh-er bati nibhlo aji, dik je dekhi na.
[Ami] Dibaratro marchi chokro, disha pachi na.
Kul pailam na.

(My brother boatman, I have not been able to find the shores. Black clouds are clotting and I have no direction to follow. The river is so dark and beautiful. I have unveiled my heart to be restless, but I still can't find the shores. The light in my eyes is dimming and I can't see my destination as I go around in circles.)

[*Sagar had also started to sing the song along with Mohsin. Feeling shy, he stops. Mohsin smiles.*]

Mohsin: You have a nice voice. Want to learn this song?

Sagar: Yes.

Mohsin: Sing along with me, then. [*Makes Sagar sit by his side.*] *Naiya bhai! Sujon naiya re!... Kul pailam na.* Yes, that's exactly the turn. But don't make it classical. Just get a grip on the tune. Yes, there you are! Good!

[*In excitement, Mohsin brings himself close to where Sagar was sitting. As they sing, they hear the door being knocked. Alarmed, Mohsin stands up quickly. Sagar, too, is startled. Mohsin returns to his old hiding place behind the boxes. Sagar opens the door very carefully. Enters Shankar and Khitish Babu. Khitish Babu is a jovial person. Shankar comes straight to the table.*]

Khitish: Hello, my legal broher! Busy with music?

Sagar: Yes.

Khitish: After Nero, it's you.

[*Sagar walks up to shut the door.*]

Shankar: Don't shut the door. There's mail in the letterbox. [*Shankar picks an envelope out of the letterbox that is attached to the door. Looks at it and says—*] It's yours. [*He gives it to Sagar. Sagar tries to open the envelope and Shankar goes to shut the door.*] You should have been more careful.

Sagar: What?

Shankar: Everybody around could hear the two of you sing. Not just this, the clothes of that boy are scattered all over the place in the drawing room. Are you out of your mind?

Khitish: What's the matter?

Shankar: Hello, where are you? It's alright. You can come out. Don't stay in that room because it has open windows.

Sagar: He is not in that room.

Shankar: I am so satisfied.

Khitish: What's the matter, boys? Lift that veil of secrecy.

Shankar: Khitish Babu, a Muslim boy was chased into our lane this morning. I was certain at that time – I haven't grown too old to lose memory – that the door was not bolted from inside.

Sagar: Mohsin.

Khitish: Mohsin.

Shankar: Of course, Mohsin! Where are you Mohsin? Are you hiding behind the boxes? Come out brother. Let's get to know each other better.

[*Mohsin comes out. Shankar watches.*]

Sagar: Jamai Babu, Mohsin belongs to Dhaka, the same place you have come from.

Shankar: You have a very nice voice.

Mohsin: Were you listening?

Shankar: Didn't get much chance to listen to your song. I knocked on the door the moment I heard some sound.

Khitish: Poor chap. How would he get out of this neighbourhood?

Shankar: Don't worry. We will make arrangements in the evening. But [*suddenly he grabs a corner of Mohsin's dhoti and addresses Sagar.*] you rascal, you have been very generous in giving my only clean dhoti to him. What am I going to wear now?

Sagar: Aw, come on. Get real. But what kept you for so long?

Shankar: I was in the clutches of Khitish Babu. First, he perched himself on the hotel bed, wagged his tail, and drank a dozen cups of tea. Then he went for a bath. I kept sitting in the room, listening to his tongue flossing and off-key singing. Thereafter, we went out but he stopped his journey near the Park Circus playground.

Khitish: When this brother-in-law of mine talks, it seems as though he owns all the finest perceptions in the world. But, what is becoming increasingly clear is that, he is turning into a slow and old philosopher. A bachelor judge in our Dhaka court and he share striking similarities.

Shankar: Alright. Get the affidavit done.

Khitish: What?

Shankar: I knew from the very beginning what he has in mind ever since he started describing the good qualities of his cousin sister to me on the way. No problem. Get an affidavit done by her.

Khitish: What affidavit?

Shankar: Alright. Let me say. But you can't file a case later for any breach of contract. I am saying this without prejudice. Get an affidavit done by that girl. If we have children, the responsibility will be hers.

Khitish: O God! What are you saying?

Shankar: I will make a small correction. The responsibility to raise them will be her. My responsibility ends at being just a husband. Have you read Sukumar Ray?

Khitish: Why?

Shankar: It is the same old story of Baburam, the snake charmer. In Kolkata, these days, thousands and thousands of unmarried young men have a fascination for playing with snakes, the kind that do not bite, or raise their hoods, or even hiss. Or else, can we afford a luxury like marriage in these trying times? And yes, do not deliberately forget to make that lady declare her right age in the affidavit. I know what would happen later when the ruse of her being a minor would be used.

Khitish: What I can make out from your words is that even your bones have gone soft. All you need is the warmth of a caring face.

Shankar: Dada, you need not be profane.

Sagar: Let's have lunch. I am famished.

Shankar: Khitish Babu, why only bones, even the marrows have softened up. What you did was just a tap to figure out the condition. A steady flow of deep sighs escapes from my bosom when I hear about girls. How long can I keep the tumult inside me on a leash all by myself while the night draws long?

Sagar: What's all this, Shankar? Mohsin hasn't eaten anything yet.

Shankar: Oh! Alright. Haji Mohammad Mohsin, let's go and sup. I am taking him with me. You guys can follow. Well, Mohsin, let me drill this into your head. You are not Mohsin. You are my brother-in-law's kid brother Sachin.

Mohsin: Whose? His?

Khitish: My kid brother Sachin? Look here, Shankar. Can't he be your first cousin twice removed or second cousin thrice removed, or something like that?

Shankar: No, that's not possible. Come, Sachin Da.

[*Collecting the clothes that were lying in a pile on the table, Shankar puts them away to a corner of the room, and leaves with Sachin.*]

Sagar: He is a rascal.

Khitish: Yes, he is a happy-go-lucky rascal. His sense of humour hasn't left him. He is truly a nice young man.

Sagar: Any news of Mili?

Khitish: I haven't received the morning mail. Of course, I went out early.

Sagar: Where had you been all this while?

Khitish: I spend about a couple of hours at the Park Circus ground. You have no idea what I saw there.

Sagar: I guess there were many people.

Khitish: Yes. Those who have lost their homes and much more have been arriving there from different places since last night.

Sagar: It was quite cold last night.

Khitish: All through the night they arrived. Thousands and thousands of women and children in tattered clothes walked into the empty ground and settled under the Royal Poinciana and Flame trees. Many women were lying next to the park fencing on the sidewalks, clutching their torn burkhas and whatever else they could salvage from the mayhem. They were not sleeping. They were shaking. Their eyes looked subdued and mirrored despair; their lips blue from the overnight dew. Why these things happen, Sagar? Why?

Sagar: Why?

Khitish: This is not right. I was taking rounds of the park to watch them. The relief being provided by neighbourhoods is not adequate. I joined the local people in distributing relief to those who have lost everything. The situation was constantly reminding me of Dhaka. What if similar fate awaits Mili and our child? Relief may or may not reach them. What if they are no longer... I am going for lunch, Sagar.

[*Khitish leaves and Sagar was about to follow him when he remembered the letter he had received. As he was set to pick up the letter from the table, there was a knock on the door. He closed the door to the interior of the house and opened the main door. He found a tipsy Dasrath and Choudhury standing at the threshold.*]

Choudhury: It is late afternoon and time for you to leave me, Dasrath.

Dasrath: No way. This search must be done with a heady tenor.

Choudhury: But why are you at Sagar's place? Neither is he here, nor has he been hidden by Sagar.

Dasrath: You can never tell. Our minds can betray us. You think I feel happy after killing them? That is not the case with me, Dada. I rush to kill, come back to cry in my own sob-story, and then rush back again.

Choudhury: I have to go now.

Dasrath: [*Dasrath doesn't let him go. He pulls Chouhdury into the room.*] I could hear a song being sung in Sagar Da's room a while ago. As there is a curfew outside, it would be great to listen to songs inside this house.

Choudhury: You go ahead and listen. I am not interested.

Dasrath: A Pathan has vanished into this neighbourhood. His friend, probably, was not a Pathan. On the one hand, the evening is growing darker. On the other, you are planning to go home happily. You have some guts!

Choudhury: That's the reason why I am telling you, Dasrath. God save us! Start your search operation, if you must.

[*Shankar enters the room.*]

Shankar: Sagar, everybody has now settled for lunch. I see! You are out to serve the nation. Have you got your quarry?

Dasrath: No, Shankar Da. I suffered a fifty percent loss. I am still looking for the other one.

Shankar: Alright. Come Sagar, let's go and have lunch. See you soon, Choudhury Da.

[*They leave.*]

Choudhury: You heard that he hasn't had his lunch yet. Let's go and scout the other end of the lane before it gets too dark.

Dasrath: Let's listen to a song first. What kind of a person are you? Rabindranath Tagore had said one who doesn't like music can kill.

Choudhury: Is that so? In that case, don't listen to any song until you find the other Pathan. I have invested a lot.

Dasrath: Let's go. Sagar Da, by chance, has anybody taken shelter in your house?

Sagar: Why?

Dasrath: I thought I heard two voices. What a lovely song… Consigning a body to the river or something

Choudhury: Don't you have any sense? God save us. Sagar is my partner in funding your liquor and you think he is going to provide shelter to a Muslim?

Dasrath: You have a point. But it is also likely that Sagar Da has shown mercy and is planning to give that Muslim guy fresh clothes so that he can slip away unnoticed. Sorry, Sagar Da. Please do not mind. I know you well. You are not the kind who would do so. Your hatred for Muslims is genuine

Choudhury: Besides, his younger sister is in Pakistan. God forbid, nothing happens to them in Dhaka. Anything can go wrong during the riots. I guess you haven't yet received any information about your sister. See you, Sagar.

Dasrath: We will listen to a song after we come back.

[*Dasrath is unsteady on his feet as he tries to leave. Choudhury holds him and takes him out. Sagar opens the envelope. His face turns pale after he reads just one line. His eyes begin to reflect a sense of helplessness. He drops the envelope on the table. Then he grabs the edge of the table forcefully. Choudhury notices him from outside. He walks into the room, alone.*]

Choudhury: What happened?

Sagar: A letter from my sister Mili, from Dhaka.

[*Choudhury looks at Sagar and then returns to Dasrath.*]

Choudhury: Dasrath, you go. I will join you soon.

Dasrath: Why? You have plans to listen to songs alone?

Choudhury: No. I need to speak to him.

Dasrath: I see. You are going to have a private conversation with him. Some money matters, I am sure. Very well. I am not going to take a slice out of your business. After all, you have been there, done that. I will be waiting for you in front of Bhimey's house. If I get my prey tonight, you have to buy me hashish.

[*Dasrath leaves. Choudhury shuts the door and walks up to Sagar who, by that time, had begun reading the letter again.*]

Choudhury: What has she written? Is she alright?

Sagar: [*Stops reading the letter.*] Dhaka's atmosphere is intolerable. Mili is all alone there. Her every moment is terror-stricken. She wants me to tell my brother-in-law that he should leave for Dhaka immediately. A letter from her may reach him after he returns to the hotel. The situation in Dhaka has made even a courageous girl like Mili to live in a state of fright. She can't sleep in the night. Dhaka has been burning over the past few days. She may have to leave home with whatever she can in order to save herself. And then, she has her child. What's going to happen, Choudhury Da?

Choudhury: You first go and eat. Already it is too late for lunching. If you don't eat now, you will suffer from excess bile secretion. On top of it, all these hassle. Let me go and organize the search operation. This is really a serious matter.

Sagar: Choudhury Da, the situation in Dhaka is affecting my mind. What would happen to Mili? Perhaps, she is already—

Choudhury: We will sit down and discuss the matter later. Now you shut the door and go for lunch.

[*Choudhury leaves. Sagar shuts the door and starts reading the letter again. He appears shocked as he reads. Shankar enters.*]

Shankar: Has Dasrath left? Is the door shut? Come. [*Mohsin and Khitish Babu enter.*] Didn't I warn you Sachin to crouch when you pass that window? Why don't you listen to me?

[*The moment Sagar saw them come, he hid the letter. He now walks towards the interior of the house, looking completely rudderless.*]

Khitish: Shankar, somewhere deep inside, I do have this feeling that a letter has come from Dhaka. Let me return to the hotel.

Shankar: Not just you, Sachin would also have to leave.

Khitish: I am becoming increasingly restless by the moment. The work at the High Court is taking too long to be completed. It's a strange situation. The zamindar is here, his documents have to be handed over to him here, but his property is in Pakistan.

Sagar: [*He was listening.*] If anything happens to Mili, I will die. My parents and my elder brother are no more. Mili is the only one now whom I can call family.

Shankar: Had she been in danger, she would have definitely found a way to write to us.

Khitish: Still, an element of uncertainty remains. There is no male member in her house in Dhaka at the moment.

Shankar: In spite of all this trouble, you would not quit Dhaka.

Khitish: Bangla belongs to Bengalis. I don't accept such narrow-minded demographical partitions.

Mohsin: This is exactly what my father says. We are Bengalis first. Everything else can follow.

Sagar: I will lose my senses if something happens to Mili.

Shankar: Go and eat. [*Sagar leaves.*] Sit down, Khitish Babu.

Khitish: But for how long?

[*He sits.*]

Shankar: Alright. Don't be so impatient. Dasrath will pass our house to go to the other side of the lane. After that, we will exit the neighbourhood by using the road next to the market. [*He strums the tanpura.*] The charm of melody is so all-pervading that it helps calm down even a rough man like me.

Mohsin: Yes?

Shankar: Would you like to sing? I can't sing but melodies and tunes keep reverberating in my heart. Khitish Babu?

Khitish: What?

Shankar: Shall we?

Khitish: Alright.

Shankar: Come on Sachin, start. Sing the song what you were teaching Sagar, that *Dariyai kul na pai... hai re amar mon-er kotha*—What are you thinking about?

Mohsin: No, nothing.

Shankar: Weren't you?

Mohsin: [*Smiles softly.*] I was thinking about a strange connection. I was in Kolkata for the first time—about four or five years ago. I couldn't take a tour of the city because I was stuck in Chitpur due to the riots, like what has happened to me this time. One day, when the riots subsided a little, I took a tram to Tollygunge to see a friend. I suddenly started liking the city and got off somewhere on the way, probably at the Rashbehari crossing. I would have been killed that day had it not been for another young man. The name Sagar is not common, isn't it?

Shankar: No.

Mohsin: His name was also Sagar. I would never forget him.

Shankar: Won't you sing?

Mohsin: Give me a start.

[*Calmly and oblivious to his surroundings, Mohsin begins to sing – 'Dariyai kul pailam na'. Continuing to sing, he comes near the table and sits on it. Sagar walks into the room, wiping his hands with a towel and perches on the boxes. Shankar gets up, leaving the tanpura, and walks up to a corner of the room. He picks up the discarded clothes of Mohsin and takes out a few small bills and some money from the pocket of the shirt with blood stains. He looks at Mohsin and keeps the money on the bed. As he prepares to leave the room with the chits, he signals to Sagar to use the tanpura. Sagar picks it up. Khitish Babu is lying on the bed. Mohsin continues to sing. Unmindfully, Sagar opens the window to the left. He brings out the letter and reads. Contoured spasms of seeming hatred mark his face. He is looking at Mohsin in a strange manner, as if a deadly serpent is eyeing its prey. He hears a sudden noise and looks outside. His eyes seem to be aflame. He looks at Mohsin again begins to sing loudly, so much so that Mohsin is taken aback. Sagar keeps on singing. Encouraged, Mohsin joins in too. A somber chorus breaks out. All of a sudden, the alarmed face of Choudhury can be seen outside the window. The door violently banged thrice. Shankar, who was coming into the room, stopped in his tracks, numbed. Khitish Babu jumps up on the bed. Sachin, who had raised her voice to a higher octave, suddenly becomes silent. Mohsin takes a step towards Sagar. Palpable fear can be seen on his face.*]

Mohsin: You are with me!

[*Sagar opens the door brusquely. Dasrath runs in. With a trembling hand, Sagar points at Mohsin. Dasrath pounces on Mohsin like a hungry feline and drags him out of the house.*]

Mohsin: [*As if not in his senses, keeps on saying.*] Are you with me? You are with me!

[*Mohsin comes back to his senses after he is dragged out of the room. He screams out for Sagar. Choudhury and Dasrath take him away along the lane to the left. His terrifying screams for help begin to fade out, as if the flames of a burning earthen lamp are spiraling down to death. With his eyes shut, Sagar stands in the middle of the room. Emitting a bestial scream, Shankar sits on the bed. Overcome by maddening rage, Khitish Babu rushes to Sagar and tries to throttle him.*]

Khitish: What have you done, you beast? What have you done?

[*Sagar slowly drops the letter to the floor.*]

Sagar: I am sure Mili is not alive any longer. Sagar has not killed Mohsin. He can't. I will kill anyone who says that. I am a Hindu and I have exacted revenge for the crimes Muslims have committed against thousands and thousands of Hindus.

[*Khitish was reading the letter.*]

Khitish: [*Shouting.*] Nothing has happened to Mili. She is worried and wants me to be with her now. Sagar, how are you going to live henceforth with what you have done? How do you expect me to treat you as a human being? You, rascal.

Sagar: Don't think about me. Consider me whatever you may.

[*Sagar collapses on the floor in a heap. Shankar picks up a piece of paper from the chits that were kept on the bed. Outside, the evening is deepening. Shankar reads out from that piece of paper with an unaffected voice...*]

Shankar: Mohammad Mohsin, c/o Taslim Ali Mian: M.A. Headmaster: Singhasan High School. Village: Singhasan... Mohsin! Singhasan.

[*Outside, Mohsin's disembodied voice can still be heard renting the air. A soft breeze seems to be blowing, rustling up the leaves of the trees. The curtain drops.*]

— Darkness —

Third Scene

[*It's the same old room with minor cosmetic changes. The clothes-stand, now placed along the rear wall and in front of the window, is facing the audience. The bed has been moved to the right. A cover has been placed on the table and a curtain hangs from the door. Sagar is standing exactly where Shankar was in the previous scene. He has a piece of paper in his hand.*]

Sagar: [*Reads.*] Singhasan! Oh!

[*He covers his face with his hands and sits down. Shankar comes in, looking elated.*]

Shankar: Sagar, The United Front has got absolute majority. I heard it on radio in the morning.

Sagar: [*Raises his face.*] Have they?

Shankar: Of course! Hey, won't you get ready? Khitish Babu will arrive anytime soon. I have to take him to auntie in Serampore today itself.

Sagar: You go to auntie's place with Jamai Babu.

Shankar: Come on! It was hard to get leave from office. I could manage just a small window of opportunity to find some free time from the work of the Organisation that I am immersed in. One of these days, we need to go for an outing away from Kolkata.

Sagar: But Shankar, you do realize that this—

Shankar: Singhasan. Yes, I know. I have been hearing this name for the past four years and I realise what you are trying to say.

Sagar: I can't go, Shankar.

Shankar: Forget all that. Is there a limit to what people did in Kolkata during the riots? There is a reason why I have entered politics. I have been through so much! From time to time, the beast in us wakes up.

Sagar: It's not from time to time. Shankar, you know that I keep losing sleep. I have also lost appetite. In fact, I don't feel like talking to anyone these days. All I can hear is: *Dariyai kul pailam na...*

Shankar: You will not find the shores, at least of filthy rivers. Forget it. But the fallout has been positive.

Sagar: What?

Shankar: These riots have at least put an end to the vested interests our political bosses had been pursuing over the past sixty years. Slicing up of the country after a terrible bloodbath now makes us realise where our umbilical cord lies. We won't make that mistake again. We have been vaccinated against all these evils.

Sagar: And I am its price!

Shankar: Let's go now.

Sagar: Shankar, I am at a loss for words to make you realise. I can see that look of disbelief in your eyes, too. It is true, nevertheless, that I didn't mean to do what I did that day. All of sudden, I lost my bearing and found myself in the grip of uncontrollable rage. Then I saw him being dragged away. I heard him scream. His blood-curling screams kept spiraling in the air before fading into the darkness. But his screams keep coming back to haunt me every moment of my existence. Should I change my clothes now?

Shankar: Yes.

[*Sagar steps towards the interior of the house. All of a sudden, he begins to cry profusely and sits on the floor. Shankar keeps looking at him, without moving.*]

Shankar: I would rather go and have a bath.

[*Slowly, Shankar walks out. Sagar gets up, wipes his nose. Choudhury, who was hurrying across the house, notices Sagar and walks in.*]

Choudhury: Sagar, I have been looking for you everywhere. Whenever I come to your house, I find the door locked from outside. Once in a while I meet Shankar who tells me that you are not at home. What's so important that it is keeping you away from home these days?

Sagar: Why?

Choudhury: What do you mean?

Sagar: Why do you look for me?

Choudhury: Just well-being that makes me look for you.

Sagar: What are you doing these days?

Choudhury: Don't ask me! Since morning, I have been moving around in the neighbourhood. Don't tell anyone. I don't know what to do.

Sagar: What's wrong?

Choudhury: You know my daughter, Roma.

Sagar: Yes.

Choudhury: Some local boys are after her. What to say! Instead of being a trump card, that Dasrath has turned out to be a snake up my sleeve. On and off, they are seen near my house. They even whistle at my daughter. Worse is, Roma's hand was grabbed at the mouth of the lane yesterday and she was threatened with a knife. Being the kind of girl that she is, Roma managed to free herself.

Sagar: Who are you talking about?

Choudhury: Who else but that Dasrath. I have packed her off today to her maternal uncle's place in Enreda.

Whether she is able to continue her studies from there or not—at least her life will be spared.

Sagar: Why have you come to me?

Choudhury: Come on. You are a jewel of the neighbourhood. I am out on the streets looking for that creep Dasrath. Until recently, he was snatching ornaments from girls or proposing to them in other areas. Now he has begun to peddle his dirty trade into our own neighbourhood. Come to think of it, he targeted me as his first customer! I am not letting him go so easily even if it is at the cost of losing my job. At the same time, I am scared to say tough words to him. I get to hear that he has used the turmoil of the riots to buy a sten gun and other weapons from the Kolay Market. All his misdeeds have the backing of the big shots. He was already visiting the whorehouses. That's not important. What is of concern is that, now he is targeting women from decent homes. Even the police are allowing them a long rope. I am given to understand that specimens like Dasrath are a great help during elections. God save us!

Sagar: The inheritors of riots!

Choudhury: That's not fully true. He belonged to a decent family. At some point of time in the past, he was pursuing education, too. Gradually, he fell off the path and became a beast. This is of great concern. Riots can cause irreparable damage to society and make you believe your own self. I wasn't myself at that time. Consider your own case. Do you remember that you had handed over that

Muslim boy to us even though you had provided him shelter in your own house?

Sagar: [*Brusquely.*] Yes. Yes. I remember.

Choudhury: But you don't drink to forget that incident, right?

Sagar: I would have committed suicide, but it was not possible due to Shankar. Choudhury Da, may I say something?

Choudhury: Of course you may.

Sagar: I can't take it any longer.

Choudhury: What?

Sagar: Dasarath might have killed Mohsin, but—

Choudhury: Who is Mohsin?

Sagar: That boy who took shelter in my house. Even though I tried my best, I cannot dismiss the incident from my memory. I have stopped singing. I cannot sing anymore. With each passing day, my guilt feeling is getting the better of me and that too at a time when one Bangla's rights to be free is coming close to fruition.

Choudhury: What guilt are you talking about? What are you saying? You think everything has changed just because Pakistan League has lost in the elections and some people are rooting for Bangladesh? You think everybody is as honest and truthful as they seem to be? Come on, brother. Muslims will be Muslims. They are like snakes. You cannot trust that race, and you think you cannot bear the burden of being responsible for a Muslim's death? You are being naïve. What you have done deserves blessings.

[*Sagar looks at Choudhury with disbelief. Dasrath can be seen crossing the house.*]

Choudhury: Dasrath! Hey Dasrath!

[*Dasrath comes near the door, looking tense.*]

Dasrath: What?

Choudhury: I was looking for you.

Dasrath: I am sorry that I misbehaved with your daughter. I swear I was so inebriated that I could not recognize her at first. The moment I did, I let her go. The remnants of my loyalty for you still remain.

Choudhury: That doesn't mean you would not spare even decent girls.

Dasrath: Of course. But it was a mistake on my part to trouble your daughter. I saw you sending her off to Enreda this morning. That was a wise move. Her life would have been spoiled has she remained in this rotting city.

Choudhury: Dasrath, what are you doing to yourself? It's a pity that you have brought yourself to such a pass. I hear that you are hiring cabs in the night to travel around in the city.

Dasrath: I do a lot of things. After all, people like you had initiated me to the life I am leading now

Choudhury: People like us?

Dasrath: Of course, people like you. You have used the riots—

Choudhury: Look at him! Finally, I am responsible for your misdeeds. You have chosen your own path. I only got the work done.

Dasrath: Now let me do some work of my own. You get lost from here. I have things to discuss with Sagar Da.

Choudhury: Great!

Dasrath: One more dialogue and the dagger will be unsheathed. Just disappear.

[*Grimacing, Choudhury brusquely shakes the outer fold of his dhoti and leaves. Sagar keeps sitting quietly. Dasrath behaves in an unusual manner. He shuts the door, turns back and looks at Sagar.*]

Sagar Da: [*Unmindfully.*] Yes?

Dasrath: You all are well-read people. I want to know about something from you.

Sagar: [*All of a sudden.*] Choudhury is a beast! He is a lethal snake.

Dasrath: Yes. He is venomous. Not just him, his entire creed is like that. They are such terrible lower class people.

[*Silence prevails for a few moments. Dasrath walks towards the interior of the house.*]

Dasrath: Is Shankar Da home?

Sagar: He is having a bath.

Dasrath: Please tell me, Sagar Da.

Sagar: What?

Dasrath: [*Dasrath sits next to Sagar.*] Nothing much, Sagar Da. I only want to know why did this happen?

Sagar: Which one?

Dasrath: Look at me, Bhimey and our ilk. After 1946, everybody around started saying that there was no greater a deed than killing a fellow human being. Those of us who began to kill were being held and held in high esteem. We got hooked to killing. An old man used to sell goat milk in the neighbourhood. Every morning we could hear the chimes of the small silver bell that hung from the neck of the goat. He had been selling milk for twenty years. He used to believe that nobody would kill him ever, with or without riots. One day, in the small hours, I heard the bell chime. I grabbed the hatchet that was given to me by the neighbourhood big-shots and tip-toed out of my house.

[*Combing his hair, Shankar arrives.*]

Sagar: Then?

Dasrath: I turned an intersection and found him. I held him by his flowing beard. He looked at me and said: 'Dasrath, you?' Those were his last words. I sliced his windpipe in one swift strike. As I tried to run away, my feet got entangled in the rope that the goat was leashed to. The goat had begun to bleat. Sagar Da, I returned home and began to throw up and cry. But then, people were deferring to me, worshipping me. That did not stop me from crying. I have killed so many people. I lost count after 168. [*Begins to cry.*] I have become restless ever since and keep running around to find peace of mind. I need to be intoxicated in some way or the other to forget the faces of those I have killed. Everyday, I need newer vices to keep my blood boiling. It's become like a disease. Poison is running through my veins. The doctor has said that it is a dirty disease that leads to a painful death. This disease wears away limbs and some other parts of the body. I am gone! [*He controls himself.*] I am not going to live. I don't wish to live anymore although I know that I have to commit a new crime everyday as long as I exist. Yet, I cannot but ask you and Shankar Da a question. I am only twenty-four. Couldn't I have had a different life? [*He leaves an oblivious Sagar alone and rushes to Shankar.*] Why did this happen to me? Why? Shankar Da, please answer.

Shankar: Are you taking medicines as prescribed by the doctor?

Dasrath: No.

Shankar: No money?

Dasrath: I care a damn about money. Medicines can't mitigate that pain.

Shankar: Don't be mushy. Have your medicines and take injections. Diseases such as these can be medically cured now. The medical science has made impressive progress.

[*Khitish enters with a bag in his hand.*]

Khitish: What treatment are you talking about?

Dasrath: [*Calms down upon seeing Khitish.*] I will leave now, Shankar Da. I have understood what you have said.

Shankar: Yes. We live, feel pain, and then we metamorphose into a new being. Death is not a solution, for death doesn't benefit anyone. There is a different path for penance. Dasrath, it's alright. After all, it's alright.

[*Dasrath leaves.*]

Khitish: Hey you, our political expert. You have been delivering grandiose speeches on conscience. Now salute.

Shankar: What do you mean?

Khitish: I am your leader. I am we. It means, East Bengal.

Shankar: Yes. Definitely!

Khitish: Didn't I tell you that I am not going to move an inch from here? You have to know that the soil on which you exist is the one you have used to grow. There's no other way. This, however, is the first step. There are many more steps to climb.

Shankar: I can make out from your appearance that you haven't had the time to bathe or eat. We can leave for Serampore after you wash up.

Khitish: Your wish is my command, comrade Lenin. Now tell me my legal brother, why are you sporting a face like that of the Asian Seabass fish?

Sagar: [*With a forced smile.*] No, No!

Khitish: I will take you along with me to Dhaka this time. Or else, Mili would not let me into the house.

Shankar: For the time being, please go for a shower. You spend too much of meaningless time.

Khitish: Sure, my master.

Shankar: Did you hear what Dasrath had to say?

Sagar: Yes.

Shankar: No matter the disease, he would live. One day, he would forget his past and be of aid to humanity.

Sagar: Shankar, I want to live, too. I will go to Pakistan.

Shankar: Why not?

Sagar: I will visit Singhasan!

Shankar: Really?

Sagar: I will confess to Mohsin's father. I will tell him that I have come here for restitution.

Shankar: You want to create a drama? This is madness unheard.

Sagar: Don't stop me, otherwise I will turn into another Dasrath. I beg of you, let me go to Singhasan. Let me go there and seek their pardon.

Shankar: Don't be adamant.

Sagar: Shankar!

Khitish: Shankar, Sagar, both of you have to come with me. By sitting here, we cannot imagine what is happening in Dhaka. Suddenly someone seems to have freed Dhaka from the dark veil it was covered with. Free winds of change are blowing over the city. We are professing our love for Bangladesh anew. We are reveling, gathering and organizing literary conferences with renewed vigour.

Shankar: It seems you are all deepening your roots.

[*Sagar brings the tanpura down, sits on the bed and listens to their conversation.*]

Khitish: We have taken the first step. I know many odds still remain to be defeated. Yet I feel that you could have partaken in the novelty of the free spirit that is associated with taking the debut step. My cousin Paresh is flushed with happiness these days.

Sagar: The tanpura has gathered dust. Even the strings have become rusty. Shankar, couldn't you have kept it in good shape?

Shankar: Strange! You don't like anyone else to touch that tanpura. Now you are talking rubbish. I haven't seen the tanpura in your hands for long. How come today?

Sagar: [*Smiles coyly.*] It feels good again to play the tanpura.

[*He bends down, strums, and listens to the sound the instrument produces.*]

Khitish: [*Pointing at Sagar.*] That monkey is hung up on Bangladesh. I would be very happy if he came with me. Since Paresh is flying around like a wind-blown crow, I have to stay back at home. If you are with me, I can leave Mili in your care and focus on the bridge competition about to be held at our Bar Library. Why don't I get the passport and visa done? I have some connections. What do you say, Shankar?

[*Shankar signals to Khitish, asking him to keep quiet. Sagar, with his eyes closed, is singing: 'Naiya bhai! Sujon naiya re! Dariyar kul pailam na.' He keeps on singing and stops when his voice escalates to the fifth harmony, exactly where Mohsin had stopped four years ago. He then opened his eyes and sits like a stone.*]

Khitish: That song!

Sagar: That Mohsin and his song! Shankar, conscience can make humans act as characters in a play. That play is then named Life. I am going out with Jamai Babu to the passport office. You can stay back.

[*He walks away quietly. Khitish steps close to Shankar.*]

Khitish: I don't know where the scar inside Sagar is taking him to.

Shankar: He wants to make a fresh beginning. Let's see how tough he is.

Khitish: Where are you going?

Sagar: For the time being, to the dining room. Come. In a few days, we will be in Mohsin's country and in village Singhasan. I am curious to find out where my journey would take me thereafter. Let's go. My body is here, but my soul is there. What awaits me at the next turn?

— Curtain drops —

SECOND WAVE: Fourth Scene

[*Singhasan. An old concrete house with walls painted blue. To the left of the stage, and diagonally, runs a verandah. Two closed doors. The verandah ends deep into the house near high banks. Beyond that bank is a river. A bent palm tree overlooks the river. It swings with the wind from time to time. To the right is a thatched hut. The structure of the house and its surroundings bear the unique trait of a small Bangla town. To the extreme left of the verandah is a worn-out reclining chair. At a little distance, a small lantern is burning. Sitting on the floor of the verandah and beside the lantern is an aged, landless Muslim worker, otherwise called Mahinder in Bangladesh. He is snoozing off. The Sun is sinking on the other side of the river, turning the land crimson. Evening shadows are lengthening on the house. The progress of the scene will be in sync with nightfall. The Mahinder yawns loudly, wraps himself with a shawl, and turns to a side in order to get sound sleep. Through the door to the left, a tall old man in a torn lungi appears with a confused look. He stands next to the Mahinder and shouts—*]

Old man: What's this? Hey you Fakra, Fakiruddi rascal!

Fakir: [*Scratches his ears.*] Yes?

Old man: [*Startled.*] Is it you who have you kept it?

Fakir: Yes. [*Turns to a side.*]

Old man: Why?

Fakir: What have I kept?

Old man: That bundle of books. It was on the shelf.

Fakir: No, I haven't.

Old man: You only want to sleep all the time, whereas I cannot find the books.

Fakir: Don't shout.

Old man: What did you say?

Fakir: I asked you not to shout. It is not right to shout in the evening. [*Yawns.*]

Old man: Who is the head of the family? You or me?

Fakir: I really don't know.

Old man: Look at him! Hello, where are you? Hello?

[*His 'hello' comes out from the right. She is small and petite, and walks using short steps. She chews beetle leaf most of the time. In the dimly-lit evening, the aura of calm happiness that surrounds her wouldn't make it far-fetched to consider her as a personification of universal motherhood, and not as a common human being. But she always uses an admonishing tone when she speaks. She is Mohsin's mother and the old man is his father.*]

Mother: Why are you calling me?

Father: Fakra has removed my bundle of books from the shelf.

Fakir: Who said I have misplaced it? [*He stands up.*] Look here Boujan, Bade Mian is hollering at me since yesterday.

Father: He has certainly kept the books in a heap somewhere. How terrible!

Fakir: Don't turn it into a terrible affair.

Mother: Stop your harangue. Didn't you keep it in the trunk yesterday, saying the books were very important?

Father: Oh!

[*He is visibly embarrassed.*]

Fakir: He doesn't know what he does these days.

Father: Enough! That is the third chapter of Bikrampur's history.

Fakir: Keep them on the shelf with a dab of vermilion powder.

Father: I said enough!

Mother: Go and change. If Jaba sees you in that torn lungi, she would start shouting.

Father: I almost forgot. Jaba is supposed to come home today. She is taking the steamer.

Mother: I am glad that you remember. Thank Khuda for small mercies!

Fakir: Boujan, divorce him.

Mother: Let go of my feet. Where are you going?

Father: I am going, OK? Perseverance is a commodity for struggle in this family.

[*He leaves.*]

Mother: Fakra?

Fakir: Yes?

Mother: Did you get to hear the whistle of the steamer?

Fakir: Didn't enter my ears.

Mother: There are days when it whistles from as far as that Samareshpur lighthouse. [*Climbs the banks.*] The river is so beautiful. I see it everyday and yet it comes back to me as new every time I look at it.

Fakir: After all, this is the property of your father-in-law. I remember the day you arrived here as a bride. You had a saffron-coloured cover on your head.

Mother: You are awash with emotions. Go now.

Fakir: Where?

Mother: Go to the jetty. If Jaba doesn't find you there, she is going to throw a fit.

Fakir: While you are being so eager to see her, she is dropping her modesty and burkha to be at the rallies on the streets of Dhaka, in order to awaken the country.

Mother: Let her do whatever she is doing. You get going now.

Fakir: I am leaving right now.

[*He sits down again. Father arrives after changing.*]

Mother: Get up.

Fakir: I am going, I am going. It's a long way to the jetty. Don't feel like walking.

Father: Tell me, how much work you do everyday?

Mother: Now go. The steamer must have arrived.

[*She pushes the unwilling fakir out of the house and bangs the door shut. She walks back to the verandah. The father is perched on the reclining chair.*]

Mother: This family gets the better of me. There are only three members but I still can't manage it.

Father: Everything is ready for Iftar. We can start anytime, isn't it?

Mother: Don't be greedy. Let our daughter come.

[*She walks towards the banks.*]

Father: This Fakra is an imbecile. I was reading a very good book at the school today. The book is titled 'Mayukh' and written by Rakhaldas Babu. You know, about three hundred years ago, Portuguese colonizers used the small islands near Chittagong to attack the villages of Bengal.

Mother: Stop haranguing.

Father: Harangue?

Mother: What else is it?

Father: Alright. What are you looking at?

Mother: Darkness has engulfed the path of the river now, but a while ago, it looked so beautiful.

Father: No matter what the path is, your daughter will come.

Mother: I don't need any path. I only watch its beauty.

Father: Even when it is dark?

Mother: Don't you think it breaches everything, including darkness?

Father: Yes.

Mother: Do you know what that devil Fakra was telling me a while ago? He was reminiscing the day!

Father: How can I forget that day when you arrived here all decked up?

Mother: That was after dusk. The river was engulfed by darkness.

Father: See, you still remember the day.

[*He slowly walks up to his wife. Both of them stand still for a few moments with their back to the audience. From a distance wafts in a song sung by a woman. The lyrics are not clear. Mother places a hand on Father.*]

Mother: I don't know why I am so happy today.

Father: I have never been able to understand you. What tune is that?

Mother: The girls from Sanfalla wish their near ones well by placing earthen lamps on tiny boats made from the bark of banana trees. Then they consign them to the river.

Father: Mohsin—

Mother: What?

Father: Do you remember that song Mohsin used to sing? One that he heard on way to Bhairavbazar – *Dariyar kul pailam na?* He heard it when it was dark. True, you cannot see the shore in darkness.

Mother: My son has also disappeared in the darkness.

Father: Phooljan, don't you still have that dream?

Mother: Which dream?

Father: Our son will return to light up the house?

Mother: No Mian, he is not going to come back. I have different dreams these days.

Father: Such as?

Mother: It's about that boy Mohsin used to talk endlessly.

Father: That boy in Kolkata?

Mother: Yes, him. You know, I have this feeling that some day or the other, he will come to this house. He will stand in the courtyard and call out to me – Mother, I am here!

Father: Are your eyes moist?

Mother: Why does he not come?

Father: Maybe, he doesn't have our address.

Mother: Mohsin said he did have our address. It's us who can't find him.

Father: Where are you going?

Mother: Let me clean up Mohsin's room. The moment Jaba arrives, she will enter her elder brother's room.

[*Mother opens the door to the thatched-hut in the right-hand side.*]

Father: Don't go. From tomorrow, you would get busy with her, knitting and decking up the house.

Mother: You think that girl will do the chores? Don't you remember that she came with her fellow college students some time ago just before the elections, raised 'United Front' slogans and cried themselves hoarse? She is from this home and shouldn't have cross the limit.

Father: Let's go.

Mother: Why?

Father: I want to say something.

Mother: Is it so important that you have to say it now?

Father: I want to talk to you before Jaba arrives.

Mother: OK, let's go.

[*They come to the verandah. Father sits on the chair and Mother on the floor.*]

Father: Today, our daughter is my only hope.

Mother: Why do you say like this?

Father: Jaba told me some time back, soon after the movement.

Mother: What did she tell you?

Father: She has pledged herself to the country and to politics. She has joined the party.

Mother: O Khuda!

Father: If the need arises, she would leave the country.

Mother: I have lost my son. It seems I have lost my daughter, too.

Father: Phooljan Bibi!

Mother: Haven't we got something through all this? When those students were killed in Dhaka, didn't we shed our burkhas and hit the streets? When oil and salt went missing from the market, weren't there protest rallies? When Bhashani came to Maulana, wasn't there any effort to gather crowds?

Father: I know Phooljan.

Mother: Then why did you say it today?

Father: What?

Mother: Why did you have to tell me about her joining the party at a time when Haq is in power and '21st February' is set to become a day to remember?

Father: There's another issue that has made people sit up and take notice. A tug-of-war is on to get Haq Sahib to Karachi. Haven't you heard the speeches over Adamji Mill on the Radio?

Mother: Bade Mian, you have understood the country, but not its mother. Mark my words.

Father: Enough. I thought you would start crying.

Mother: I would cry in private. You had hidden it from me. But I wouldn't block the path of my daughter.

[*They hear a soft knock on the main gate. Both of them are startled. A big smile breaks on the face of Mother. She runs to the door.*]

Mother: I won't open the door until you tell me what you have got from the Capital for me. [*Another knock.*] Spare me!

[*As she opens the door, Sagar and Shankar enter. They are carrying a bag each. They are both a bit embarrassed and restless with stifled excitement. Shankar looks at Sagar with trepidation. Seeing a woman in front of them, Sagar is nonplussed. Shankar steps forward. Mother is equally taken aback.*]

Shankar: Is this the house of Janab Taslim Mian?

Mother: [*Makes a futile attempt to draw the tail of her saree across her head.*] Yes, it is.

Shankar: We are from Kolkata.

Mother: Oh!

Sagar: [*Takes a step forward.*] Is Taslim Mian Sahib home?

Father: Here I am.

Shankar: You must be mother.

[*He touches her feet.*]

Mother: Me? Mother!

Father: Why are you here?

Shankar: We came from Kolkata by train. We got off at the Shonaikandi station at four in the afternoon. After that, we came walking along the banks of the river. It got dark as we walked.

Father: Come inside, please.

[*They enter the house. They are both tired. By the time they entered, Mother had already given herself a makeover. She keeps looking at them. Sagar is having an irresistible urge to talk, but somehow he can't. Shankar is gradually regaining his trademark poise.*]

Shankar: You are the father.

[*Shankar touches his feet.*]

Father: [*A little uneasy.*] Bless you, Son. Let your life be full of happiness. Sorry, I didn't address you the way I should address an elderly.

Shankar: Of course you should not. We and Mohsin are of the same age.

Mother: Mohsin!

Father: Mohsin!

Shankar: Yes, Mohsin. Your son.

Mother: [*Walks up eagerly.*] Who are you? Who?

Sagar: My name is Sagar. He is—

Mother: Sagar? You there, do you know who is our guest today?

Father: Finally, our wishes have come true. Sagar—

Mother: Sagar! I have been waiting for you for so long.

[*She holds her fondly.*]

Sagar: I can't understand what's happening.

Shankar: Who did you hear about us from?

Father: After Mohsin returned from Kolkata in 1946, he kept talking and talking about Sagar and how he helped him in a crisis.

Shankar: OK.

Sagar: But how could Mohsin talk about me? I think you are making a mistake.

Mother: We don't make mistakes. I heard your mother is no more. Don't you have any feelings for me, then?

Sagar: Shankar!

Shankar: I can see that the matter has become quite knotty.

Mother: [*Holds Shankar fondly.*] I lose one son and get two. What's your name?

Shankar: Shankar.

Sagar: But—

Mother: How lovely! What is going to happen to me! [*She claps.*] My home is full today.

Father: Do whatever you may, but don't cry. Don't squat on the floor and begin to cry. You should go now and make arrangements for them to wash up. Fakra is not here now.

Mother: Yes, I shall go now.

[*She wipes her tears, turns back and kisses them on their cheeks. Then she moves towards the interior of the house. Despite their protests, she takes the bags from Shankar and Sagar and leaves with a smile.*]

Sagar: But—

Father: Sit down. Oh! The stools are in the other room. I will bring them

[*As he gets up, Shankar says—*]

Shankar: I will get them.

[*He goes inside.*]

Sagar: I am getting confused. I hope you have heard my name clearly.

Father: Yes, Sagar.

Sagar: Are you aware of the situation in which Mohsin and I had met in Kolkata?

Father: I have heard.

Mohsin: The kind of situation and what happened after that – have you heard all?

Father: Son, Mohsin told me everything in detail.

Sagar: I am getting puzzled.

[*Sagar looks at seemingly nobody in a bland manner. Shankar arrives with two stools and a book.*]

Shankar: Books are strewn all over that room. I fished out one from there.

Father: Good. Now sit down. [*They both occupy the stools.*] Which book did you get from the room?

Shankar: It is a journal of The Archaeological Survey of India.

Father: That journal contains a thesis on the Harappa civilization, the story of India's most ancient civilization. Are you interest in Archaeology?

Shankar: Yes. I have read a couple of books written by Gordon Child.

Father: In that case, give me the journal. That's only the preface. Let me get you a summary. You will find it a good read.

[*He goes inside with the journal. Sagar stands up swiftly and walks briskly to the courtyard. Shankar was quick to be by his side.*]

Sagar: I am getting stifled!

Shankar: Comedy of errors!

Sagar: Comedy?

Shankar: Yes, comedy. You wanted drama and now your life is full of it. I want to laugh.

Sagar: I don't feel like laughing. I just don't understand anything.

Shankar: A bit silly, but alright.

Sagar: What is happening here?

Shankar: Nothing wrong is happening. Do you remember that Mohsin said on several occasions that he had met another Sagar in 1946 in Kolkata?

Sagar: He had said that to me as well.

Shankar: The connection is more deeply strange. That Sagar had saved Mohsin from certain death.

Sagar: O my God! Are they treating me as that Sagar?

Shankar: Don't be funny.

[*Father comes with a book.*]

Father: Here it is. This book is a short read. It ends with Vedic India.

Shankar: I love to know about all this.

Father: You will not have the same affinity for gathering knowledge.

Shankar: Did you say something?

Father: I said you would no longer love to know about all this. These days, people try to find an escape route the moment they see me because they think I try to make them wise whenever I get to trap them.

Shankar: Uncle, in that case, you and I share the same profession.

Father: Are you going to run away?

Shankar: Yes, tonight itself. I am told there's a train at 10 pm.

Father: My dear, you have not been able to gauge Khuda's wishes. You are already in communion with him. This is the month of Ramzan. Eid is just round the bend, and you think you would be able to leave tonight?

Sagar: We have to leave today. By the way, did Mohsin talk about me in 1946?

Father: Yes.

Sagar: See—

Shankar: [*Interrupting Sagar.*] You have a formidable collection of books. I never imagined I would come across so many books in a village.

Baba: They are my only asset.

[*Mother arrives.*]

Mother: Sagar, Shankar, the towels are ready. Go and wash up.

Shankar: Which way? Come, Sagar

[*He takes an unwilling Sagar with him.*]

Mother: My heart is full with happiness.

Father: Phooljanbibi, there isn't any pain in this world that go waste. They come back as happiness some day or the other.

Mother: True. They return taking strange paths. Didn't I tell you, today will be a day of happiness? No idea how soon they would leave.

Father: They are planning to take the night train to Dhaka.

Mother: I will remember that.

[*Sagar and Shankar arrive.*]

There is no arrangement for food right now. You have come to a Muslim household in the month of Ramzan. We have to do the Iftar together.

Shankar: Not to worry. We had eaten at a tea stall on the way.

Mother: My daughter is also arriving today. All of you should sit for a meal together, alright? Let me lay out the food.

[*She leaves.*]

Father: So you will leave tonight!

Sagar: Yes Sir.

Father: In that case, would you be able to discuss?

Shankar: We can do that now.

Father: Where would you go from here?

Shankar: Dhaka.

Father: Do you have anyone there?

Shankar: Yes, our sister and brother-in-law.

Father: What is the name of your brother-in-law?

Shankar: Khitish Sanyal. He is an advocate and lives in Gendaria.

Father: Near the iron bridge?

Shankar: Yes, in Sharfatgunj.

Father: OK.

Shankar: Do you know him?

Father: I don't know him personally but a brother of his goes to the same college as my daughter. He was here at the time of the elections.

Shankar: Isn't your daughter coming today?

Father: She is about to come.

Sagar: [*Moving about the place.*] Is there a river that side?

Father: Yes, the Padma.

Sagar: This house has an unusual location. It is so close to the river. That river is very wide, isn't it?

Father: Yes.

Sagar: So wide that it is difficult to see the other side of the river.

Father: Almost like that.

Sagar: The house, indeed, has an unusual location. What are those that are floating with lights on the water?

Father: Hindu girls have probably made a wish and released tiny boats made from the bark of a banana tree.

Sagar: A song is also being sung at a distance.

Father: Those girls are singing after making a wish.

Sagar: Shankar, I was telling you on the way that the voice modulation in these tunes is akin to traditional folk yodeling of Europe.

Father: Do you sing?

Sagar: Very little.

Father: What about you, Shankar?

Shankar: Spare me. No, I don't. But you are a famous pakhwaj player.

Father: That was once upon a time. I was just a pakhwaj player, not famous.

Shankar: Why don't you play these days?

Father: I am not in the mood anymore. Neither do I have the opportunity to play, nor any need.

Sagar: Uncle, what's there on that side?

Father: Paddy fields.

Sagar: Do you store paddy in this room?

Father: No, no. Mohsin used to stay in that room. His mother has kept the room tidy even to this day, if it comes to be of any use some day.

Sagar: [*Suddenly steps forward.*] Uncle, let me tell you—

Shankar: [*Interrupting Sagar.*] Uncle, shall we begin our discussion?

Father: O yes. Let's go inside then. Come, Sagar.

Shankar: No, let him move about this place. He doesn't have much thirst for wisdom.

[*Addressing Sagar.*]

Sagar, there is no benefit in destroying the paradise that comes to you without being asked for. I discovered this after a long thought. The main thing is, it's alright.

[*Shankar and father go out. Sagar keeps standing quietly for a while. Then he walks slowly towards the thatched hut and opens a small window. He then lifts the lantern and begins to peep inside the room. With her hands behind her, mother tip-toes in from the right. Looks for Sagar. She spots Sagar and goes near him.*]

Mother: Khoka!

Sagar: [*Startled.*] Who's there? Oh!

Mother: [*Looks around and then brings out a bowl from under the tail of her saree.*] Eat this.

Sagar: What?

Mother: Thickened milk layers.

Sagar: You want me to eat milk layers?

Mother: Why should you? Look at yourself. Your everyday city life has turned you into a cactus. Eat.

[*She goes up on her toes and makes Sagar eat the milk layers from the small bowl. Sagar keeps swallowing. She wipes his face with the tail of her saree.*]

Mother: Wasn't it good? Our mynah cow is black in colour. Milk produced by black cows is very sweet. The cow delivered a calf last month. I can't make out whether the calf is down with jaundice or not.

Sagar: O!

Mother: Come, you and I sit on the banks of the river down there. Will you come?

Sagar: Isn't your daughter coming?

Mother: O yes! In that case, let's sit here. [*They sit. Mother runs her finger through Sagar's hair.*] The breeze is very nice here.

Sagar: Yes. It induces sleep. But then, there is no sleeping either.

Mother: Yes.

Sagar: Mother!

Mother: Yes?

Sagar: Shall I say something?

Mother: Tell me.

Sagar: You have to promise that you won't be hurting.

Mother: I have received more than enough pain. It seems the country is coming to terms with the need for peace and hence, my life is becoming complete. You know, the people of my country are crossing obstacles, one after another. Now we need peace and calm.

Sagar: You have such deep concerns for the country?

Mother: Yes, I have.

Sagar: You have, perhaps, not moved out of Singhasan in the past ten years.

Mother: More than ten years. In my whole life, I went out of Singhasan only thrice.

Sagar: Still—

Mother: My crazy son, one doesn't need to travel distances to see the world. Delve deep in your soul and you will find the world. Would you like to hear a poem?

Sagar: Sure.

Mother: *Nanan boron Gabhi re bhai, aki boron dudh*
Bhuban bharmiya dekhi aki ma-er poot

(The cows are of different colour but their milk is white. I see the world to realize that we all belong to the same mother.)

Sagar: Mother! There's something I cannot resist telling you.

Mother: Tell me.

Sagar: Mother, the Sagar Mohsin had talked about—

[*Shankar arrives out of the blue and says—*]

Shankar: Mother! Great! So it has started?

Mother: What?

Shankar: You have started to shower him your affection privately. Am I the one that which the cat dragged in?

Mother: No, no. You are my gem, too.

Shankar: What was that you are hiding? What was that bowl for?

Mother: Where?

Shankar: [*Goes near her.*] Bring it out. I am telling you, bring it out. I see. It looks like some sweet dish made from milk.

Mother: It's just a small amount of thickened milk layers.

Shankar: Impossible! I can't tolerate this. I am leaving this house.

Mother: Here is another crazy son of mine. Don't shout. If the old man gets to hear, there will be problem. He would want it too, even though he gets an upset stomach after drinking milk.

Shankar: Then go and get some for me quickly.

Mother: I am bringing for you.

[*She leaves scared. Sagar turns towards the river. Shankar walks up to him.*]

Shankar: So you have not been able to say it yet. I become tense every time I leave you alone.

Sagar: It's like a dream. Where we were a day ago and where we are now.

Shankar: You were running around in a manner as if you were under a spell. How would you be able to see everything with that state of mind?

Sagar: And the sunset? I remember the vast stretches along the banks and the knotty, distant villages. One or two palm trees are spiking up in the horizon and the smoke from the locomotive billowing to create patters in the sky. My mind is so restless now.

Shankar: And after everything, we arrive in a home like this. A house like this, a mother like her, a father like him. I am sure the daughter, too, will be just like this.

Sagar: [*Suddenly.*] Shankar! I had forgotten everything. Now it seems that I will explode to death.

Shankar: Don't lose your senses.

Sagar: In my senses or not, I have to clear the false impression they are under now, and I have to do it firmly.

Shankar: Look here, at times some issues monopolise our brains, prompting us to see emotions as responsibilities and then responsibilities seem to be falsehood. People are now—

Sagar: That's the reason why I need to tell them the true story. I, too, want to drown in this affection. If I don't tell them, the entire gamut of events will become an unbearable joke.

Shankar: Sagar, you will be inviting disaster!

Sagar: Come what may, I will emerge pure from all this. You can't stop me.

[*Mother comes.*]

Mothere: Hey, my other crazy boy. Here, eat it. Not much was left.

Shankar: Give me. [*He takes the bowl.*] Mother, we have to leave today, right now.

Mother: What are you saying?

Sagar: Yes Mother. If you allow us, we will return. But we will leave today.

Mother: I won't let you go.

Sagar: Mother, please call uncle here. I need to have a word with him.

Shankar: Mother, Sagar has gone barmy and what he is saying is making no sense.

Sagar: I can't keep it down any longer.

[*Father comes.*]

Shankar: Uncle, Mother, Sagar is going to say many things. All false!

[*Sagar shakes off Shankar and comes forward. There is a knock on the door. Father and mother snap to a state of alert and look at the door. The voice of their daughter Jaba can be heard.*]

Jaba: [*In the background.*] Father... Mother, open the door.

[*A big smile surfaces on Mother's face. She runs towards the door and opens it. Jaba dashes into the room. She tries to hug her father but stops. Fakir, with a trunk on her head, follows Jaba into the room. He, too, stops in his tracks, seeing new people. A surprised Jaba looks at Sagar and Shankar. She is ordinary looking and appears docile when one chances upon her. She also appears to be a thoughtful person. The condition of Sagar and Shankar is unspeakable.*]

Fakir: What's the matter?

Mother: [*Through her pursed lips.*] Jaba, any idea who they are?

Father: Shankar, this is our daughter. Her name is Gulshan Banu. She stays in Dhaka these days. She did her BA last year. She is now deeply involved in your Left politics and is a leading member of the United Front.

Shankar: Begumgul...

Jaba: ...Shan. Gulshan Banu.

Father: Would you know them? He is Shankar and this is Sagar.

Jaba: Who?

Father: Sagar.

Jaba: Which Sagar? From Kolkata?

Father: Yes, him. Shankar is his brother.

Jaba: [*Goes near them.*] Please call me Jaba. My parents call me Jaba. My elder brother, too used to call me by the same name.

Shankar: Jaba?

Jaba: Yes, brother.

[*Shankar suddenly becomes quiet. Fakir gets the trunk down from atop his head to the floor and sits on it.*]

Father: These gentlemen are planning to leave tonight.

Shankar: I mean, we should leave.

Mother: Forget it.

Shankar: I mean, what's the harm in leaving tonight.

Jaba: Shankar, it is you who seems eager to leave.

Shankar: Not me. It's Sagar.

Mother: Forget it! Jaba, get ready for the Iftar.

[*Mother leaves.*]

Father: Hurry up, everyone!

[*Father leaves.*]

Jaba: Shankar, I am going now.

Shankar: Alright Gul.... Jaba.

[*Jaba leaves.*]

Shankar: What's on your mind, Sagar?

Sagar: What would Jamai Babu think?

Shankar: I am wondering if I should write to Jamai Babu to come. No, forget it. Let's run away today.

Sagar: Run away?

Shankar: What else can we do considering the way you are behaving?

Sagar: I will tell them the day we leave.

Shankar: When?

Sagar: The day we leave.

Shankar: So, the first sight has....

Fakir: [*He is still sitting on the floor.*] My name is Fakiruddi. I am Fakiruddi Sheikh, a loyal and purchased slave of Bade Mian.

Sagar: Really?

Fakir: Yes. I used to call Mohsin Chote Mian. I will use the same name for you.

Shankar: What would you call me?

Fakir: I would call you Mazan Mian.

[*He picks up the trunk and walks into the room.*]

Sagar: [*He had climbed the banks while the conversation was going on.*] This house has an unusual location. It is right on the river.

Shankar: What all are you looking at?

Sagar: Looks like a dream. It's dark. From among the darkness comes the faint sound of the river's flow. I had met Mohsin long ago and today, I see her sister. [*Shankar stands next to him.*] The tune of the song sung by the Hindu girls is rising. It's a chorus by many girls who are lending tune to strange folk lyrics.

[*Jaba was passing through the verandah behind with quick steps. Her movement becomes sloth as she looks at them. But she hasn't noticed that her father, too, has stopped while he was passing her from behind.*]

Shankar: That tune of the folk songs...

Mother: [*In the background.*] Khoka, Khoka. O my second Khoka. Come quickly.

Sagar: My country... so powerful... so peaceful!

[*Sagar turns to see Jaba and her father. He stands coyly. Shankar gets off the high embankment.*]

Father: Jaba!

Jaba: I suddenly felt as if I was lying down in the steamer and having strange dreams. That's why—

Father: Don't enter your elder brother's room now.

[*Father walks away slowly.*]

Jaba: No!

[*Jaba stands on the banks. The surge of the Padma waters increases. Female voices from a distance keep their song on. Her face is lit up with a sense of contentment.*]

Shankar: My country. How powerful it is! How powerful it is!

[*He turns with a full swing and runs into the house. The waters of the Padma continue to flow in gay abandon.*]

— Curtain drops —

Fifth Scene

[*A few days have passed. The curtain goes up in step with the call for prayers from a distant mosque. The first rays of the Sun spread across the eastern skies. The Padma is now flowing silently. A thin darkness covers the stage. On the verandah, Sagar and Shankar are lying next to each other. A rooster sends a wake-up call. Sagar sits up and takes a look at the crimson skies. He appears mesmerized. He reaches out to Shankar and shakes him.*]

Sagar: Shankar! Shankar!

Shankar: Yes!

Sagar: Take a look at a beautiful dawn-break!

Shankar: Sorry brother, I couldn't sleep the whole night because of mosquitoes.

Sagar: Come on! Let's go and stand beside that date tree.

[*He shakes him again.*]

Shankar: [*Gets up swiftly.*] If you have to go there, you go. Who's asked you to wake me up? Split from here now, or else there will be mayhem!

[*He lies down again.*]

[*The volume of the call for prayers rises. Sagar looks out, again. He walks slowly to the high banks and slowly disappears in the slope. From a distance, one can only occasionally see his head or hands near the date tree, making it clear to the viewer that Sagar is sitting close to the tree. Mother arrives with a mat and lays it out in the front of the stage. After wiping her face and hands, she places her hands on her lap, kneels, and begins to pray with a soft, trembling voice.*]

Mother: Allah, your kindness is seamless. I hope that my prayers are answered. You are my only savior in this ruthless world. O the Emperor of the universe, it was you who had told me the secret about the love for country. You took my Mohsin and yet you haven't left me empty. Your kindness is seamless. Let my prayers be answered. Is that the reason why you brought these boys to me?

Your benevolence has delivered what your blow couldn't. In the brotherhood of man, one human saves another. Is that the message you have sent to me through them? I have become a mother again and I realized why we add or subtract. I am a pure Muslim and I have learnt to see your path. I have become a Bengali. I have just one thing to ask. Would Mohsins give their lives in every age to accomplish truth at karbalas? The driver of the universe, do you need a martyr in every age? Wouldn't your high flag display any other colour than the blood that comes out from the sliced hearts of the brothers and mothers? This world has been dealt with too many blows. It now deserves some peace. Please consider its case. Your kindness is seamless. I hope that my prayers are answered. Amen!

[*She keeps sitting in that posture for some more time and wipes her tears. After that, she rolls up the mat and leaves it next to Mohsin's room. Near the slope of the banks, Sagar sits up. He is trembling with excitement. He quickly comes to the centre of the stage. He turns to go to the right. Shankar sits up.*]

Shankar: Mother's voice is so amusing and sweet. It felt so nice to hear her voice in the thin air of the morning.

Sagar: Why did she say all this?

Shankar: The purity of her soul became clear.

Sagar: *Nanan boron gabhi-re bhai aki boron dudh,*
Bhuban bhormiya dekhi aki ma-er poot.

Shankar: What is this?

Sagar: Ma had recited this poem to me the day we arrived here.

Shankar: *Bhuban bhormiya dekhi aki ma er poot!*

Sagar: Do we have to submit in this manner?

Shankar: Yes, we have to. This is called trial by fire. This is what gives rise to purity.

Sagar: You should spread the word around. They burn to become heaps of ash. Shankar, let's go now. Jamai Babu must have...

Shankar: As desired by Uncle, I have written to Jamai Babu, asking him to come. He will be here either tomorrow or the day after.

Sagar: Each show of affection is like a whiplash. I will leave today itself. Before I leave, I will tell Mother everything.

Shankar: And what would you say to Jaba?

Sagar: Jaba?

Shankar: Yes. You have to explain to Jaba as well.

Sagar: [*Says as he turns around to walk away.*] O!

Shankar: Where are you going?

Sagar: To the river. I will pause there for a while. My head is reeling.

Shankar: Wouldn't you reply?

Sagar: It is your responsibility to explain to Jaba, not mine.

Shankar: Really? Are you saying this because Jaba was scolded in front of everyone yesterday?

Sagar: This is not desired of you.

Shankar: Really! None of you are looking into my problems. Do you know what she did to me last night? Mother gave me some sweet porridge solely for tasting. Jaba had me seated on a piri. Do you know what happened after that? When I woke up, I realized that I had no clue to what had happened in the preceding five minutes. The porridge was all over the floor. I also realized that the piri had betrayed me. Four beetle-nuts had been placed under the piri and they worked as wheels the moment I had sat upon it. Wouldn't I be livid if I see her laugh after that incident?

Sagar: Perhaps.

Shankar: Later, she was pressing clothes standing next to the oven. The handle of the iron was wrapped in a piece of cloth. While talking with her, I surreptitiously removed the cloth. You should have seen the manner in which she danced around after she tried to pick up the hot iron for pressing. She got the handle wrapped in that cloth again and came towards me with the red-hot iron. When I realized that the destination of that iron was my back, I ran out of the house. But she followed me. When I was planning to get out of the village, Mother came and took Jaba away, sermonizing her all the way back on the absence of any civility in her. That was like music to my ears.

Sagar: Then?

Shankar: Then nothing. I have to be careful today.

Sagar: You think she would get back at you?

Shankar: No doubt about that. You don't know girls of her type. They come straight from the trees. Where are you off to?

Sagar: To the river.

Shankar: What all is there that you have to see it everyday?

Sagar: My own mind.

Shankar: I, however, haven't seen my own sleep yet. Let me try again.

Sagar: You will do that sitting?

Shankar: I will do that from a half-seated position. Constant disturbances are robbing me of deep sleep. Life is full of troubles!

[*Sagar walks towards the banks. Shankar leans against the wall and shuts his eyes. Jaba, with a bucketful of water, comes in from the right. As she tries to cross the stage quickly, she notices Shankar and stops walking. Jaba scratches her chin and thinks. Then she quietly goes behind Shankar and pours the water from the bucket on him. A blood-curling scream emits from deep inside Shankar. He sits up, stunned. Jaba disappears to the right. With a war-cry, Shankar jumps onto the centre of the stage. Father arrives from the left.*]

Father: Could you please hold these books for a while? Are you returning from the river after ablution? Let it be then.

Shankar: What?

Father: Were you wearing a Piran or did you slip and fall? But your clothes are not muddied.

Shankar: Sorry?

Father: You did go to the river for ablution, right?

Shankar: Maybe.

Father: [*Looks at him with complete amazement.*] Anyway, I just got the history of Gour from the school. It's very interesting!

Shankar: Yes, extremely interesting!

[*Jaba brings out a portable bed from Mohsin's room and sit on it.*]

Father: Especially the ninth century. It seems you are not concentrating.

Shankar: No, Uncle. I am really finding it very interesting.

[*He gets up to the verandah.*]

Father: What are you doing there?

Shankar: I am trying to figure how my bed can be rolled up

Father: Your sense of humour is greater than mine.

[*Mother comes.*]

Mother: Jaba, Fakra went out hours ago to arrange a car for Shovan Mian. He is not back yet.

Jaba: He will be back anytime soon.

Mother: Shankar, your bed is there.

Father: I will roll it up. He doesn't know how to roll up a bed. What's this?

Mother: What happened?

Father: Wet.

Mother: Wet?

Father: His bed is wet.

Mother: Wet? Shankar, you have water on your body. Your piran is sopping wet.

Shankar: Yes, I know.

Father: Let me keep these books in the room.

[*Father leaves.*]

Mother: Son, I fail to understand you. Go inside. Otherwise you will catch cold.

[*Shankar nods and walks away.*]

Mother: Jaba!

Jaba: Yes mother.

Mother: Put these on the fences for drying.

Jaba: Give.

[*She leaves and father appears with a book in his hand.*]

Mother: Jaba is a girl from a household. I don't like the way these two are mixing. After all—

Father: I don't have such worries about Shankar.

Mother: Neither me. But what would the neighbours say? The entire neighbourhood saw how they fought with each other yesterday.

Father: I have some other worries about Shankar.

Mother: What?

Father: I wonder whether he is a little mentally off or not. The way he looks and talks—

Mother: He fetches water from the river and comes up to pour it on himself. I don't know, really.

[*Jaba comes.*]

Jaba, cook the rice fast. I have to do the dishes.

Jaba: Alright, mother.

[*As Jaba leaves, Shankar enters. They lock eyes.*]

Mother: Shankar, come, sit here.

Shankar: Of course.

Mother: You take care of him now. I mean talk with him.

Shankar: Of course.

Mother: Did you say something, son?

Shankar: Nothing much.

Father: Sit down. Where's Sagar?

Shankar: On the other side of the embankment. Let me find out.

Father: No, no. It's alright.

Shankar: No, no, let me see anyway.

Father: You sure?

Shankar: I am thinking.

Father: Then go.

Shankar: Shall I sit down?

Father: Better you had sat down. We could have deliberated on some matters.

Shankar: Deliberations?

Father: Don't you remember that just a little ago, we decided to have a discussion on the history of Bangla literature?

Shankar: O.

Father: The history of Bangladesh is so beautiful.

Shankar: Bangladesh!

Father: Yes, Bangladesh. I am sure you remember that country. It's your country.

Shankar: O, you are talking about that Bangladesh?

Father: For the time being. But it is important to know history.

Shankar: Yes.

Father: Why?

Shankar: What?

Father: Why is it important?

Shankar: Why?

Father: Why do we read history?

Shankar: Why?

Father: So that we learn from the past and take the right step forward.

Shankar: Right.

Father: For instance, when eminent personalities of Bangladesh leaned towards history about fifty or sixty years ago, there was a definite purpose behind their move.

Shankar: O.

Father: The British have tried to drill into our heads over 200 years that we are worthless. Therefore, the moment we were blessed with science, we began on a war-footing to prove to them that our civilization is older than theirs. In fact, you are worthless. So what was the result?

Shankar: What?

Father: We could convince the world that India would once again be on a high pedestal in the global arena. And why are we studying history today?

Shankar: Why?

Father: That's because we realise now that we had talked a lot of rubbish earlier. We are saddled with many wrong ideas. The first mistake was not being able to find a place for ourselves in the flow of humanity. In fact, the primary flow of history is transfusion of cultures, which is about cross-pollinating minds and exchange of goods. The waves that touch the Indian shores are the remnants of waves from the gulfs of the five continents. The second mistake was that, we forgot that the history of Bangla is the history of farmers.

Shankar: Farmers!

Father: Most Bengalis are traditional farmers. On the surplus on their harvest thrives Jaidev's, Chaitanay's and Alivardi's Bangla. The entire country is like a cauldron. For thousands of years, this cauldron has been emitting an aroma which is Bengalis' and Bangla's. And this historical cooking is the result of the hulls drawn on soil by millions and millions of farmers.

Shankar: Where is that article you wrote on this subject?

Father: You mean the uprising by the ryots? That is at the school. I tried to portray in that article how genuine campaigns for improving the quality of farm life had been shown as religious fanaticism. Would you like to read that?

Shankar: Yes.

Father: Let's go then. We must get over with it before Fakiruddi comes.

[*Jaba arrives.*]

Jaba: Father, where are you heading to?

Father: To the school building. Oh!

Shankar: [*Stealing glances at Jaba, who was moving about at a distance.*] What?

Father: Nothing. I mean that water issue. Let me get my shawl.

[*He goes into the room.*]

Shankar: Nobody can blame me if I kill you now.

Jaba: Not so easy.

[*Jaba prepares to run. Shankar attempts to jump at her. Father comes and Shankar nearly lands on his shoulders.*]

Father: Have you gone mad? I guess you should visit the doctor.

Jaba: Even Lattu Kaviraj can help him with a dab of cooling hair oil.

Shankar: I am all fire and brimstone now.

Father: Did you say something?

Shankar: No. Let's go.

Father: Let's go. How far one can go, Khuda! [*Sagar comes from the banks of the river.*] Where were you, Sagar?

Sagar: I was sitting on the sandy stretch next to the river.

Shankar: Were you able to see your own mind, finally?

Sagar: A little. By the way, where are you going?

Shankar: To the school. [*As Shankar and Jaba lock eyes, he makes a face at her and slaps himself. Says—*] Ok, I am going to the school now.

Father: Don't lose your temper. We need not go to the school. What do you say?

Shankar: No, Let's go.

[*He leaves the room like a shot.*]

Father: O Khuda!

[*Then he follows Shankar out of the room.*]

Sagar: [*Sitting on the cot.*] Why is Shankar so antsy like a leashed horse?

Jaba: [*From the verandah.*] That's because I poured a bucket of water on him.

Sagar: Water?

Jaba: He is jumping like a horse because of that bucket of water.

Sagar: O My God!

Jaba: Why?

Sagar: No mental relief would exist anywhere near any house that you may choose to live in.

Jaba: Maybe not, but there would be peace.

Sagar: Aren't peace and relief synonymous?

Jaba: A huge gap exists between peace and relief. Relief means security, something like not taking any risks.

Sagar: Don't you like security?

Jaba: I hate it. No work in this world can be done without taking risks.

Sagar: At times, I wonder where you were all these years. Why haven't we met before?

Jaba: There's a thought that keeps striking my mind, too.

Sagar: What?

Jaba: It's difficult to imagine that I do not know you from the past. It seems I know you for ages, as if from the beginning of life.

Sagar: As back as that?

Jaba: As new. Where did you go?

Sagar: I was walking aimlessly and found myself on a stretch laded with silvery sand. That was a new surprise for me at the turn of the river. I consider myself so fortunate.

Jaba: Why?

Sagar: I have never noticed the diversity of my country before. Now my focus is intensifying. I now planning to walk the villages of my country and encapsulate their myriad offerings from one end of the spectrum to the other.

Jaba: Would you only see?

Sagar: I will learn all the uncommon songs of this land.

Jaba: What purpose would it serve?

Sagar: I will learn them. That's all. That would be some achievement.

Jaba: You may end up learning some songs. Not all.

Sagar: Maybe, I will take you along. You will take risks and I will learn song. I will do 'some' and you will keep 'all'.

Jaba: Wish we could travel together.

Sagar: You know, the worse thing about good plans is that they remain as plans. This is quite impossible, isn't it?

Jaba: Not really.

Sagar: You mean both of us can travel together?

Jaba: Unless the situation changes.

Sagar: From the banks of the river, the villages seemed to reveling in festivities and celebrating life. Is this a normal way of life here?

Jaba: Normal life is now riddles with misery. The villages appear to you the way they did because of very important turn of events.

Sagar: Very important?

Jaba: Yes, the triumph of the United Front. The whole of East Bengal is on the threshold of a political awakening. I don't know why, but we are suddenly so deep in love with Bangladesh.

Sagar: You were talking about ominous portents of Haq Sahib's departure to Karachi.

Jaba: They are trying to buy him out, but he can't allow himself to be sold.

Sagar: Then?

Jaba: Either fascism in the garb of Islamic Shariyat will invade us, or a true democracy will take over the reins.

Sagar: Governor's Rule?

Jaba: Yes.

Sagar: Then?

Jaba: Then what? An all-pervading spirit of celebrations will sweep these villages for some time. A vocal Pakistan today is paving the path for a numb

	Pakistan tomorrow. It's just that the path will flow like the River Falgu that flows beneath its riverbed.
Sagar:	Beneath the soil?
Jaba:	Yes. Beneath the soil.
Sagar:	What would happen to the people?
Jaba:	They, too, would have a subterranean existence.
Sagar:	Even you?
Jaba:	Even me.
Sagar:	Beneath the soil?
Jaba:	I have pledged my life for the soil of this country. So what if I am beneath that soil? My friends have fallen to their bullets on the streets of Dhaka.
Sagar:	But you can come to Kolkata. Don't you need a job?
Jaba:	I do. There will be many who would go to Kolkata, but I am not going to desert this land.
Sagar:	Wish I were sharing that premise with you.
Jaba:	What?
Sagar:	My life would have found a new meaning if I were able to join your movement.
Jaba:	Are you getting an urge to do so?
Sagar:	My mind is being overcome by apprehensions!
Jaba:	That should not happen. Anyone who wants to be on my side has to fight for the land we call our own.
Sagar:	I have heard that before.
Jaba:	Then?
Sagar:	Even then, I get ominous feeling in my guts. Besides, my mind is restless these days.
Jaba:	Don't be restless.

Sagar: Jaba! I have much to say.

Jaba: Let them be preserved inside you. You don't have to say them today.

Sagar: It's so difficult to hold them back. I will explode to death.

Jaba: Don't you realize that this is not the time?

Sagar: But Jaba. [*Goes near her.*]

Jaba: [*Stops.*] I am not ready to hear them today.

Sagar: But conscience is gnawing me. How can I keep these words hidden from you anymore?

Jaba: Let them stay hidden. Let them.

Sagar: Jaba!

[*Sagar holds Jaba's hand as she was about to leave. Fakiruddi arrives.*]

Fariruddi: I see, Chote Mian is here! Oh! My legs are packing up?

Sagar: Fakir Uncle!

Fakir: Yes?

Jaba: What's the fate of Shovan Mian?

Fakir: I just saw him leash the oxen to his cart.

Jaba: Take the mat with you to lay it out in the cart.

Fakir: Yes.

Jaba: Go now!

Fakir: Why you are you after me all the time?

[*Mother arrives.*]

Mother: Has the rice been cooked? Hello, Prince Fakiruddi.

Fakir: Tell me.

Mother: I just wished you. Finally you get the time to come!

Fakir: Yes.

Mother: The job is getting done, right?

Fakir: Yes. The bullock cart is on the way.

Mother: Get a container filled with drinking water. They would need it on the way.

Fakir: Alright.

Mother: Go get it!

Fakir: Come on! You people are constantly pestering me. [*He gets up.*] I will complete the work and park myself in the workroom. Strange! The moment you see me, you remember work.

Mother: Where are they?

Jaba: At the school.

Mother: [*Squats on the floor of the verandah.*] I just finished washing some utensils. What's Sagar up to?

Jaba: He says that he will travel from village to village in order to see the country and learn local songs.

Mother: On foot?

Jaba: That's what he plans to do.

Mother: Some boy! [*Places a fond hand on Sagar.*] Mad for his country, mad for songs. Well, Sagar, you haven't sung for us yet.

Sagar: I don't know any song that can be sung here.

Mother: You only know popular and modern songs? Ah! Moshin was such a good singer!

Sagar: He was truly a good singer.

Jaba: Have you listened to him sing?

Sagar: Just one.

Mother: Which one? Dariyai kul pailam na?

Jaba: That was his favourite song.

Sagar: It is my favourite, too.

Jaba: Do you know that song?

Sagar: No.

Mother: Hey son, why didn't you tell us before? I have been so restlessly waiting to hear that song for so long. Sing.

Sagar: That song?

Jaba: Please sing.

Sagar: No! Aren't we supposed to leave for some place?

Jaba: So what?

Mother: Let it be. Let me not hear that emotional song in the daytime. Sing that song to me in the night while sitting on the banks of the river.

Sagar: That song is my—

Mother: That was my son's song. You know that song and so you have to sing it. Where is that burnt smell coming from?

Jaba: Is the rice burnt?

Mother: You are always dancing around, Jaba. Go get the rice-cooking pot off the oven. Nothing works in this house if I don't take personal care of it. Where are you going, Sagar?

Sagar: I am going out to check whether the car has arrived or not.

Mother: Don't worry. Fakruddi will let us know. I want to know about something from you.

Sagar: Tell me.

Mother: Did Shankar ever get a head injury?

Sagar: Why?

Mother: Is he suffering from mental disorder?

Sagar: Mental disorder and that, too, Shankar? Are you crazy? He is too clever.

Mother: I found he had drenched himself with water. I found his bed drenched. He has very strange looks in his eyes.

Sagar: Your daughter.

Mother: What do you mean?

Sagar: Jaba poured a bucketful of water on him.

Mother: Jaba!

Sagar: Yes, it is her. That was probably an expression of her love for her Shankar Da.

Mother: What nonsense! I wouldn't have realized women could be so dangerous had I not seen my own daughter. A dacoit!

[*Shankar comes reading a letter.*]

Mother: Son Shankar, Jaba did that to you—

Shankar: What?

Mother: Jaba—

Shankar: I am going to kill her.

Mother: You better do that. I entrust that responsibility with you. I cannot show my face to you. Let me see if things are ready or not.

[*She leaves.*]

Shankar: Sagar, where are you going?

Sagar: Since Mother has left Jaba's fate in your hands, there's no reason why I should stay here.

Shankar: You are harping that line. Can't you figure out that Jaba?

Sagar: Jaba is coming this way.

Shankar: Let her.

Jaba: Brother Shankar, please listen.

Shankar: Is anybody listening to me now? On the one hand, I am being pampered here. On the other, secret messenger are being sent to the doctor.

Jaba:	Brother Shankar, please, please listen to me. I beg of you.
Shankar:	Now I am going to break into the dance of destruction and leave for the forbidden land.
Jaba:	Before you launch that programme, listen to me just once. [*Asks Sagar.*] What don't you tell him?
Shankar:	What is he going to tell?
Jaba:	That you are not listening to me. There are times when I am not beside myself.
Shankar:	So what do I have to do?
Jaba:	Forgive me this time.
Shankar:	Really? [*He picks up the cot and swings it above his head.*] Alright, I forgive you.
Jaba:	I have never seen another specimen like you. I was feeling sad.
Sagar:	Are you planning to burn the rice once again?
Jaba:	This time, Mother is going to have my neck. While I am away, you keep brother Shankar amused.

[*She departs.*]

Shankar:	Keep me amused! Hasn't she learnt her lessons?
Sagar:	Don't go after her, Shankar?
Shankar:	Why?
Sagar:	I am not liking your childish behaviour anymore.
Shankar:	Why?
Shankar:	That's because I got you wrong.
Shankar:	Did you also think that I have a mental problem?
Sagar:	I just thought—
Shankar:	Understood. Now forget it.
Sagar:	Forgive me, brother.
Shankar:	Alright.

Sagar: It's not alright!

Shankar: It's alright. You and your ilk are like that.

Sagar: Like what?

Shankar: Neither is it easy to make mistakes that you do, nor is it effortless to pay back with a free mind. People like you are the heroes of mundane plays and novels.

Sagar: What about people like you?

Shankar: We are the kind that does not figure in plays. At the most, we could run parallel to the scripts. Everything is alright in our times.

Sagar: Do you people see everything that is happening in the world as right?

Shankar: No. But we are ready when we face a new situation. We shout slogans – 'It's alright'. We are the eternal dewdrops on a lotus frond. We sparkle and roll, but we never stick to anything.

Sagar: You know Shankar, Mother was asking me to sing moments ago.

Shankar: That's a nice idea!

Sagar: She wanted to hear *Dariyai kul pailam na.*

Shankar: Did you sing?

Sagar: I will die if I sing that song.

Shankar: Have you lent a thought to the main issue?

Sagar: Which one?

Shankar: That how would you have Jaba in your life? Have you thought about it with a clear mind?

Sagar: No. Shankar, I wonder what would happen to me?

Shankar: What is it about?

Sagar: About Mohsin. Do you think she would treat me as a human being after she gets to know what I did to her elder brother? Besides—

Shankar: Besides?

Sagar: Her and my societies are different.

Shankar: Yes.

Sagar: Would her parents accept the idea?

Shankar: Big question.

Sagar: And my society—

Shankar: I am your society. The problem is arising from within you.

Sagar: Who said? No, that's not right. But, after all, she is a Muslim. What would Jamai Babu think?

Shankar: Ask him that question.

Sagar: How?

Shankar: Here is a letter from Khitishbabu. He will be here the day after tomorrow. But he is not going to be the one who will have a family with Jaba.

Sagar: I cannot understand what I want.

Shankar: Speak to your mind about what you are aspiring for.

[*He leaves.*]

Sagar: Shankar, wait! I am scared. [*He finds nobody around and sits down on the cot.*] Oh! God!

[*At a distance, the laborious sound of the wooden wheels of an oxen driven cart can be heard.*]

Fakir: [*In the background.*] Chote Mian, Shovan Mian's cart is here!

[*The sound of the wheels is close. Sagar stands helplessly.*]

— Curtains came down —

Sixth Scene

[*Same scenario. Two days later. It is dusk. A sense of sloth relief prevails. Fakiruddi is snoozing off at the same spot on the verandah. Beside a lantern, mother is weaving patterns into a sheet of cloth. A little away, Jaba is sitting on the cot and reading a book.*]

Mother: [*Lifts her face.*] Shankar and your father haven't returned from Dhaka with that brother-in-law!

Jaba: Maybe, the steamer has not been plying.

Mother: Where's Sagar?

Jaba: He is sitting next to the river.

Mother: He is not his own self for the past two days. Any idea why?

Jaba: No.

Mother: I can't figure out the way his mind works. Does Sagar know that you may leave today?

Jaba: I told him in the late afternoon. He wants to come along with me.

Mother: Where?

Jaba: With me.

Mother: How is that possible?

Fakir: What are you saying?

Jaba: Wouldn't you let us go together? Or will you gather a posse of villagers and say that your daughter is being kidnapped?

Mother: Jaba!

Jaba: Mother, it was you who had sung that song—

Nanan boron gabhi re bhai, aki boron dudh
Bhuban bharmiya dekhi, aki ma-er poot

Mother: True. I believe in those words.

Jaba: Then?

Mother: I don't know. Just stop it now. Sagar is strange.

Jaba: Why?

Mother: He has still not sung that song.

Jaba: Shall I call him?

Mother: Why?

Jaba: So that he sings. I guess that song will remain unheard considering the possibility of our departure today.

Mother: Eid is just round the corner. Can't he wait for a little while more?

Jaba: No.

Mother: You go now.

Jaba: Mother.

Mother: Yes?

Jaba: You didn't appear to be affected.

Mother: When?

Jaba: When I told you that Haq Sahib is returning from Karachi and I have to leave home.

Mother: No, that didn't affect me.

Jaba: Why, Mother?

Mother: That's because I don't know how to stop you.

Jaba: If you had a way, would you have stopped me?

Mother: I wouldn't allow myself to be affected by worries for small things when there is a greater cause to fight for.

Jaba: Mother!

Mother: I am finished, but I am pledging my daughter to the country. I hope she stays in fine fettle.

Jaba: Mother! You know, what's coming up?

Mother: You tell me.

Jaba: We will get authentic information when Jamai Babu from Dhaka comes. I will leave immediately.

We are expecting Martial Law anytime soon. This would lead to random arrests, torture and injustice.

Fakir: We give a damn.

Mother: What did you say?

Fakir: It's not possible to molly-coddle every new regime every time. This time, we will create havoc.

Mother: But you are so lazy!

Fakir: I, too, have the fire in me.

Jaba: You are the first recruit of my army. Would you be able to sail a boat and take me across the river?

Fakir: Of course!

Mother: But why aren't they coming?

Jaba: There was no steamer today.

Mother: I told him repeatedly to take Fakra with them, but he wouldn't listen.

Jaba: Mother!

Jaba: Wish we could listen to that song!

Mother: Fakra, call Sagar.

Fakra: Yes.

Mother: Go now.

Fakir: Yes, yes, I am going now. [*He gets up grimacing.*] Chote Mian!

Sagar: [*In the background.*] What, Fakiruddi?

Fakir: Boujan is calling you.

Sagar: [*In the background.*] I am coming.

Fakir: [*Returns.*] He is coming.

Mother: Jaba, has Sagar said anything else to you?

Jaba: [*Raising her face.*] What?

Mother: The boy is so nice, but he always seems to be lost in something.

Jaba: So tough!

Mother: What did you say?

[*Sagar arrives.*]

Sagar: Mother, hasn't Shankar come with Jamai Babu yet?

Mother: No.

Sagar: Jaba, do you want to cross the river in the night?

Jaba: Yes.

Sagar: Do you know that storm clouds are gathering?

Jaba: I may not go today.

Sagar: But you may need to go today.

Jaba: Once I get to hear from Jamai Babu about the situation in Dhaka, I would decide whether it would be safe for me to stay here or not. After all, I am a marked person!

Mother: Sagar, do you want to accompany Jaba?

Sagar: I am thinking. Mother, I could sense the palpable tension in the air while I was sitting on the banks. The breeze is not blowing and the sails of the boats are hanging low.

Mother: Why aren't they here yet? I can only hear whispers in the air. Wish I knew for certain what was happening.

Sagar: Jaba, what have you decided?

Mother: Sing that song.

Sagar: Song?

Mother: Let's go to the riverside.

Sagar: Let me not sing that song now.

Mother: No. Come with me.

Sagar: Shall I?

[*Father arrives.*]

Father: Shankar has lost his way.

Sagar: What does that mean?

Father: Before he went to the jetty, Shankar said he wanted to visit the school building once more.

Mother: Was it him or you who had said that?

Father: I mean, we both said that. As a matter of fact, obstacles like these are not unexpected.

Sagar: Which obstacles?

Father: Obstacles on the way to the nation's progress. This, however, is temporary and expected. It is difficult to identify the right path and even more difficult to take a step on that path.

Sagar: You—

Father: Yes, this is the truth. You see, since time immemorial, Bangladesh is continuing to flow in its peopled demography. Yet, we have not been able to do away with social ills like class and religious differences. When we look at ourselves from a distance, we feel as if that those differences have finally been banished. But our own way of life belie that belief. Such as—

Mother: Where have you left that boy?

Father: What?

Mother: Where is Shankar?

Father: Shankar?

Mother: Has my question entered your head?

Father: Oh! Yes! Shankar said he would find his way back and asked me to write the last point. In fact, we were both caught in a very interesting part of the discussion. A little later, when I came back, I met Taher, the son of the steamer's pilot. I asked him whether he had seen Shankar receive the guest from Dhaka. He said there were some passengers but Shankar wasn't there. He said quite firmly that Shankar wasn't there. He must have lost his way.

Mother: He has lost his way and you have come back home to unleash your speeches!

Father: No. I wanted to go out but returned when I saw the dark clouds gather at a corner of the western skies. It may rain.

Mother: Tell me, what kind of a human being are you?

Father: Enough, enough. Jaba, could you please fetch me the umbrella? I will go out.

[*Jaba walks away.*]

Mother: You will go out again?

Father: I have to look for him.

Mother: Why can't Fakra go?

Father: No, no, he wouldn't be able to do it.

Mother: And then, I have to send someone else to look for you. Let's engage ourselves through the night to look for one another.

[*Jaba bring the umbrella.*]

Father: I would set everything right. Actually, Shankar is not in his senses anymore.

Mother: Stop talking.

Father: Enough, enough.

[*He leaves.*]

Mother: Look at my fate! My life with him is such a waste. I wonder whom my father had given my hand to!

Fakir: Don't try to cry at this age.

Mother: Let go of my feet!

Jaba: But you sing that song.

Mother: Yes, sing.

Sagar: Shall I?

Mother: Sing the way Mohsin used to.

Sagar: Mohsin?

Mother: Yes, Mohsin.

Sagar: I have been repeatedly trying to tell you that many memories, events and sagas are associated with that song.

Mother: And I have been telling you repeatedly as well that I am firmly tethered to that song for many reasons.

Sagar: It will hurt if I sing that song.

Mother: It will hurt if I listen to that song. [*Pulls him.*] Let's go.

Sagar: [*On the embankment.*] Mother, this song brings back all the memories.

Jaba: What did you say?

Sagar: Nothing. See, the clouds are flexing their muscles.

Jaba: It's going to pour.

Sagar: And you want to be in the rains alone?

Jaba: Won't you sing?

Sagar: Shall I sing?

Mother: Sagar, please sing.

[*They look at each other. Sagar turns his back towards them, covers his face and looks for a start. Mother and Jaba sit at a distance and below. They train their eyes on him. Sagar looks twice at them hesitatingly, closes his eyes and starts: 'Naiya bhai, Sudan naiya'. With a full voice, he sings the whole song. Fakiruddi gets up slowly, comes close, and watches Sagar in awe. Mother sits with her eyes closed. Jaba walks up, collects the sheet of cloth her mother was stitching and the books and dumps them on the verandah. She then returns to her earlier position. Sagar raises his voice to the point where Mohsin had stopped years ago. He opens his eyes. His eyes bear a lost look. He looks at Mother and Jaba sharply.*]

Jaba: Finish the song!

Sagar: There is no end to this song! [*He clutches his chest and screams.*] The upheaval inside me is unbearable!

[*He runs along the embankment and disappears.*]

Mother: [*Opens her eyes.*] Where are you going son, leaving me behind?

Jaba: [*Holds her mother.*] Mother!

Fakir: [*Springs up.*] Chote Mian!

[*Runs after Sagar.*]

Jaba: Leave him alone. Too much pain is trapped inside him. Haven't you felt his pain?

Mother: What is that pain that is hurting him so much?

Jaba: I don't know. I am scared.

Mother: [*Stares into the vast openness.*] It's going to rain soon.

Jaba: That corner of the sky is really dark like ink.

Mother: I still cannot understand this world. Happiness comes to you only to vanish, like a light being switched on and off. I have no clue to the ways of this world.

Jaba: Let's go.

[*Quietly, they leave. Fakiruddi and Sagar appear on the embankment.*]

Fakir: I have a clue to what you have in your mind. You want to kill me.

Sagar: Bhuban bharmiya dekhi, aki ma-er poot.

Fakir: We need real men these days. Why would you take lives?

Sagar: Only if I could rid myself of the hangover of that dream that exist in darkness.

Fakir: You showed the way and so I changed.

Sagar: I have finally realized that everything is hiding inside me.

Fakir: Share with humanity the hidden treasure that you have inside you.

Sagar: I am responsible for what happened to Mohsin. I am the reason why I have been burning from inside for these four years. I am the problem behind accepting Jaba. You know Fakir, the one who my wisdom had perceived as true was the one my mind could not accept. This is my tragedy. Hindu, Muslim.

Fakir: You have shown us that there is no difference between Hindus and Muslims.

Sagar: Oh! Pity me!

[*He covers his ears with his hands and runs away. Fakir takes a step forward.*]

Fakir: Go. You want to be all by yourself at this moment. Go and sit in the darkness.

[*Jaba comes.*]

Jaba: Uncle Fakir!

Fakir: He wants to be left alone. Don't bother him now.

Jaba: Who?

Fakir: My dear Jaba, Mohsin has come back!

Jaba: My mother shares your opinion after hearing him sing.

Fakir: What is your mother doing?

Jaba: She is crying. In fact, weeping. But—

Fakir: Tell me.

Jaba: We will go to the abode of Sonaullah.

Fakir: Let me bring the boat and tether it to the embankment before the rain arrives. Would you be able to steer the hull while crossing the river?

Jaba: I can. [*Shankar arrives, his clothes muddied.*] Shankarbhai!

Shankar: Don't tell me!

Jaba: What happened?

Shankar: I didn't know where exactly the jetty was. I only had a direction. As I walked, I reached a huge field. I thought I would take a shortcut through the field after I saw some lights on the other side of it. I kept circling in the darkness. Where's Sagar?

Fakir: Don't look for him. He wants to be left alone.

Jaba: Fakir Uncle!

Fakir: I will be back right now. Be ready, dear Jaba.

[*He leaves.*]

Shankar: It seems I can signs of life in Fakiruddi!

Jaba: The sleeping giant is awakening!

Shankar: When did that revolution happen?

Jaba: When Sagar was singing.

Shankar: Really! That song – Dariyai kul pailam na?

Jaba: Yes.

Shankar: What happened next?

Jaba: Shankarbhai, would you tell me something?

Shankar: What?

Jaba: What is there inside Sagar?

Shankar: A very kind heart.

Jaba: Not that. There's—

Shankar: What?

Jaba: Why did he suddenly stop singing and run away?

Shankar: Did he run away? To where?

Jaba: To the banks of the river. You know what's gnawing at him. Won't you tell me?

Shankar: I know why he dashed like that. But I won't say a thing.

Jaba: But much of my future course of action depends on—

Shankar: I know that, too. Still, I won't say anything. It's only Sagar who can tell you.

Jaba: But when is he going to do that?

Shankar: I really don't know. Does he still want to go with you?

Jaba: He is only saying that.

Shankar: The only hindrance is the lack of harmony between the either ends of our minds.

Jaba: In spite of that, I was ready to push away the hindrance and move forward.

Shankar: It is not always possible to shake off hindrances. One has to wait.

Jaba: Especially when I am the only one who is ready, isn't it?

Shankar: Neither you nor I have an idea about who's preparing how and where. Will you give me your word?

Jaba: Tell me.

Shankar: No matter the pain or the obstacles you face, never banish reason and logic from your life. Jaba: Why did you say that?

[*Sagar returns. He is looking calm.*]

Sagar: Shankar!

Shankar: [*Startled.*] Who? Oh, you! I will go now.

Sagar: Hasn't Jamai Babu arrived yet?

Shankar: Are you serious about accompanying Jaba?

Sagar: Of course! After returning to Kolkata, you would rejoin work and politics and I would end up singing with nowhere to go. It's better that—

Shankar: Were you sitting near the river?

Sagar: Yes. I was sitting on the banks that were flooded with a faint light from the stars. On the other side, the clouds were gathering. You know what I saw?

Shankar: What?

Sagar: A dream. Uncle was talking about the flow of humanity in Bangladesh. I saw that flow. I am gripped with a strange feeling.

Shankar: Caused by a dream?

Sagar: Yes, caused by a dream. History is a dream and a reality as well.

Jaba: Shankarbhai, won't you wash up?

Shankar: Don't drive me away. I would go anyway.

[*He leaves.*]

Sagar: Jaba!

Jaba: Yes?

Sagar: Aren't you happy that I wish to come along with you?

Jaba: Weren't you singing while you were sitting on the banks of the river?

Sagar: Yes, I was humming. I added a few stanzas, too.

Jaba: You wanted to say something.

Sagar: You know Jaba, when I was sitting there, I felt as if I was washing myself clean of all the differences...

Jaba: Are you talking about the religious differences between Hindus and Muslims?

Sagar: Yes.

Jaba: These two words are my greatest concerns.

Sagar: What?

Jaba: I begin where these two words end.

Sagar: I, too, have reached that beginning after crossing long distances. That change was holistic from inside. As I began loving the traditions and heritage of my country, I found myself here.

Jaba: Is this what you wanted to tell me?

Sagar: Even this. I have much to say but I cannot arrange my thoughts to express properly.

Jaba: I want to know something from you?

Sagar: What is it?

Jaba: Why did you suddenly stop the song and dash off?

Sagar: Jaba!

Jaba: I am scared.

Sagar: Are you afraid of me?

Jaba: I am afraid for you. What is that pain you are suffering from?

Sagar: I am not being able to tell you.

Jaba: I want to hear.

Sagar: I am scared.

Jaba: What or who are you afraid of?

Sagar: If I tell you, you would never want to see me again.

Jaba: What is that story that you cannot tell?

Sagar: Jaba, would you accept me and take me along with you?

Jaba: Say that!

Sagar: Would you accept me as your companion?

Jaba: What are you saying!

Sagar: I can't take it any longer.

Jaba: Look into my eyes. Can you?

Sagar: [*Looks her into the eye, calmly.*] I did not save Mohsin's life.

Jaba: You did not!

Sagar: The Sagar Mohsin had met in 1946 was another person with whom I share my name. That was not me.

Jaba: Not you!

Sagar: I came to know Mohsin in 1950, the year he died.

Jaba: Stop now!

[*She moves away to the other side.*]

Sagar: I am going to tell you everything today.

Jaba: Tell.

Sagar: Mohsin was apprehended from my house. One Sagar saved him while another gave him away. I am that Sagar.

Jaba: Sagar!

Sagar: At that point of time, I could only think that I was a Hindu who exacted a revenge on a Muslim. Later I realized that one was a Bengali and the other, a human being. One Bengali had

	led a human being to his death for no reason. I am a beast!
Jaba:	Sagar!
Sagar:	For four long years, pangs of remorse and a deep sense of guilt were incinerating me from inside. After that, I came here. While on the banks of that river, I realized I had wrong. I realized how false perceptions have devastated my life.
Jaba:	Sagar! [*Look at him with her eyes wide open.*]
Sagar:	I am a firework that faded prematurely into the sky.
Jaba:	Four years ago, you had—
Sagar:	In the end, I came here.
Jaba:	But why?
Sagar:	To do penance.
Jaba:	Did you want to tell my parents as well?
Sagar:	I had thought of telling everyone. But I couldn't.
Jaba:	Thank you for sparing two old persons their lives.
Sagar:	Jaba!
Jaba:	Were you here for penance or did you have plans to kill again? Aren't you satisfied after killing one human being?
Sagar:	Jaba!
Jaba:	You are a Hindu and you have killed a Muslim.
Sagar:	I had similar thoughts.
Jaba:	What do you want now?
Sagar:	Forgiveness.
Jaba:	A Muslim is standing in front of you.
Sagar:	What?
Jaba:	A Muslim is standing front of you. You can seek her pardon. This Muslim knows that she, too, has to seek pardon on behalf of her race.

Sagar: Jaba!

Jaba: Forgive me, I suddenly became weak in the mind. Expressing of repentance or reparation cannot be rushed into. Life is like a flowing river from which small islands appear following years of silting.

Sagar: I wonder how you are being able to use such strong logic as you speak.

Jaba: Something is making me do it. Life was mercilessly snuffed out of someone who was so dear to me. But you are alive. Everything is for those who are living.

Sagar: People die different deaths. The way I killed Mohsin is different from the manner in which her sister slayed me today.

Jaba: Sagar!

Sagar: Jaba, you took biting revenge!

[*A knock can be heard on the door.*]

Khitish: [*In the background.*] Is this the home of Taslim Mian?

Sagar: Jamai Babu!

[*Sagar opens the door. A tired Khitish with a bag in his hand, enters.*]

Khitish: Hello, my brother-in-law! [*Looks at Jaba.*] Haven't I seen you somewhere before?

Jaba: At your Dhaka home.

Khitish: Yes, along with Paresh. Sagar, you know of Paresh, who is a cousin from my father's side.

Jaba: Please sit down.

[*Shankar enters in changed clothes as Khitish sits.*]

Shankar: Hey, Khitish Babu!

Khitish:	Don't behave like a monkey! Aren't you in the same league as Paresh? Your days are over.

[*Mother arrives.*]

Mother:	Who is this gentleman?
Shankar:	My Jamai Babu from Dhaka.
Mother:	Jaba, get some warm water ready for him to wash up.
Khitish:	What did you say?
Mother:	Has Haq Sahib returned from Karachi?
Khitish:	[*Gets up.*] Shankar, Sagar, you must take the night train to Kolkata. Iskander Mirza has declared.
Military	Rule.
Jaba:	What?
Mother:	Military Rule?
Jaba:	I have sent Fakiruddi Uncle to get the boat.
Mother:	You have, already?
Jaba:	Let me get ready. [*Addressing Shankar.*] I have followed your advice and strengthened my mind with logic

[*She leaves.*]

Mother:	Oh! Allah! Jaba has to leave.
Sagar:	Khitish Babu!
Khitish:	What?
Sagar:	Military Rule means—
Khitish:	Virulent despotism, torture and injustice. The Cabinet has been disbanded. Combing operations will be launched in Dhaka from tomorrow. The United Front workers are now running to the villages to take cover.

Mother: Sheer darkness! Come. Let me hand you the water for washing up.

Khitish: Let's go.

Shankar: Mother, in the mean time, bring the suitcases to the other room. We have to pack.

[*Mother and Khitish leave.*]

Shankar: Hey!

Sagar: What?

Shankar: Have you told her?

Sagar: I spilled everything out.

Shankar: What did she say?

Sagar: Say what?

Shankar: Has she agreed?

Sagar: Shankar, the sister has avenged the brother.

Shankar: What did she say about you accompanying her? And—

Sagar: And?

Shankar: Yes, when you told her, what did she say?

Sagar: I didn't ask her.

Shankar: You didn't ask her?

Sagar: No, I forgot completely. Sorry, I just asked once but she didn't reply. Shankar!

Shankar: What?

Sagar: Did she only turn her disdain for me into forgiveness?

Shankar: You haven't told me what exactly transpired between the two of you. How can I say?

Sagar: Shankar, she is leaving today. In fact, right now.

Shankar: Before she leaves...

[*Jaba arrives in the red saree that she was wearing in the fourth scene.*]

Jaba: Shankarbhai, would please let me touch your feet as per your Hindu tradition?

Shankar: Why so, you monkey?

Sagar: Jaba!

Jaba: Sagar, I wanted to say something to you but I was not able to say it properly.

Sagar: To me?

Shankar: I will slip away from here.

Jaba: No, you stay. Sagar, I have not been able to pay my respects to you.

Sagar: What are you saying?

Jaba: Misdeeds are not unusual. But not everybody can devote their life to righting the wrongs they once did. You have done that.

Shankar: That's because of his propensity for dramatization of situations.

Sagar: Jaba? Jaba, I, too, have a question for you.

Jaba: What?

Sagar: Where did you get the strength to suppress the pain I inflicted on you?

Jaba: I owe that to love, my love for those who are living.

Sagar: Was that possible only because of love? Jaba!

[*Father comes in, panting.*]

Father: I couldn't find Shankar. Oh! You are here! A storm is building.

Shankar: Storm?

Father: Yes, the clouds are hanging precariously low now! Jaba will have to face when she leaves.

Shankar: She is not going alone.

Father: Yes, Fakiruddi will be with her.

[*Fakiruddi waits with the oars near the boat.*]

Fakir: Chote Mian, I have brought the boat to the pier. The sky is acting up. You have to hurry.

Shankar: Uncle, this is Khitish Babu.

Father: Welcome, Sir! Please do not mind, I am squirming in embarrassment.

Mother: Fakra, load the luggage.

[*Fakir goes inside.*]

Shankar: Where are our suitcases?

Mother: In the east room.

Shankar: Sagar, let's go and pack up.

[*Both of them leave.*]

Mother: Jaba, you are leaving in the darkness to come back shining into this home!

Father: Phooljan Bibi! The clouds have begun to clot.

Mother: Do you see tears in my eyes? I will wipe my eyes dry. Let them go and return in peace. Let my countrymen be happy. Let peace shower on us from all sides like the rain.

[*Sagar reappears.*]

Mother: Son Sagar, why did you rush out that time? You know, Sagar sang for us today.

Father: Sagar-er kul pailam na?

Khitish: That song?

Mother: You know that song, the one that my Mohsin used to sing?

Khitish: Yes.

Mother: You all are so close to my heart!

Father: But Sagar didn't sing for me.

Mother: Sing for him Sagar. Let that old man not be deprived of that song. [*Addressing her husband.*] You know, when I was listening to Sagar sing with my eyes closed, I had a vision of my son.

[*Fakir arrives with the luggage and climbs the embankment.*]

Fakir: Utter Gazi's name and be prepared to leave, dear Jaba.

Sagar: Jaba!

Jaba: What?

Sagar: You are leaving now, but you haven't yet answered by question.

Mother: Does Sagar wish to go with Jaba?

Sagar: Yes. Jamai Babu, I have decided to accompany Jaba.

Khitish: What?

[*Shankar arrives with a suitcase in his hand.*]

Sagar: For this time, I want to go with Jaba.

Father: What is he saying? [*Addressing his wife.*] Why don't you reply?

Khitish: Sagar, are you out of your mind? Why you talking nonsense?

Sagar: [*Takes the suitcase from Shankar.*] Khitish Babu, you used to say that Bangla belonged to Bengalis. And Uncle, what happened to that Bengali flow of yours?

Father: Look here, Sagar. I am confused. While I don't want to say 'no' to you, my mind is not agreeing. I mean, people around would read between the lines if you and Jaba leave together. I cannot bypass my society. If you must go, you go.

Jaba: Father!

Father: See, I have grown old. Don't rush me. I can't stand it.

Sagar: Jamai Babu!

Khitish: I wasn't prepared for this situation. I have to think, as much as you have to.

Sagar: Why?

Khitish: Sorry brother, I don't have the gumption to tell you. But there is a difference. I cannot support the idea of plunging into darkness without comprehending that element.

Sagar: Mother, what about you?

Mother: I want to see and understand why harmony and contrariety exist side by side.

Sagar: Why are you all so morose? Jaba, this is your reality. The colour changes when personal life is threatened. I feel like screaming and running away from everything. Shankar, Jaba, go wherever you have to go with your reality. I will live with my dreams.

Shankar: Reality cannot be wished away! Sagar, give me the suitcase.

[*He takes the suitcase.*]

Jaba: Shankarbhai!

Shankar: Now is the time to wait. They are willing to co-exist but unite. Let them live with these conceptions. Let their sacrament be assaulted day after day. Only after that shall these people be seamless. Come down, Sagar.

[*He holds Sagar by the hand and climbs down.*]

Jaba: Shankarbhai!

Mother: [*Climbs to the embankment and raiser her hand to bless.*] Fakra, hail Bard!

Fakra: [*Begins the Islamic religious chant.*] Gazi, Gazi, Badr, Badr!

[*Jaba pauses for a few moments.*]

Jaba: You are saying we have to wait even though there is no reason or logic?

Shankar: Yes. This is the bane of progressive reformers.

[*Jaba covers her face with both her hands and climbs down.*]

Sagar: Shankar, I still haven't had a clear reply from Jaba.

Shankar: How soon that reply comes would depend on how strong your backbone is. Everybody has to be jolted out of stupor. And with your soul between your teeth, you have to scream: This is injustice, this is false. You know it but you still can't rise. You have fallen and sunk!

Sagar: Mother?

Nanan boron gabhi re bhai aki boron dudh.
Bhuban bhormiya dekhi aki ma-er poot.

There can't be a greater lie than this! Humans can be so pretentious!

Mother: No! [*She runs up.*] Fakiruddi, turn the boat and bring it to the pier.

Father: What are you doing?

Khitish: Why are you calling the boat back?

Mother: I will not allow the blood of my heart to be maligned. Humans are not fakes. We are pure.

Jaba: Mother! [*Wraps her arms around her mother.*] I knew, Mother. I knew.

Sagar: Hey Shankar, the suitcase?

Shankar: Here it is. [*Climbs.*] So, does that mark and end to your search?

Sagar: Now is the time to walk the roads.

Khitish: But mother, aren't you showing haste?

Father: Please don't stop her.

Shankar: You want to leave now? Alright, I will stay with my land, with my human Mother!

Jaba: Will you go to Kolkata, Shankarbhai?

Shankar: Yes, back to my workplace.

Mother: Sagar, I won't be able to listen to you sing again!

Sagar: Do you want to listen to it now?

Jaba: But the sky is threatening.

Sagar: I will sing from the boat at the top of my voice.

Father: Leave now! There's a long way to go.

Sagar: Yes, let's go. We will be passing through complete darkness. I have to sing using a high pitch so that the harmonies of my song reach even home forecourts.

Jaba: Watch your steps.

[*They descend.*]

Mother: The air is moist. It's going to rain now.

Khitish: Shankar!

Shankar: [*Gets off the embankment.*] Yes?

Khitish: It seems you are the hero of the piece.

Shankar: That is not true. Let's go.

Khitish: Where?

Shankar: Let's find out if Sagar has begun to sing the song. We can then sit down for dinner. After that, what?

Oh! The night train! Khitish Babu, any idea what awaits us at the next turn?

Khitish: Next turn?

Shankar: Yes.

Mother: My dear... I... I...

[*Shankar grips her hand.*]

Father: [*From the embankment.*] He has begun to sing.

Mother: Has he?

[*She runs up to the embankment. They can here Sagar sing the notes in an expressive voice.*]

Naiya bhai!
Chakrapath-e ghuira mor mon roilo udash –
Batash tobu abhash-e dai notun bhor-er bash.
Byathai amar buk je bhange asha bhange na
Shath-e ache hajar manush, toofan dari na.

(I am awash with emotions as I go around in circles. The wind indicates that the dawn is not far away. My heart aches but my hopes continue to rise. I am not scared of storms because I am walking with a thousand people.)

[*Suddenly, a flash of lighting streaks across the sky. The clouds begin to rumble. They look up to the sky. A chorus of a hundred voices has joined the singing. The last stanza keeps breaking on the stage like high waves. Four persons are standing still. Roughing up the date tree, the storm arrives.*]

— Curtains —

3

Agony

Preamble

Jwala was written in 1950 against the backdrop of a series of unfortunate incidents during that period. A little before this play was written, many people in the eastern Indian city of Kolkata had committed suicide in a span of one month. The characters used in this play are among those who took their own lives. All the characters have been inspired from real life incidents except the lunatic. From that point of view, this play could be considered as a documentary.

Considering the backgrounds of these characters, it wouldn't be amiss to see an element of pain and misery behind this play. I would be grateful to those who may want to keep that in mind. It would be of much help if one can keep John Strindberg in mind while staging this play. Strindberg, a Swedish playwright, was known for combining psychology and naturalism to create expressionist drama. Besides, he had successfully used colloquial and realistic speech in his plays.

Translator's Note

The play was written in the aftermath of Partition that had split the Indian landmass into three parts –West Pakistan, India and East Pakistan. In the original script, the author used colloquial language mostly based on Bangla dialects used in the erstwhile East Pakistan, which is now Bangladesh. Even though it is not possible to have the unique flavor of the dialects truly reflected by the English script, I have tried to keep the dialogues colloquial and close to what Ritwik Ghatak had written in Bangla, without sacrificing repartee or sense. But some meaningful changes were required to be made in the names of some characters, such as *Bodhu* and *Khoka*. *Bodhu* in Bangla means a young, married woman but there is no one word for that in English. Therefore, I have used 'woman' instead of *Bodhu*. Similarly, a young boy is usually called *Khoka* in Bangla. To make it clear that the character is a young boy, I have used 'boy' and not *Khoka*. However, during the course of the play, the 'woman' also calls the 'Boy' as *Khokon*. In most parts of West Bengal, a young boy is often lovingly called Khokon. There are other subtle changes I had to introduce because some portions in the script would make no sense to the reader if they were transliterated. For example, some feelings and emotions require just one or two words in Bangla to express, whereas the whole sentence in English needs to be deployed for the same purpose.

Characters

Shefali Bandopadhyay (referred as Woman and Bodhu in the play): She is the wife of Kalidas Bandopadhyay, who is the yardmaster of the Kalighat station on the Kalighat-Falta rail route. Shefali had taken her own life. She had doused herself with kerosene and set herself on fire because she could no longer withstand the misery of her unfed children.

Khokon (referred as Boy in the play): He is a landless boy. It was so painful for him to witness everyday the increasing pecuniary distress being faced by his mother and sister that he jumped in the front of a speeding train at a railway crossing near the Howrah Station.

Purno Babu: He was employed by the General Post Office. At the age of sixty, he was fired from his job without any prior notice or explanation. In extreme penury, he survived only on water and did the rounds of offices at the Dalhousie Square, searching for another job. But he couldn't get any. Completely hapless, he jumped to his death from the third floor of the Burma Shell building.

Bhola: He was a labourer at a jute mill in Barrackpore. As he worked at the mill, almost invisible jute fibres would enter his lungs. As a result, he began suffering from tuberculosis. He went from one hospital to another to find treatment but not one admitted him. So he killed himself to get relief from pain.

Peon: He was working with the erstwhile Presidency College. He had a burning desire to pursue Education so much so that he enrolled with the Ripon College by the dint of his own efforts. He didn't get his dues cleared from Presidency college which made him a broke.. On the one hand, he had an examination to write and on the other hand, Ripon College would not let him do so unless he paid the exam fees. Later, when he went to the Principal of Presidency College to demand what was legitimately due to him, was insulted and driven away. The next day, his body was found hanging from the ceiling of a room in the premises of Presidency College.

Lunatic: A lunatic inhabiting the sidewalks near the crossing in Kolkata's Hedo area.

[A small piece of pale land dotted with undulation; at the end of the stretch is an old, barren Indian Gum-Arabic tree (called 'Babla' in West Bengal), completely burnt out by the thunder strike. It's lifeless, high branches seem to be cursing the skies. The smoky, misty land disappears behind the tree into sheer emptiness. One or two thorny clutters of cacti silently announce their ominous presence. To the left are the still and opaque waters of a long-unused pond reflecting low light. From the pond has risen a thin layer of mist that lay coiled in emptiness. Not a soul to be seen anywhere on that rough pasture that wears an unearthly, lost look. It is still, lifeless and without even any suggestion of a breeze. Silence descends as the curtain goes up. The sound of thunder reverberates, casting a ghostly light that makes everything look pale for a moment.

A twisted voice could be heard continuously, like a wail repeatedly slicing the silence of the pasture. The Babla tree begins to tremble. Shadows, like apparitions, speed across the rough pasture, as if the sun is being eclipsed by flitting clouds. The atmosphere appears cursed and demonic. Suddenly, from the other side of the pond, a dark shadow comes up racing in serpentine movements and appears right in the middle of the stage. From the shadow's wavy and long hair, one can make out that it is of a woman. The woman is emitting blood-curling screams until she stops moving. As she stops, a flash of lightning illuminates her face. She appears to be a lovable housewife from a middle-class home. But badly burnt flesh from half of her face is hanging loose. Burn marks in black and white can be seen on her body. Her saree is half-burnt and her right hand is raised towards her face in an obvious sign of fear.]

Woman: Ohhh! It's burning! It's burning!

[*Suddenly, a thin voice of a youth rises from seemingly nowhere.*]

Voice: And then?

Woman: Huh?

[*She looks around to trace the source of the voice. The voice begins to chuckle.*]

Voice: Surprised?

Woman: Yes.

[*She finds no one around but from near her feet sits up a young boy of fifteen, covered by nothing but a soiled loincloth. The errant locks of his curly, unruly hair are stuck to his head, smeared with blood. His face is criss-crossed by narrow rivulets of clotting blood. Only his eyes are sparkling from beneath that ghastly countenance. The boy stretches his arms into the air to break slumber and yawns. Then he looks at her.*]

Boy: You have just arrived, isn't it?

Woman: [*Shakes her head, as if in a trance.*] Yes.

Boy: Who are you?

Woman: Me? I am Shefali, Shefali Bandyopadhay, from the Kalighat station.

Boy: Alright.

Woman: What is this place called? And who are you?

Boy: I am Khokon. I have arrived here only recently.

[*Looks around, as if she is under a spell.*]

Woman: Where have I come? Oh!

Boy: Is it hurting? Sit down. The burning sensation that you feel in your body would subside soon.

[*He runs his hands on her shoulder to soothe her.*]

Woman: Feeling so strange. Perhaps I am, I am…

Boy: …dead! Don't you realize that? Those who take their own life are the ones who arrive here. It seems you committed suicide by setting yourself on fire. I was nowhere near firc though.

Woman: Oh! That fire! That rancid, burnt smell! Yes, I was completely insane that morning. Do you know where Kalighat is?

Boy: Yes, the temple of Goddess Kali in Kolkata. Yes, I know.

Woman: That Kalidasbabu is the yard master at the Kalighat station. He draws eighty rupees a month as salary.

Boy: Is that the reason why you had set yourself ablaze?

Woman: No. We were a family of seven with five off-springs, and just eighty rupees a month for sustenance. You wouldn't understand all that. It's better to lead a beggar's life.

[*The boy is curious.*]

Boy: Beggar?

[*The woman explains.*]

Woman: There is no pride or self-esteem to protect if you are a beggar.

Boy: Alright, you complete your story. Then I will say mine.

Woman: I have no words to express the kind of pain a peopled, lower middle-class family goes through everyday. With each passing the day, the children were getting increasingly sick from malnutrition. They were caught between life and death, like dying embers. I couldn't breastfeed the one that was an infant because I had become barren. I had terrible mood swings. I became easily irritable and ill-tempered. My mind and heart were tied in knots.

[*The woman starts writhing.*]

Boy: What? Are you feeling the burning sensation again?

Woman: No, no. That sensation is no longer there. It's over. But why do those painful memories still invade my mind. I can't get over them. I just can't!

[*The boy shakes his head.*]

Boy: Now, now, this is not going to work for you now that you are here. Then?

Woman: I had borrowed some milk for the infant and went to the kitchen to heat it up. The children hadn't eaten anything since yesterday. Nutu, my third child, came and stood near me. Nutu is a little fond of food. He has never eaten anything decent in his life. He came and said: 'Mother.'

[*The woman's eyes become tearful.*]

Boy: Please, don't be weak.

[*The woman regains her composure.*]

Woman: Nutu said, 'Mother, I want to eat.' Upon hearing that, I just couldn't control my rage and gave him a mighty slap. Soon, Nutu began to thrash around in pain. Khuki cried out: 'Mother, O Mother, look at Nutu. He is not alright.' I was at the end of my wits. I lost my temper completely. I slapped all of them and drove them out of the room – those famished children I had given birth to! I sat down with my back to thc door and began to cry. Tell me, is there anyone who would care to know why I was crying or understand how deeply I was hurting?

Boy: Was there anyone else in that room?

Woman: I don't know. I was crying. I kept on crying. Have you ever hated or berated yourself?

Boy: No.

Woman: Disdain gripped me and I saw only sheer darkness ahead. There was a Jerry can of kerosene in the room and, somehow, the oven was still burning. Somehow.

Boy: Hmm. So you set yourself on fire?

Woman: I used the fire on my body to extinguish all pain. No more struggles to stay alive. Yes, I did the right thing. Yes, of course.

Boy: So this is it! Hmmm.

Woman: It was still hurting when I arrived here. But now it's gone. Ah! This is peace, isn't it?

Boy: What?

Woman: It's like taking an afternoon dip in the dark, opaque water of this pond. All pain gets washed away.

Boy: Here?

[*The woman answered with an element of doubt in her voice.*]

Woman: Yes. That's the reason why I came here.

Boy: The pain has subsided, right?

Woman: Yes, sort of. But I really don't know.

Boy: You talked about your pain. Will you listen to my story?

Woman: Sure, I will.

Boy: You spoke about beggars. I was a beggar myself.

Woman: Oh! Really? Then I guess...

Boy: Let me tell you my own parable of agony. You know, I had my mother and an elder sister. We all had arrived from East Pakistan. We used to beg on the streets to make our ends meet. My mother and sister were not able to get alms but people used to give me a bit of loose change but that was not enough. I used to park myself at a tea stall next to a platform at the Howrah rail station. I used to cry then, but not now. There was no food to eat. Acute hunger was sapping all my energy. I used to collapse on the ground often. I felt as if I was being throttled from all sides. You all talk about living life. Believe me, I know what life is all about and what struggle for existence is. Besieged with emotions, I used to cry, too. It was then that the huge train was rolling into the platform, whistling its arrival. I didn't think twice. I jumped in front of the train. There was a screeching noise, and it was all over in a moment. And then, here I am.

Woman: How does it feel to be here?

Boy: When I arrived here, I felt exactly the way you did.

Woman: And now? Please tell me.

[*The boy kept quiet for few moments.*]

Boy: My mother and my sister used to love me so much. Believe me. You know, I keep remembering my mother. She is etched in my memory. Come what may, I can't forget her. She really used to love me deeply and cared for me as much as she could. I don't know how they are now or what they are doing back there. Are they still alive? Are they... I don't have anyone who could let me know about them. The pain of not being able to find out about them has made me so tough and brusque.

Woman: Tough?

Boy: Yes, tough. Or else, I won't last long here. Do you think you have left your Nutu with a bride back there? You think you have brought Khuki and Khokon along in your cradled arms? Maybe, your infant child cries endlessly without you. Separated from you, they must be hurting deeply, like I hurt inside without my mother. Maybe, this pain is much deeper than we can imagine.

Woman: Stop! I am not going to travel to the past. Why should I? After all, I am not going to take care of them anymore.

Boy: That's precisely is the reason why you would burn more intensely. You and them, both. You cannot just subdue memory. Fond recalls will torment your mind forever. My Grandpa used to say.

Woman: Neither can you forget, isn't it? Even if you try and escape from reality, memories will haunt you.

Boy: Yes.

[*The woman keeps her hand on the heart.*]

Woman: What's this? What's happening all so suddenly?

Boy: What?

[*The woman cries out.*]

Woman: I want to go back. I want to go back, I want to....

Boy: Be quiet. I was also as disturbed as you when I first came here. That's the malaise of this place!

Woman: Can't you hear? They are crying, weeping. All are crying in that world! Nobody can stop me. I have to go. Oh! Why did I kill myself?

Boy: All doors to that world are shut. There's no way back. You just cannot be there anymore. I wouldn't have been here had there been a way.

[*The woman's face was trembling. She looked at the boy for a moment and began to weep in spasms. She sits on the stone and covers her face. The boy walks towards her, wanting to place an arm on her shoulders. But he stops in his path, turns and sits down on the ground at a distance from her. The woman rose her face.*]

Woman: Khokon.

[*The boy stares into the distance.*]

Boy: Yes?

Woman: Come to me, please. Come to me. [*The boy walks up to her.*] Tell me, what shall I do? Someone please tell me. Oh dear!

Boy: Let me tell you. Come on, come with me. Look upwards.

Woman: Why?

Boy: Just do it. What do you see?

[*The woman is too excited.*]

Woman: It's red! The sky here is so starkly red. Why is it so red?

Boy: That red is the colour of pain the sky holds in layers. That's what Grandpa says. Can you see the swamp there? If you go behind the swamp and look up, you would find a small opening in that the red sky. The red is not endless, as it seems from here. From that opening peeps a slice of blue sky. I often go and stand behind the swamp. Far away, I can see that slice of blue lie quietly in that vast expanse. Beneath that blue sky is another world where pain and happiness share space. I feel that world which vibes with me using that blue pathway. I feel so strange!

Woman: I... I want to see that too.

Boy: Let's go. Yes, we have to do these to forget. We have to make our minds strong. But can we?

Woman: Sorry, what did you say?

Boy: Forget it. Let's go.

[*Together they walk deeper into the stage. At a distance, the woman stops, turns and looks at the boy. The boy, too, has stopped in his tracks.*]

Woman: What happened? Won't you come?

Boy: Just a moment. Wanted to say something.

Woman: What?

Boy: Your... you know... you.... Ok, let's go.

Woman: Come on, tell me.

Boy: Well, nothing really. I mean, something keeps circling inside my head. You have nobody now but you once had everyone. Same here, with me. That's what I wanted to say.

Woman: Well... what do you want to say?

Boy: No, forget it.

[*He turns his head, takes two more steps forward. Puzzled, the woman keeps moving ahead. All of a sudden, the boy calls out in a muffled voice.*]

Boy: Mother, O mother, see, see! See the sky, see the blue!

[*The woman was startled.*]

Woman: What did you say?

Boy: We can see only a little bit from here. Please take a look.

Woman: What did you call me as? You said something, didn't you?

[*The boy smiles.*]

Boy: Oh! That? I wish I could call you Mother. My heart wants me to call you Mother.

[*The woman spoke faintly, almost in whispers.*]

Woman: Mother!

[*Then she spoke loudly.*]

Woman: No!

Boy: But why?

Woman: I am not a mother. I can't be a mother. I am not your mother.

Boy: Do you have a feeling of melancholy? Are you forlorn, Mother?

Woman: Still...

[*Wears an impish grin, runs to the woman and cradles his arms around her. Gently runs her fingers through his hair and then raises her head to stare into the distance.*]

Woman: We have to live after death. Isn't it, Nutu?

[*The boy looks at her in complete surprise. The woman is embarrassed.*]

Woman: Umm ... Khoka.

Boy: Yes, Mother. Come, come. The blue sky is awaiting us on the other side.

[*The boy holds her hand and walks away from the stage. The stage is empty. Then, from the other side of the hillock, a poker-faced old man with white hair is seen coming up. As he reaches the top of the hillock, his appearance changes, as if he is in a trance.*]

Old man: There! It's gone! The windows gone! Second floor, first floor, ground floor! A road is coming up fast. A road! No, no, no, no, no, no, no!

[*Once his excitement subsides, the old man sits down on the hillock. A teardrop each rolls down his cheeks. A man, who is a labourer and aged 24 or 25, appears and looks at the old man with wide open eyes. Seeing him, the old man stands up, evidently embarrassed, and uses a corner of his tunic to wipe the tears.*]

Labourer: Alright, Purnochander! Now fasten your armour and be ready all brothers.

Purno: Bholanath, don't ever sing that song here. Do you understand the meaning of the lyrics?

Bhola: Why? If I feel like singing that song, I will. So what if I do not understand the meaning of the song. So, why were you crying? Remembering your grandson?

Bhola: Alright. But why do you worry so much? If you do so, you would lose your bearings.

[*The boy and the woman enter.*]

Boy: There is another person who lives here. He is a peon. He was employed with some college. He had to die because he wanted to pursue education. And there's Grandpa! Grandpa, here's Mother, I mean...

[*Purno didn't even look at them.*]

Purno: Later. I will listen to everything later. Let me think. You see, know thyself. Know your soul. How does that help make both ends meet? I mean, it's alright to have a soul. Knowing thyself is fine. But what happens to your life, family?

Boy: So you are thinking about your grandson, right? It seems you are getting increasingly pinned down by these thoughts. By the way Mother, this is whom I call Grandpa. This is him. Do you remember I told you about him? I don't know what kind of work he had at the post office. But then, he jumped from the terrace of a tall building. It is said that he had about a dozen dependents. By the way, he is extremely wise. He knows a lot.

Woman: He knows everything?

Boy: Yes, absolutely everything.

[*Purno notices the woman.*]

Purno: Who, who are you?

Woman: Sir, I am Shefali. I couldn't take the pain any longer! I am not so literate. I know nothing. That's why I perished in the flames.

Purno: But why did you set yourself on fire?

Woman: I couldn't sustain the pain of extreme penury anymore. My husband used to get just eighty rupees as monthly pay. On top of it, I had five children. You can well understand what this situation can cause in a Bengali household...

Purno: No, no. I didn't mean that. I just wanted to know why you chose to die by setting yourself ablaze. There are other means to end life.

Woman: What else could I have done? I know little about these things. Nobody ever told me what to do.

Purno: You could have drowned yourself. You could have jumped from the roof of a building. Or, while walking on the road, you could have simply flung yourself in the front of a speeding car.

Woman: True. Even I used to think along the same lines. Has anyone ever thought about those nattily dressed women who hit the streets every evening? Has anyone ever cared to find out how many of them, like me, were burning from inside, like the glowing embers of a forest fire? All we can see is the façade that sports a sham smile. Their tears of pain have remained imprisoned deep inside them. They never surfaced for anyone to notice. Nobody ever cared to delve deep to feel their pain.

Purno: Yes, yes. Right. Consider my case. I didn't do all that. Instead, I jumped from the terrace of a four storey building.

Woman: Oh!

Purno: It's so simple. As I jumped, the road below began racing towards me. Your concentration becomes so intense at these times. The windows on the building were passing me with great speed, one after another. And then, there were many. Ah! Forget it. Everything was over in a moment. I don't have my ribs anymore. They're completely shattered, pulverized.

Woman: You know, death by fire leaves a stench. The flames…

Boy: ….they spiral into the air, as if in a malevolent dance. Isn't it?

Woman: Yes, and then comes extreme pain. As it begins to happen, you want to run and scream. But later, when the flames wrap you gradually like a serpent, you feel at peace. You are numbed. It is at that point your entire past flashes in front of you in flitting moments of recall.

Purno: What was on your mind at that moment?

[*The woman gave a blushed smile.*]

Woman: It's so strange that I remembered something that happened long ago in my life.

Boy: What Mother?

Woman: I used to be quite sprightly and cute when I was four or five. At our village home in the night, when I used to cry, my father would pick me up and hold me close to his chest. He would pat my back gently and sing to sleep. The way he used to cradle me … I would melt into his chest. And those lullabies! I don't exactly remember the lyrics but at the same time it seems as if I do. I was remembering the entire scenario though. The dark night, a few stars sparkling in the sky, and the lazy strain of the melody inducing deep sleep. This was the last thing that came to my mind as the end came. Strange, isn't it?

Purno: Yes, strange, strange indeed. Sit down. I just want to tell you about something.

Woman: Yes, please.

Purno: Look at Bhola. He used to be a labourer at a jute mill. He didn't realize that, while working, he was all the time inhaling the thin and deadly fibres of jute. It was not long before he began suffering from tuberculosis. Instead of taking care of Bhola, the owner of the mill sacked him. Without a job, Bhola went from door to door for help, from one hospital to another. But he couldn't get himself admitted into any. Thereafter...

Bhola: I began to bleed profusely from the mouth. I was spewing blood everyday and had nowhere to go. To end the misery, I hung a stone from my neck, tied up my feet and jumped into a canal. I am completing this old man's sentence quickly because if you let him tell my story, he would meander a lot to create a full-length tragedy to make you cry. Nothing more, nothing less. Alright boss, I have to leave now.

Purno: How do you feel being here?

Woman: Pardon me?

Purno: Do you now have a sense of finality in your mind?

Woman. No. Not at all.

Purno: Hmm. You are still a captive of your earthly memories and they are causing you great pain. I am no exception.

Woman: You mean there isn't any place where we can rid ourselves of our earthly ties and live in peace?

Purno: Don't say that. There has to be a place where peace is awaiting us.

Boy: Grandpa, remember? You used to talk about a place?

Purno: Yes.

Bodhu: Where is that place?

Purno: Well, there is a place, a beautiful world. All this while, I have been trying to find the gateway to that world where peace and contentment exist together. There has to be a place like that.

Woman: Please, tell me where? I can't take it any longer, here.

Boy: Why?

Purno: I don't know where.

Boy: Then it doesn't exist.

Purno: You must not say that. A world like that was envisioned by the Upanishad, by ancient India, too. From time immemorial, we all have been dreaming about a world where no miseries would exist. The quest is still on. We have to find the path to that world. You may leave now.

Boy: Why?

Purno: Let me think. I have to find the pathway.

Woman: Alright. We would just say a few words and then leave.

Purno: What do you want to say?

Woman: I took my own life to rid myself of the pain I was suffering; of the miseries I was going through. But why can't I?

Purno: You tell me.

Woman: I can't summarily dismiss my children from memory.

Purno: Hmm. Thoughts about the future are still chasing you. You didn't perish with your death.

Woman: Maybe. Tell me, if this is really the path to being delivered of pain, then....

Purno: But your sons are also hurting, agonising.

Woman: You mean, even they would have to seek salvation this way? Oh!

Boy: What did you say, Mother?

Woman: Just think about them Khoka. How would your mother, your sister, my sons, his grandson and granddaughter survive? How would you make them live without miseries?

Purno: Not just them. There are hundreds and thousands of people who are burning the same way as us. I have seen it with my own eyes. They, too, are gripped by the same thoughts, that there is no way out. Like us, even they would one day end taking their own lives.

Woman: What path did you say everyone has to follow?

Purno: The path that we have taken. We have shown them the path.

Woman: No.

Purno: What do you mean by saying 'no'? Haven't we screamed to the world that, to end all miseries, you have to take your own life? You, me, Bhola, the peon, Khoka, we all have raised a clarion call to the world at large. We have told the world: Whoever wants to defeat pain, including the children of those who die everyday at the hands of all-pervading distress, please take your own life. Please be life's greatest foe. No more struggle. No more agony. That would be deliverance. As if it was gospel.

Woman: Why would my children die? I never wished them death.

Purno: Liar!! Of course, you wanted them dead. It's us who have shown them the way and shone a light on the path that leads life to its end. We strove to convince them that solutions to all problems lay in perishing. We told them that peace will prevail once everything is over.

Woman: Believe me, I didn't want this. I really didn't. I ran away because I felt I was getting throttled. The noose of distress was tightening around my neck with each passing moment. Let them live in peace, and let the humankind blossom.

Purno: Not possible. Everything will be shattered.

Boy: You carry on. Meanwhile, I will go and take a look at the blue sky in the middle of the red expanse above us. [*The peon walks in reading a book.*] Hey peon, you still read books?

Purno: There you are, peon! Listen. I had asked you something some time back. What happened to that?

Boy: [*Addressing peon.*] Don't worry. Grandpa goes off the mark like that once in a while. That's the time when you shouldn't be near him. I will go and look up Bhola.

Peon: Yes.

Purno: Speak now, peon.

Peon: Newton said, to every action there is an equal and opposite reaction. That's the Third Law of motion. In some other book I had read, can't recall exactly which one, that much concerns have been shared, much discourse have taken place over the problems that plague the world, but the need of the hour is to change the world and the way we perceive it. Did you get that? Change.

Purno: Come on, why aren't you replying? You, too, have become another Bhola.

Peon: No, I am not like Bhola. I have read a lot. See, I am reading Romain Rolland now but it's of no use. For the world, we have not been able to set an example of courage that is required to battle odds and overcome them. We are cowards!

Purno: Who says? Who has the guts to say this?

Peon: That's what the world will say about us. There wouldn't be any compassion for us either.

Purno: No! We are martyrs! Let me tell you this: in your lexicon, we are martyrs as we are being crushed to death with stones. How could you then knife in the back the legacy of memories that we leave behind?

Peon: You are new to this place, aren't you? Another tired river! That reminds me of what Swinburne wrote in the 'Garden of Proserpine': Even the weariest river winds its way somehow to the sea.

Purno: Look here, this woman was compelled to set herself on fire. What would you call her? A coward?

Woman: But then, I never wanted my children to perish. I only felt that no matter my death, let my children flourish in life.

Purno: But did that happen? No. It's just the opposite that has happened, isn't it?

Peon: Whose death are you talking about?

Purno: I am talking about our progeny. I am talking about those who are alive, those who are burning in agony.

Peon: Yes. I know for sure that similar feelings are doing the rounds of their collective minds. Right now, so many people of our country are thinking that taking one's own life is perhaps the only way to be unchained from sufferings. Just imagine! How amazing it seems, isn't it? On the streets, inside homes, at workplaces, so many people are thinking on these lines. And what did we do? Instead of lending them the courage to fight, we paved an easy escape route for them.

Woman: But, what possibly could we have done?

Peon: We could have risen like the jumping flames of a fire. We could have tried to expose the source of oppression and despotism. After that, well, I really don't know what we could have done. You know Sir, once in a while, I remember Hamlet – Time is out of joint, oh cursed spite, that I was born to set it right! The entire age is horrendous, sick and diseased.

Woman: I don't know. I am suddenly nervous.

Peon: I know sister, I know that feeling. Even I experienced the same feelings.

Woman: By the way, what made you do that? What was the reason behind what you did?

Peon: I wanted to pursue education. But they didn't let me. I was employed as a peon with the Presidency College in Kolkata. I toiled hard on my own and passed Matriculation. After that, I got myself admitted to a college. But they just couldn't stand the progress I was determined to make. I wanted to know about the world we live in. I wanted to scout the many mysteries the world had to offer. I had a burning desire to know the unknown. Maybe, you would not realize how intense this dream was. Just imagine! There's so much to learn and so much to know. I feel science is like endless poetry, constantly keeping us wrapped in its myriad offerings. Nobody ever cared to open the door to education for me. That's why I say, Grandpa, when I was turning the pages of a thin book, I realized how true its words were! What is the history of Man? It is of class struggle.

Purno: I just can't figure out which way you are going these days. Don't think so much. Don't immerse yourself in books so deeply. Your mind may go into disorder.

Peon: No, No. It is in disorder but I have to set it right. I realize that there are hundreds and thousands of people in the world who are like me, wanting to rise in life with fierce determination. Should all these people slowly die while being on their quest for knowledge? Would my ilk be completely erased from the face of the world? Why can't these obstacles be removed once and for all?

Purno: But, my dear, if you feel so much, why did you take your own life?

Peon: Wait, wait. There is no room for ridicule. I did have second thoughts. But I was helpless as I was completely alone. What could I have done? The demons have spread their tentacles far and deep into the world. I am ... I am extremely weak.

Purno: Is that the reason why you chose to leave the world in the hands of these demons?

Peon: Look, life is not like a book. You feel fine when you read stories of struggle and triumph. But reality is far removed from the pages of books. What could

I have really done?

Purno: Why, you could have…err.

Peon: The rest is silence!

Boy: Who's there, who??

Woman: Is somebody coming?

[*The sound of lightning strikes reverberates.*]

Purno: Take cover everyone, take cover!

Boy: Mother, Mother, go to sleep now. Sleep.

[*Everybody lies down on the ground. The stage is empty. In the flashes of the thunder strikes can be seen mist slowly spiralling from the stage which has suddenly fallen silent. Then a lunatic appears, wearing only a tattered piece of cloth. He runs to the top of the hillock from where he flails his arms like a traffic policeman. The woman tries to get up but the boy stops her from doing so.*]

Boy: Mother, Mother, it's a Man!

Lunatic: Hey You! Keep to the left. You there, the cart-puller, what an idiot are you! Peeep!!!!

[*Purno pulls himself up and stands behind the man.*]

Lunatic: Come on, clear the road. Hey you, private car, this way, this way.

[*The lunatic turns to find Purno behind him.*]

Lunatic: Please don't mind, I am just a lunatic.

Purno: Why?

Lunatic: What?

Purno: Why are you a lunatic?

Lunatic: Call me a lunatic and I am a lunatic. Call me whatever. You can call me a stupid goat or even a hand-drum. You know the hand-drum's beats like this: tak dhinita tak dhinita tak dhinita.

[*Soon, everybody stands surrounding the lunatic.*]

Lunatic: Who are you all?

Boy: We are the dead. But you are not.

Lunatic: No way. Nobody can kill me. But, of course, you could say that a lunatic is worse than the dead.

Peon: Did you get it Purno?

Purno: Yes.

Peon: His soul is dead like his brains. He lives in a body, but his mind has committed suicide under extreme distress.

Purno: Just because we are dead we cannot say anything about the pain that drove us to take our own lives. And he is not even alive, so he can't speak a single word about himself, right?

Lunatic: Yes, I can. Of course, you may think what can a lunatic say. But I park myself daily at the crossing near the square waterbody at Hedo. If you go there right now, you would find me sleeping in the shades on the sidewalks. It's afternoon now, so the railings that surround Hedo are casting diagonal shades. In front of me, the tea stall has downed its shutters and the boys who run the shop have neatly placed the chairs on the tables to create space so that they can have a siesta, which is what they are doing now. You know, these boys tease me a lot.

Boy: But does that complete your tale of pain and hurt?

Lunatic: Doesn't it? I used to be at the Hedo crossing, asking for alms, and moving around without a piece of clothing on me—naked, dirty and laughing out loud at no one. In other words, I am profusely crying.

Peon: You are still there. Among all these cities, this one...

Woman: So sad! Where's your home?

Lunatic: I don't know. I know nothing. Even if I know, I won't tell you. Why should I? If I do that, even those who are close to me, those who are my own, would be driven to insanity by you!

Woman: Why are you hurting so much?

Purno: Whom are you asking?

Woman: I am asking everyone. Why is there so much sadness, so much pain? Does anyone have an answer?

Peon: There is one person who has the answer. I don't know where he is now. Rabindranath Tagore used to say: 'The darkness of the night has faded' and Romain Rolland said: 'I will not rest!'

[*He picks up the book.*]

Purno: I have read Rolland's depiction of Ramakrishna. It's beautiful!

Peon: Do you want to know what Rolland had said. After surpassing all pain, he said: 'Tranquil peace. Sleep, my head is alive and agitated. Sleep, my bloodied underfoot. You have toiled too hard. The path was tough and laden with danger. In spite of that, the path was beautiful. At every turn of that path, I have redeemed the worth of my struggle. What I have received after that ... 'And then I will be history'. But I couldn't. [*Smiles.*] I couldn't.

Boy: What does he say all the time? I just don't understand. Mother, would you come along with me to the other side of the swamp?

Woman: No. I don't feel like doing anything.

[*She keeps sitting with her back towards the boy.*]

Boy: Another blow from the disease!

Lunatic: Listen to me. This is all meaningless banter. You may think what can a lunatic say. Still, let me say: Be insane. Everyone be insane. Drive yourself to insanity as quickly as possible. Only then would you realize how cool life is. This is what I tell the traffic on the road. You know, they listen to me.

Purno: You mean things quieten down after you become a lunatic?

Lunatic: Your Highness, shall I say it with fear or without?

Woman: Please say, how does it feel to be a lunatic?

Lunatic: Keep to the left. [*Walks up to the woman.*] I will tell you privately. It feels tangy to be a lunatic. Kind of sour, you know.

Purno: Means?

Lunatic: With a dash of salt and pepper, lunacy doesn't taste so bad. It's like a spicy mish-mash of fried chickpeas and groundnuts.

[*He resumes directing traffic.*]

Purno: He is just being mad. Is there any hard and fast rule that you have to be a lunatic even after committing suicide?

[*Purno shakes his head.*]

Purno: If somehow I had found Hiranyavarnam Purusham Adityam, I would have survived.

Peon: Let me quote our immortal poet:

Tomorrow and tomorrow and tomorrow,
creeps into this petty pace from day to
day to the last syllable or recorded time.
all all our yesterdays have lighted fools the
way to dusty death

Lunatic: You know [*addressing the woman.*], I do remember from time to time. Between the two ends of a black curtain, one or two steps onto the sidewalks. All rubbish! I want to drive them away but they don't leave. That's when I cry, yes, that's when I cry.

Woman: And then?

[*The boy stands behind the woman holding her hand and the lunatic becomes fidgety and addresses the woman.*]

Lunatic: You know, it's a great relief that these thoughts don't imperil my senses for long. I keep forgetting. And I don't want to think. It hurts inside my head if I brood on these memories. The pain is unbearable! Of course, you can say... Oh! My God! What's that?

[*They can hear Bhola sing: 'Now fasten your armour, and be ready all brothers'. The lunatic wants to run away but the boy wraps his arms around his waist.*]

Lunatic: Ah, keep to the left. Imbecile! Can't you see who is coming?

Boy: Who?

Lunatic: [*Addressing the woman.*] You don't know the people for whom that song is like an anthem. Come on, let me go. You stupid, idiot, creep.

[*The lunatic starts crying.*]

Boy: Bhola is coming.

Lunatic: I don't care. They are the people who believe in these songs. The moment they arrive, they would ask us to work, toil and fight.

Purno: Alright. Don't be afraid. As a matter of fact, Bhola doesn't understand the inner meaning of that song.

[*Bhola arrives and steps away to a corner.*]

Bhola: Everybody thinks I am so cut and dried. As if I am tied up in knots. But blood still rushes out from deep inside my chest.

Lunatic: As if we don't know your kind!

[*Bhola looks at the lunatic and the woman.*]

Purno: Well, for example, If you sing the song: 'If I am proven wrong someday'.

Lunatic: There was a time when I used to sing that song. Now I sing: 'My love is but a gentle garland'.

Purno: One and the same. Have you ever wondered what this song really means?

Lunatic: Never. I tried a great deal but could never fathom the inner meaning of songs like these.

Purno: That's exactly how the inner meaning of 'Now fasten your armour, and be ready all brothers' never reaches Bhola.

Bhola: Who's this?

Purno: The new resident. He is going to stay here.

Lunatic: No, not me. Of course, you can say what made me come here in the first place? Frankly, I just came here on a pleasure trip. I have to return to Kolkata to control road traffic. After all, my body is still lying next to Hedo.

Bhola: Good enough. By the way, peon, I was telling you about the burning sensation inside my chest, throat and also about profuse bleeding from the mouth. I was feeling all this when I was sitting there. You know, you have imperilled me. You are asking me to think. That's worrisome. I had been going from one place to another for one whole year. I have never caused any harm to anyone. There was hardly any food to eat. I was so famished. As a result, this disease held me with a pincer grip. Tell me, what was my fault that I had to go through such misery? Forget it. Let me not talk about myself. But those who are still back there – my wife, my father, Gautam – do they also deserve the same fate as mine? Would they, too, hang like me? Would they jump into the air and nothingness, and then flies circling their faces?

Peon: What's the point in telling me all this? I was alone, too.

Bhola: What else could I have done? I could have become a robber. I could have launched a looting spree. I care a damn. I have no sympathy or respect for anyone or anything. I could have created mayhem. These thoughts had never crossed my mind before, do you understand? Never.

Purno: Don't talk rubbish, Bhola. Doing these would have not fetched you the desired ends. That you are dead has proven to be a better proposition than you being alive.

Peon: Besides, you couldn't have done all that all by yourself.

Bhola: A dagger, a dagger! A good dagger is very expensive. But then, I would not be able to fathom your mind. You died of despair and I, of sadness, deep sadness.

Woman: May I say something? You guys are well-read people, you have seen a great deal.

Peon: What is it, sister?

Woman: What would happen to our children?

Bhola: Who knows…

Woman: Would they also burn and vanish like us?

Bhola: Peon would now start talking about uprising again. Hey old man, isn't this all meaningless?

Purno: There is no meaning to your own self as well. Try to understand your mind first. This song is actually urging us to find our true calling. It is sending you a message – 'Now fasten your armour, and be ready all brothers …whatever, whatever …For we who die of hunger'. You got that? Do you think you deserve to sing this song after what you did back there on Earth?

[*Bhola ran his fingers across his chin.*]

Bhola: Yes.

Bhola: We are not to talk about the pain we experience here. Not at all. Isn't it, Grandpa?

Peon: Who's going to tell me where is that world Rolland spoke of, where everything is available for everyone, where knowledge is for everyone to share?

Purno: That world exists but the path to reach it doesn't. I don't know the way. We can't go there.

Bhola: Now fasten your armour, and be ready all brothers …whatever. Hmm.

Peon: There was a person called Gayotte. He was mad. He once said: 'In the beginning, there was action!'

[*The lunatic suddenly begins to sing in a manner as if he is mourning. He started singing.*]

Lunatic: All alone in this world I travel
Who will shine a light with a marvel?

[*Bhola suddenly raises his voice.*]

Bhola: Hey, listen. Everyone come close.

[*Everybody reaches the centre of the stage. The lunatic stops singing.*]

Purno: Why are you behaving strangely?

Peon: Bhola, what happened to you?

Woman: What is that look you have in your eyes, Brother?

Bhola: Wait, dear, wait. All of you will get it. You there, lunatic, [*He pulls the lunatic close.*] whatever you were singing, sing again.

Lunatic: Oh that?? You almost gave me the creeps! Didn't you know, nobody ever wants me to sing? I really like you.

[*Bhola was stern.*]

Bhola: Sing.

Lunatic: 'All alone in this world I trave'.

Bhola: What a song! Hats off!

Purno: Now, young man, tell me what you are trying to say? You can leave the preamble for later!

Bhola: Old man, when exactly did you think of dying?

Purno: When I could no longer shoulder the huge responsibilities all by myself.

Bhola: Ok. Peon, you?

Peon: When I could no longer stand the injustice, I began to hurt and sulk deeply, and ...

Bhola: ...tied a noose around your neck when nobody was around. What about you, sister?

Woman: Set myself on fire when I was alone in a room.

Bhola: You, Khoka?

Boy: You already know, I jumped in the front of a train.

Bhola: And I? I went around in solitary circles, tied a stone around my neck and jumped into a canal. Sing that song again, please.

Lunatic: Of course, you may think what might a lunatic would have to say. Yet, let me tell you that nobody else has ever asked me to sing so often.

Bhola: Now sing.

Lunatic: Please don't be annoyed with me. 'All alone in this world I travel'.

Bhola: Now stop! It's flawed at the beginning. All alone we travelled in that world, not in this world, as the song suggests.

Peon: Absolutely right! Hey Bhola, you are a small-time labourer and yet you could see the flaw, whereas we are so well-read but we still missed it.

Bhola: I really don't know. I just felt a spark in the head.

Purno: The picture is now becoming clearer to me. We committed the same mistake. We must band together now. But then, what's the point in doing that now?

Woman: Why are you so despondent? Our children still exist in that world. They will live if they unite.

Bhola: You bet!

Woman: Really? Would they find a way out of pain?

Bhola: No doubt about that.

Woman: Why has this dawned upon us after we arrived here? How would the world back there get to know what we are thinking now?

Boy: Not to worry. We have a messenger. Hey lunatic, aren't you returning to the Earth?

Lunatic: Of course!

Boy: Would you carry messages back?

Lunatic: Sure… of course, you can say. I don't know how to think.

Bhola: We will do the thinking for all of us.

Peon: Everything.

Purno: All you have to do is to lend us your body.

Woman: Your calling is to burn all pain. Give us your body and deliver the world of its pain!

Boy: Lunatic!

Purno: You dunderhead!

Lunatic: Now that all of you are asking, I am lending by body. But my pain is no less than yours. I amhurting as much. It's all piling up, you know, piling up like trapped smoke.

Bhola: Listen, do you see the blue opening in that red sky? Use that opening to go back to the Earth. Go there. Go to that world where our parents, brothers, sisters and wives are spending their days in pain.

Lunatic: Whooooshhhh… and land at Hedo. What do I tell them?

Woman: You have to tell them that nobody shall die in a fire again. There are no suicides anymore.

Boy: Tell them, come what may, be united and fight the odds together.

Purno: You have to let them know that the time to wait for miracles is over. Do not jump from roofs. Wake up and be counted.

Bhola: Tell them that do not let your pent up frustration burn you anymore from inside. How long can you shed tears in private, all alone? How long do you want to be a human separated from human beings?

The perpetrators of injustice will perish. That day of reckoning is not far. All you have to do is to espouse the human cause.

Peon: Tell them all this. You must also send out this message: People with compassion, please listen. Much misery and anguish exist in the world. Hundreds and thousands of human beings are silently agonizing, hurting and burning in pain. Gather all the pain and sufferings and throw them out like filth.

Purno: It's there in our mythology, like the ribs of Dadhichi the sage.

Woman: I have wept and wept. My cries went unheard and the drops of my clotting tears, unseen.

Bhola: Go and carry our message with you.

Lunatic: Shall I? Alright. I will tell them not to fade out with insanity. I will tell them: Friends, my countrymen, bring wisdom back! What I will do is, I will manage traffic right at the four-way crossing in the afternoon. I will stop everyone and shout Halt! Here is news for you. Keep to the left, keep to the left!

Purno: Go now. Take to the morbid world the news of life.

Lunatic: Here I go. I will go through that blue slice in the red sky and land in the middle of Kolkata. Come on Manuaaaa, let's go.... peeeeeep peeep, chug chug chug chug... keep to the left, keep to the left.

[*He takes two quick full-turns and goes like a shot. The Indian gum-Arabic tree in the rear begins to tremble. A pale burst of lightning streaks across. Everybody turns around towards the backdrop and waves at the departing lunatic.*]

Boy: Mother, humans will be humans.

Woman: Khoka, I feel as if sparks of lightning are running through my veins.

Peons: Ah! Tranquillity! It's quite far from here, but it is there. It has to be.

[*Bhola starts singing, his voice off-key.*]

Bhola: 'Now fasten your armour, and be ready all brothers'-

[*Thousands of voices in the backdrop begin to sing this song. Bhola's voice fades into the rising crescendo—*]

Now fasten your armour
And be ready, all brothers,
For we who die of hunger
Death is not a danger,
Blow the trumpet of liberty
And raise the flag of might,
You can hear the call of the war
And let's be there to fight
On your guard, farmers!
Workers be ready,
On your guard, my brothers,
Let's keep the boat steady.

— Slowly, the curtain drops —

Ablaze

4

Translator's Note

This play uses figurative messages by means of posters and blends screenshots with stagecraft towards the end to drive home the point it is making. Much of the dialogues are colloquial, with a smattering of Bangla slangs. In the course of translation, two dialogues that figured in the Fourth Act, could not be translated into English because of the use of the Bangla word '*Bon*'. The word '*Bon*' in Bangla means both 'Sister' and 'Jungle'. One of the characters addresses the lead woman in the play as 'Bon', whereas in the preceding Acts, the word 'Sister' was required to be used. There are also songs in Bangla and hymns in Sanskrit that have been left unchanged because they are difficult to be transliterated. An English word that may create confusion among readers is 'pipegun'. The pipegun used to be a countrymade weapon that became famous in the hands of anti-social elements in West Bengal during the late '60s and '70s. The gun, with no butt, used to be made from iron pipes and had to be re-loaded every time a shot needed to be fired.

First Act

[*As the curtain goes up, another curtain, black in colour, can be seen covering the rear of the stage. The stage is lit up by sudden bursts of lights. A poster drops down from above. On the poster it is written: 'The purpose of the play is to bust masquerades.' A woman can be heard singing in the background.*]

Sachimata go, ami char jug-e hoi jonomdukhini.
Satyajug-e chilam Sita, Treta-te Draupadi
Dwapar-e chilam Shakuntala, Koli te ei Bishnupriya.
Ma go, ami char jug-e hoi jonomdukhini.
Amai dakhar keho nai, jibon galo tai
Tobu ami jogot chalai, Shochimata go.

[*The song is being sang in chorus—as if the song reverberates in the entire stage. Still there is neither any prop nor any actor on the stage. From the left wing, enter Taracharan Tarkabagish, the old teacher along with his wife Sachi and daughter, Bishnupriya. Taracharan looks at the surrounding listlessly.*]

Taracharan: Sachi! It's been such a long time! No idea in what state it is now. [*Taracharan turns to the left.*] Here it is! This is that hut, Sachi, this is that hut! So Sachi, we return after ages. This is my land, my abode. We have to keep it close to our heart. 'Bengal's' chapter is over. Even in Jalpaiguri in North Bengal, where I went to, I found human beings are turning themselves into an endangered species. The village school, housed in this hut, that has been a paternal legacy, may redefine our lives again.

Sachi: I wonder if we would ever get that life back after so many years. Bishnu was just a little girl then. She has now grown up, really grown up.

Bishnupriya: [*Meanwhile, began doing a merry jig.*] Oh! Come on Mother, I really don't understand this growing up business. I just want to play, as I love to play. The world is such a nice place to live in. It is amazingly beautiful! Everything here is so beautiful. The skies, the fields and the rivers are so mesmerizing. Isn't everything so beautiful,

Mother? I will play, yes Mother, yes. Playing is beautiful. This is what life is all about.

Taracharan: Alright precious, you keep on playing without having to worry about anything else. You would not know why we had to return to this land after so many years. Why should you? You keep on playing. You belong to this land of your ancestors where you grew up. This land, the sky and the rivers are yours. Where else would you get such happiness? This is where you have to be free like a skylark.

Sachi: Let's clean up the hut. No idea in what shape the hut is in now.

Taracharan: Yes, let's go.

[*From the left of the stage enters Sushovan, who was once Taracharan's student. He touches Taracharan's feet as a mark of reverence. Taracharan takes a close look at Sushovan and says—*]

Hey Sushovan, how you doing? You have really grown up and you look so smart. What are you doing these days?

Sushovan: Sir, I work as a reporter with a newspaper. I heard you were here and so I came.

[*He touches Sachi's feet too.*]

Taracharan: There is my daughter with whom you used to play around when the two of you were children.

Sachi: Bless you long life, Sushovan. I guess you have not seen my daughter for many years. She has really grown up, my lovely daughter.

[*Sushovan looks at Bishnupriya. Coyly, Bishnupriya stands to a side of the stage.*]

Sushovan: You look quite pretty, Bishnupriya. But why haven't you learnt to walk?

Bishnupriya: [*Turns around in a swift movement.*] That's because I have learnt to dance and sing. But I see that you have not learnt to stand.

Sushovan: [*Smiles.*] Haven't we begun by locking horns? We could leave this 'friendly' banter for later.

Bishnupriya: We are simple and rustic village people. We find it difficult to blend with urban disposition.

Taracharan: Not to worry, Bishnupriya. You will get used to it soon. So Sushovan, what brings you to this village?

Sushovan: Sir, we have been tipped off about goods train wagons being rampantly stopped on the tracks and broken open by miscreants in this area. We also have information that commodities are being smuggled in from Bangladesh. All this and much more prompted my Editor to send me here for coverage. But I still don't understand why you had to come back.

Taracharan: Bangladesh is in the grip of smugglers and lawlessness. Anti-social elements have spread their tentacles far and wide. The biggest problem involves women. These criminals have little regard for women. Even my daughter Bishnupriya – why just Bishnupriya? Almost all women are in a similar situation.

Sushovan: I know about all this.

Taracharan: Is knowing everything? Shouldn't there be a way out? What about remedy?

Sushovan: One has to wait, Sir.

Taracharan: Wait? But for how long? We can't wait for ages, my dear. Man, after all, is mortal.

Sushovan: Alright, Sir. Let's not talk about it now. What do you plan to do here, now?

[*Sachi is dusting the floor of the hut and Bishnupriya is busy arranging things. Taracharan and Sushovan are engaged in a conversation at the edge of the stage.*]

Taracharan: I have plans to rebuild this village school.

Sushovan: Sir, that is an excellent idea! I think that would be the right move at this moment. You need to start by sowing the seed of knowledge and wisdom. Let that seed blossom from this soil.

Bishnupriya: [*Sings an ancient love song.*]

Debota galo bairey
Ghorey keu nai rey
Kothai shukh, kothai dukh
Ka ke kothai pai re?
Ami Bishnupriya
Amar Bishnu kothai galo re?

Sushovan: [*Looks at Bishnupriya and says to Taracharan before leaving—*] I will return after scouting this area for information for a few days. I will come and meet you again once my job is done.

[*Bishnupriya runs up to him. Music starts.*]

Bishnupriya: You sure you'll come back?

[*Both are caught in a frozen frame.*]

Sushovan: Yes, I will.

[*He leaves.*]

Sachi: My daughter has an intelligent mind.

[*Sachi leaves.*]

Taracharan: She is a simple and innocent girl.

[*Taracharan leaves. Bishnupriya can be heard singing: 'Debota galo bairey' and Raja and Rana enter the stage from the left. They begin to clap in sync with the song's rhythm. Bishnupriya turns around to take a look at them. The entire stage is flooded by lights.*]

Raja: Encore! Encore! Once again, Encore!

Rana: Ah! It seems I am overcome with feelings.

Raja: This is what we call the charm of Vrindavan!

[*Feku enters.*]

Feku: Wow! She is a fantastic piece. Where did you get her from?

Raja: Shup up, you stupid chap! She is the daughter of Taracharan Tarkabagish. That chap had left this place ten years ago. The duffer has now returned.

Rana: Whatever be the case, this broad has really become saucy.

Feku: If we can fix her up with the guards and drivers of goods trains, we don't have to worry about money anymore.

Raja: She is some piece, man. If we can use her for smuggling goods from Bangladesh, nobody is going to ask us anymore for cash cuts. We can also use her for our own purpose.

Feku: You bet! But yes, we are now the youth of Bangladesh. We don't have to think about these cash payments and bribes. We will get everything in order.

[*A stunned Bishnupriya is looking at these boys, without understanding a word of what they are saying. Raicharan enters from the left.*]

Raicharan: Here I am. Raicharan Dhara. I am the nephew of the Station House Officer at the Town Police station. But that's a bluff. Neither do I know him, nor anyone from his family. But I have to keep this masquerade on to get some money out of these creepy village specimens. Please don't give me away, or else I would not be able to rip them off. I am their friend, philosopher and guide. Hey you, Raja, Rana, Feku Mia, you should do well to remember that a goods train from North Bengal will stop at the junction at two in the morning. You have to give me the correct amount of goods you offload and whatever has been the share of the loot so far will remain the same.

Feku: Yes, yes, of course! We know that you don't work for less than fifty percent.

Raicharan: My dear, do you think that I get to keep the entire fifty percent? I have to dole out cuts. I would consider myself lucky if I get even twenty percent. Whatever remains goes to my seniors.

Raja: Take a look here, boss. We have a fresh girl here, young and ripe. If we can get her on board, a lot of kickbacks can be done away with.

Raicharan: Don't get into that business. That may invite trouble.

Feku: Bloody hell! You have a point.

[*Bits and pieces of conversation waft in from the background: 'We don't understand your politics'... 'You talk too much'... 'Just shut up'.*]

Raja: Now scram, all of you. The keepers of morality are coming.

[*All of them leave. Enters Durgacharan Nayratna, Raghudev Sarbobhoumo and Utpal Vidyabhushan.*]

Durgacharan: Old man, the last twitches of Vietnam are still burning. Where are you, Americans? What would happen to Lon Nol in Cambodia? Has it ever crossed your mind? Hey you, Raghudev Sarbobhoumo and Utpal Vidyabhushan, won't you say anything?

Raghudev: Brother Durgacharan Nayratna, you should start to right new wrongs now. All problems in Algeria have been solved. But what would happen to Argentina, now that the CIA has got its President Allende overthrown and killed?

Utpal: You better stay trapped in these stupid thoughts. It seems you have no idea about what is happening in South Africa, Bhutan and Rhodesia.

Durgacharan: Let's all park ourselves in the forecourt of Raicharan's house and analyse these problems threadbare in order to find solutions. You see, Indian philosophy is unfathomably deep. Only when we take a dip in it can we find the bottom. Come on, let's depart from here.

Utpal: You have only one departure to make. But if you consider Indian philosophy, we have to make departures from the times of Kurukshehtra. If you remember what Lord Krishna had said to Arjun before the start of the holy conflict – 'And the legacy of the tradition never dies…'

Durgacharan: So, according to you, wisdom is the moot point and that has left you?

Utpal: Dear Friend, it hurts as you remind me of that.

Raghudev: We must have witnesses as we discuss these matters. Who knows what we may say unwittingly! We need to keep our thoughts in place.

Durgacharan: Come on, that's why we need to go to Raicharan's place where we can immerse ourselves in such discussions. Let's go.

[*They exit the stage. Bishnupriya's childhood friend Kanika enters dancing from the left of the stage. She is being followed by Bishnupriya.*]

Kanika: [*song.*]

Pinaha Charunilbash...

Bishnupriya: Kanika, you are still as perky as ever.

Kanika: Dear friend,

Hridoi-er e kul, o kul, du kul bheshe jai...

Bishnupriya: For whom are you so restless?

Kanika: For you, friend, for you. I have been all alone without you.

Bishnupriya: Now, stop it! Will you?

Kanika: [*Wraps her arms around Bishnupriya.*] Ah! You have come back, you have returned to my life. Now let's go and set this village on fire and make a mess of the audience. It is important to make the people in the audience aware of how stupid they are. They haven't yet learnt to know themselves. They are here only to have a few moments' good time by watching us on the stage. They don't know that happiness exists inside, not outside. All say Hari, all say Hari!

Second Act

[*No sooner than the curtain goes up can be heard the whistle of a train. Rana and Raja are sitting in the middle of the stage. Feku Mia holds a pipegun and whistles some tune. After that, the noise of the rolling wheels of a train increases gradually. Feku turns and twists, as if he is performing a dance piece from Bharatnatyam.*]

Raja: Why are you jumping around like a frog, Feku?

Feku: It's normal that you won't have any clue to what I am doing. This is called Kalchur. Ok? This is not Khemta. It's the real stuff.

Rana: Why are you so pepped up?

Feku: My beloved is coming, my beloved is coming.

Raja: Who is coming?

Feku: Don't you Hindus have some folklore written by someone called Chandidas?

Chole neel saree ningari ningari poran shohit mor.

Feku: Or is it something else? Forget it. Here comes the goods train with its goodies.

[*In the background, the sound of the rolling wheels drops to signal that the train has stopped. Some people haul a few sacks and throw them onto the stage. As these boys pick them up, squads of BSF and CRPF personnel run into the stage from the right. One among them is the squad leader.*]

Squad leader: Hey, what you doing?

Raja: Can't you see that we are serving the country?

Feku: [*Muttering to himself.*] Grandpa, we are kneading the soul of your father!

Squad leader: Get the hell out of here, all of you! I am going to take custody of all these goods now.

Rana: Who are you, my dear? Are you planning to take everything away? Are we just spares? We stayed up the whole night to be here.

Squad leader: Say one more word and I will arrest you.

Feku: I am Feklu Mohammad. Which Vrindavan would you take us to? We are the new Turks here. We dance on the back of the peacock, with a bow in our hands and an arrow in the back. Don't try to be smart with us. You are now an also-ran.

Raja: Don't make the mistake of unsheathing your sword here.

Squad leader: Stop speaking from your high horse. Constables, handcuff them. I always speak the truth.

[*Raicharan enters from the left and upon realizing the situation, he swiftly pulls out his service card.*]

Raicharan: What's happening? Why create unnecessary trouble?

Raja: Just see, Brother Raicharan. No, sorry, Raicharan Sahib. We are only trying to serve the country and these so-called guardians of law are trying to throw a spanner in the works.

Raicharan: But why?

Raja: See, we picked up just a few sacks full of commodities. The people here don't get food to eat. Villages after villages remain unfed. We cannot stand this situation anymore. Our aim is to bring the smile back on these famished faces.

Raicharan: Look here, Squad leader. The goods have landed in my domain and these boys are my helpers. Let them go with these goods.

Squad leader: This is not right. You are not being wise.

Raicharan: To hell with being wise. Just do what I say.

Squad leader: [*Salutes.*] Alright, Sir.

Raicharan: One more thing. I think I am going adrift of you all, isn't it? I mean, in terms of point of view? I will settle all that soon. You boys leave this place right now.

[*The three boys pick up the sacks and exits from the right of the stage.*]

Raicharan: Hey you, come here.

Squad leader: What happened?

Raicharan: How much?

Squad leader: What?

Raicharan: How much do you want for this?

Squad leader: Sir!!

Raicharan: Come clear. How much money do you want? Let's get over with it, quickly.

Squad leader: [*Smiles.*] Sir.

Raicharan: Stop calling me Sir all the time! Or else I will turn all of you into worms. Now take care of your entire squad, OK?

Squad leader: Well, now I understand. I always speak the truth.

Raicharan: But I am a complete bluffer. This is my business.

[*Raicharan leads the vigilance squad and exits from the left of the stage. Before exiting, he claps thrice and the three boys enter smiling.*]

Rana: He is our Raicharan the guide.

Feku: Our flippant salvager.

Raja: Our philosopher.

Rana: What the hell!

Raja: How could you serve your nation if the police are after you all the time?

Feku: Well, the assignment for the night is over. We will have to wait until dawn. We are expecting

	delivery from Petrapol, Benapol and Bongaon. Hossein Mia has promised to deliver the goods on time. Aren't we supposed to receive them?
Raja:	I almost forgot. A much bigger consignment has to be received. A top heroine from Bombay is coming to perform at a dance event. Owing to the trouble and time being taken to take delivery of these small consignments, I almost forgot about the Bombay heroine. Thank God for small mercies! I remembered it in time. We don't have much time because there is no one else to but us to handle that consignment. We can't leave it to Nobokeshto's boys from the Fulila village, can we?
Rana:	If we do that, the Bombay parcel may vanish lock, stock and barrel. But if the consignment is with us, it would be fun! What was that, Bharatnatya or something you said?
Raja:	Bharatnatyam.
Rana:	Whatever.
Feku:	Moreover, she is a star of the Hindi filmdom. When she arrives, this area will burst at its seams. Unless we take care of her, all those drunken dogs will devour her.
Raja:	Like before, block tickets so that we can sell them at a premium at the time of the show. Call me names if I don't sell the Rupees Seven ticket for Rupees Seventy. Mark my words, this marketplace is so frenzied about the show that the right kind of hype can take the price of the tickets to even Rupees Hundred each.

[*From the left enters Raghudev Sarbobhoumo along with his daughter Sushma and Raicharan. Raicharan takes a dressed beetle-leaf from a small tin box and pops it into his mouth.*]

Raicharan: My wife really prepares these beetle-leaves so well.

[*He gesticulates to Raja to take a look at those who came in with him.*]

Raja: She is new and nice.

Rana: I am looking after this case.

Feku: First file the case.

Rana: Hey Pandit Sir, where are you going with 'Mother'?

Raghudev: Not anywhere really.

Raja: The news about her arrival is already in circulation.

Raghudev: Means what?

Raja: It means that you are splitting from here, now. You can't be present as long as we are here. After all, we do have responsibilities, don't we?

Rana: [*Gesticulating at Sushma.*] especially when it comes to taking care of public property.

Raghudev: I didn't get than, Son.

Raja: Only the public has the right to public property.

Raghudev: Very true, but that's not happening all the time.

Rana: That's the reason why we have launched a campaign. There are some properties that we want to have for ourselves. After all, we are the young Turks of the nation.

Feku: Then let's get this property, or preserve it, as you guys say in your polished lexicon.

Raja: Right. Come 'Mother', come and light up the home.

[*Raghudev begins to tremble with fear. Sushma is stunned into silent embarrassment. The three boys begin to surround her. Helpless, Raghudev fearfully walks up to Raicharan.*]

Raghudev: You are the nephew of the Inspector General of Police. How could these boys outrage her modesty in front of you?

Raicharan: Raghudev Sarbobhoumo, you are making a mistake. This country is lawless. There is just one law that now rules this country, and that is the law of the jungle. The ethos of life here does not draw upon the lessons of Sanskrit, Gita, the Vedas or the Upanishads. The main mantra of life here is to lay waste everything and devour what that disarray produces. That's the only theme being followed by everyone in this country now.

[*Raja drags Raghudev away. Rana picks up the pipegun. Raja bring out a country-made bomb from his pocket.*]

Raja: Look here Pandit Sir, let me say a few words that would be salubrious for you should you choose to listen to what I have to say.

Rana: As they say in English, it would be good for your health.

Feku: Make him understand.

Raja: First of all, Pandit Sir, you must not leave the village. You would be in trouble if you try to do that. Secondly, we would return your daughter to you after a fortnight. We can guarantee that. If you go to the police, you would be in deep trouble. We are not going to short-change you.

We will keep paying some money as long as she is with us.

Raghudev: What are you talking about!

Feku: We mean to say that you may need money to spend on her abortion. You know, you got to pay the doctor, after all.

Raghudev: That's not possible.

Rana: If you make noise, we will force you into silence, as simple as that.

[*Rana grabs Sushma by the hand and readies to exit the stage from the right. In one swift movement, Sushma frees herself from the clutches of Rana and reaches the centre of the stage with her back towards the audience. The three boys run up to her and grab her from all sides. They say—*]

Come, Mother Sushma. You are the Goddess Bhagwati reincarnate! Bloody bitch!

[*Rana muffles Sushma using his hand as she begins to scream. The trio drags her to the right of the stage. As if nothing has happened, Raicharan stays unruffled and spits out the beetle-leaf that he was chewing.*]

Raicharan: Ah! My wife really prepares the beetle-leaf so well.

Raghudev: Is this a nightmare? Is this really happening in this country? O God!

[*They exit from the left of the stage. Slowly, dawn is breaking and chirping of birds can be heard. It's a misty morning. The stage is empty for a few moments before Bishnupriya and Kanika, holding hands and dancing, enter from the left of the stage, their hair embellished with flowers. They are singing an ancient love song.*]

Akash ato neel kano
Megh ato sundor kano
Prithibi ato bhalo kano

Pochondo hoi na.
Ato bhalo, bhalo na
Jibon ato sundor na,
Manush boro gondogoley
Eshob thik jome na.
Hoto jodi shekel-er din
Tokhon jibon hoto tin,
Tokhon ato jonmodin
Ajke sheyshob manai na.
Orey bhalobashar manush
Tui jodi shotti hosh
Tobe amai bujhte parbi
Noiley kichui bujhbi na.

[*The sound of a train can be heard. Sushovan enters with a suitcase in his hand. Kanika runs up to him and grabs him by the lapel of his shirt.*]

Kanika: So you are running away to Kolkata again? I won't let you go.

Sushovan: If you don't let me go, how would I make my both ends meet? Who would take care of my needs then? Can't be you.

Kanika: I don't care, but when you are not around...

Sushovan: ...it seems something is missing from the village?

Kanika: One who feels like that is standing there.

[*She points towards Bishnupriya, who looks visibly embarrassed. She flashes a quick look at Kanika. Sushovan fumbles for words.*]

Sushovan: I am leaving, Bishnupriya.

Bishnupriya: OK.

Sushovan: Is that all you have to say?

Bishnupriya: As if you will stay back if I ask you not to go.

Sushovan: I have some important work. I do have a lot of responsibilities to care for.

Bishnupriya: Yes, I know.

Sushovan: Bishnupriya…

Bishnupriya: Yes?

Sushovan: Do you remember?

Bishnupriya: What?

Sushovan: Do you remember those moments that we shared long ago, those sweet moments?

Bishnupriya: Not really.

Sushovan: Don't I figure in your memory when you recall those moments?

Bishnupriya: Maybe, I do.

Sushovan: When we were both children, we had once climbed a Guava tree together. I remember I fell from the tree and injured myself. See, I still bear the mark of that injury. This mark is indelible, as much as you are.

Bishnupriya: Come on!

Sushovan: Your subject bows to thee, your majesty. I will be ready when you are. I could have said much more quoting Rabindranath Tagore, but no use now. I guess this is enough. I have to go since my train is approaching. But I will come back some day. Please wait for me. Bishnu, I hope that you remember me.

Bishnupriya: Come on!

[*A moment turns into a free-frame. Then Sushovan exits the stage from the left. Kanika walks up to the centre of the stage and places an arm on Bishnupriya's shoulders. Bishnupriya looks at her and then looks up.*]

Kanika: What?

Bishnupriya: What?

Kanika: What? What happened?

Bishnupriya: Something has happened. Something definitely has happened.

Kanika: What possibly could have happened?

Bishnupriya: Something seems to be missing. There's a strange feeling of emptiness, but I can't exactly figure out what it is.

Kanika: Shall I tell?

[*Bishnupriya looks at her. Dancing, Kanika pulls her away to the rear of the stage. It is now a clear morning.*]

Kanika: Can attribute a name to your feelings...

Bishnupriya: And what that would be?

Kanika: Love. [*Kanika Sings.*]

Ami Hridoir kotha bolite byakul...

[*A card drops from above. It is emblazoned with these words: 'This, perhaps, is love'. As the two girls begin to laugh, the curtain drops.*]

Third Act

[*The curtain lifts. The film heroine from Bombay is performing Bharatnatyam. Seated in the front row at the venue are most of the characters we have used in this play so far. Towards the end, the performance depicts the journey of Nimai to Gaya, where he renounces the material world and finds his spiritual calling. This has to be portrayed as a prominent scene. Nimai returns from Gaya with a new name: Sri Chaitanya Mahaprabhu. Bishnupriya (the wife of Sri Chaitanya), in an attire used in the middle-ages, appears. She sings mournfully to lament losing her husband to spiritual mendicancy and exits the stage. Kanika and Bishnupriya (the character in this play), leave their seats in the audience and exit.*]

1st youth: That was top-notch!

2nd youth: Tell me, what did you understand from all this?

1st youth: What else but a dance performance.

1st youth: You mean it was just a dance performance?

1st youth: Of course!

2nd youth: What you watched was an Indian classical dance form. It's called Bharatnatyam. Along with it was Sri Chaitanya Mahaprabhu's transformation into a spiritual being and…

1st youth: Who cares! What matters is that, I have watched from close a heroine from the Hindi filmdom dance. Come on, let's go now.

[*The two young men leave. Raja, Rana and Feku enter from the left of the stage.*]

Feku: People from as far as twenty miles have come to watch this performance.

Rana: Imagine what would have happened had we used a loudspeaker in the villages to announce the programme.

Raja: There's much money to make from such cultural events.

Feku: By the way, where is that dancer being put up?

Raja: Let's not get involved in that.

Rana: Why so?

Raja: She would be in the protective custody of the rich and famous of this area.

Feku: That's sad. Aren't we getting a piece of her tonight?

Raja: Hey, look, look. Those two voluptuous girls are coming this way. Let's get them.

Feku: Leave that to me.

[*As Feku tries to grab Kanika, she jumps back and slaps him on the face. Thereafter, she runs away, exiting through the right of the stage. Bishnupriya, too, tries to run but Rana blocks her path.*]

Raja: Where are you going, dear girl? We need you.

Bishnupriya: Why do you need me?

Rana: Yes, we need you badly.

Feku: Without you, this night will not be over.

Raja: I have been dreaming about you all the time.

[*Bishnupriya looks at them helplessly. In the meantime, Raicharan, chewing on his beetle leaf, enters the stage from the left.*]

Bishnupriya: I can't make out what these boys want. Could you please take me along with you?

Raicharan: Dear Sister, everybody comes into this world alone. Neither would anyone accompany you when the time to leave arrives. We come alone, we go alone. Let the Almighty take a call in the end.

[*He pops another wrapping of beetle-leaf into his mouth with a dab of aromatic chewing tobacco.*]

Raja: There will be good money.

Rana: There will be sweetmeats from the shop of Ganguram.

Raicharan: The old woman at home has not used good-quality chewing tobacco today. I have to teach her a lesson when I return home today. Alright boys, keep playing happily. I will go home now. Oh! My gout seems to be acting up these days. On top of it, I have blood sugar.

[*Raicharam smiles, twirls his moustache and exits from the right of the stage. Taracharan enters from the left.*]

Taracharan: Hello boys! How are you doing these days?

Raja: We are doing fine, Sir.

Feku: What's the plan of action?

Rana: Let's get out of here. This old man can be dangerous.

Raja: Uncle, we have some important work pending. I mean, we have a meeting to attend. We will come back and see you tomorrow. Bye for now.

[*The three boys use the right exit of the stage to leave.*]

Bishnupriya: [*Singing a song based on the Raga Mian ki Mallar.*]
Kothao akta bhalo desh ache
Jekhane manush manush ke bhalobashe
Shey desh kothai jani na
Kintu tar kotha mone ashe
Akdin ei prithibi ta sundor hobei
Manush manush ke bhalobashbei
Koto hajar bochor pore jana nei
Kintu jana ache er kono marjona nei
Sheydin-er jonno ami tikey achi
Shei din ta ashar jonno ami bhalobashchi.

Taracharan: Why are you looking so down?

Bishnupriya: Father, let's go somewhere, away from here.

Taracharan: What do you mean?

Bishnupriya: Father, I do believe that this world will one day be a beautiful place to live in. For that to happen, it may take two hundred, five hundred, even a thousand years. But it is bound to happen someday. I can sense this in my heart. We all must work towards achieving that goal. We must live to usher in that special day. Let's go, Father. Let's go.

Taracharan: My dear, you may not know, but I, too, share similar thoughts. But where do we go from here? I have nowhere to go. At least here, I can arrange for us two square meals a day. I also have the ancestral home. But I don't know what our future will be on unknown shores. But what makes you say all this now?

Bishnupriya: Never mind. You wouldn't understand. It's alright.

Taracharan: What's alright, dear?

Bishnupriya: I mean, alright. Let's go.

[*Sachi enters from the left of the stage. She could sense something amiss the moment she sees her daughter Bishnupriya. Sachi walks up to Bishnupriya and places a gentle hand on her head.*]

Taracharan: [*Nonplussed.*] What happened?

Sachi: I can sense something is not right here. You go now and leave us alone. You don't need to interfere in these matters. You have spent your entire life dabbling with the Shastras and yet, you don't understand a thing. You are still trapped within the precincts of archaic custom and norms. You better not speak. Now go.

Taracharan: What's all this? Alright, I am leaving.

Sachi: I have come across enough of tomfoolery by others. No harm, if we do that for a change.

Taracharan: What are you trying to say? I don't understand.

Sachi: To satisfy your whims, you came to your ancestral house lock, stock and barrel. You then reopened the school. But what was the result? Nothing. Are you being able to protect anything?

Taracharan: At least, we are getting to eat two square meals a day.

Sachi: Is eating the end-all and be-all of life? Isn't there anything else to care for?

Taracharan: My dear wife, that's the moot point these days.

Sachi: But two square meals a day may not be of paramount importance to everyone.

Taracharan: What else can be there?

Sachi: How about protecting modesty?

Taracharan: Raghudev Sarbobhoumo is freely moving around with his own shame.

Sachi: You leave now.

[*Taracharan leaves the stage, dejected. Bishnupriya wraps her arms around her mother and begins to cry profusely. Sachi lifts the face of her daughter with a tender hand on the chin.*]

Sachi: Tell me, dear.

Bishnupriya: Oh! Mother! The situation here is so terrible, Mother.

Sachi: I know, dear, I know. But we have to live within this filth.

Bishnupriya: I won't be able to survive. I can't live like this. This is not living a life.

[*The curtain drops as she keeps on crying. A card drops down from the fly carrying a message: There are many variations to living.*]

Fourth Act

[*The curtain goes up. The whole stage is flooded with light. A card drops down from the fly. It says: 'Now witness the fate, the same fate that Awaits all in their homes Go home and find What fate holds for you...' Rana, Raja and Feku enter. They seem to be drunk as they stand in the centre of the stage.*]

Raja: We did good business right.

Rana: Yes, I have made some money.

Feku: But this Bishnupriya girl continues to nag my mind. Any idea how we can get her?

Rana: Just uproot her. That's all.

Raja: No way. We have to win her over. She is one firebrand girl and can send our business crashing.

Feku: Why are you guys being constantly driven by libido? Let's go and meet Raicharan. He is coming to a field near us. An express train is arriving from Jalpaiguri today, carrying a lot of stuff. We need to grab some of it. Let me make it clear. Sustenance comes first and then the amorous acts of life.

[*They exit from the right of the stage. Somebody can be heard singing. From the left of the stage, Bishnupriya dances into the stage, along with Kanika.*]

Kanika and Bishnupriya:

[*Sings a song based on the Raga Puria Dhaneshree.*]

Tumi gele kobe?
Kano gele?
Phirbe jobe
Tokhon tomai
Notun kore gan shonabo.
Shey gan tomar mon-er majhe
Jhumur hoey bajbe.
Sheydin tomai bhalobeshe
Pagol hoey kandbo
Tumi amar, ami tomar
Ei kotha ki bhulbo
Ei kotha ti shesh obdhi
Omor hoey thakbe.

Kanika: You monkey, why did you stop?

Bishnupriya: You were right. I am being gripped by those feelings.

Kanika: You mean love?

Bishnupriya: Something like that.

Kanika: Can you spell love?

Bishnupriya: If I did, I would have spelt it out for you right now. You are responsible for all this.

Kanika: Oh! My, My! You found your love, but what about me? When do I get mine?

Bishnupriya: Don't you have anyone special in your life?

Kanika: There is one, but inside my mind. It seems my love is continuing to come without arriving.

[*She sings…*]

Aji jhor-er rat-e tomar obhishar
Poranshokha bondhu hey amar.

[*Or another song, based on the Raga Shankara Behaag and scored by Ritwik Ghatak can be used here.*]

Shey ashche, shey aschei, mone mone.
O je amar pran-e.
Tar roop kamon bhule gechi
Kintu ta ke dekhte pacchi
O je amar bhalobashar dhon, amar moton
Ta ke ki bhalobasha jai, ta ke ki keu pai?
Amar jibonshadhon shudhu tai to,
Ei chara ar kichu nai to.

Bishnupriya: Don't sing that song.

Kanika: Why? Is it a lousy song?

Bishnupriya: Not at all, but that song raises a tumult in my heart. Besides, I am not in a happy mood today.

Kanika: Why?

Bishnupriya: I don't know.

Kanika: Are you kidding me? It's you who is immersed in love and I am supposed to stop singing this song.

Bishnupriya: I am going to kill you.

Kanika: Try me.

[*The two friends use dance steps to lock in a sham combat. Slowly, they move towards the rear of the stage. Meanwhile, from the left of the stage, Durgacharan Nayratna, Raghudev Sarbobhoumo and Utpal Vidyabhushan enter.*]

Durgacharan: Don't you have any worries about your daughter?

Raghudev: I have got her back. Forget it. Let the chips fall where they may. But isn't anybody prepared to raise a voice against the killing of Allende in South America by the C.I.A. and Nixon?

Utpal: There is no guarantee that this son of a bitch Nixon and his lackeys would not repeat their act in India.

Durgacharan: Consider the case of Diego Garcia. The whole country is protesting against the scam created out of this issue. But is anybody bothered to find a solution to this problem?

[*A smiling Raicharan enters from the left.*]

Raicharan: You are making a mistake. Capitalism didn't halt there. Have you read Leontiev? Do you have any clue to what neocolonialism is? If you did, you would have realized that this country is beyond repairs. This country has gone to seed.

[*Sachi runs into the stage from the left. She grabs Raicharan. Her hair is open and flailing; her eyes portraying helplessness and fear.*]

Sachi: [*Violently shaking up Raicharan.*] What have you done? You have disrobed the mothers and sisters of this country. Sushma has lapsed into a state of mental disorder.

[*In fear, the pundits vanish through the exit to the right of the stage. Sarbobhoumo is seted from the flock. He runs to the other side of the stage, completely confused. A mournful song can be heard: 'My Mother, O My Mother'.*]

Raicharan: Sachi Ma, You know, as a matter of fact, I mean, err, I have to analyse the matter. As we are employed by the Government, we have to wait for orders. We send files from one department to another for action to be taken. Not just this, we have to interact with bureaucrats as well.

[*Taracharan runs in. He pulls Sachi away. In that rigmarole, Raicharan scampers off through the right.*]

Taracharan: What are you doing? Have you gone completely mad?

Sachi: I can't take it any longer. I am shivering in fright.

Taracharan: Somehow, I am not being able to make you comprehend the reality. This injustice cannot continue forever. There has to be an end to this disorder. At the end, it would be:

Paritranai Sadhunang Vinashay cha dushkritam
Dharmasangsthaparnathai sambhabami yuge yuge

(This is the truth and it cannot be proved wrong.)

Sachi: But…

Taracharan: …No ifs and buts. Let's go home now.

[*Sachi rests her head on her husband's chest. Without speaking a word, Taracharan and Sashi quietly exit from the right of the stage. The moment they leave, Bishnupriya enters. As she enters, the stage is flooded with light. She is making Bharatnatyam movements. Then the three boys enter, smiling at her. Bishnupriya is startled. She stands still.*]

Raja: Ah! We are in Vrindavan now.

Rana: In the lexicon of the rich, it is called birthright.

You are our birthright. We are for new youth and new life. You have to come with us. We can't let you go anymore. The case has been filed.

Feku: Think about the support we have of influential people. So many big shots are backing us. If you create trouble, we will remove you and your parents from the face of the Earth. Come with us.

[*Bishnupriya starts shivering. She looks around, searching for an opening she can use to run away. But the trio blocks her from three sides.*]

Bishnupriya: I am like a sister to all of you. Won't you let me go?

Raja: I swear! We are enamoured by you and your body. We want to taste it, examine it.

Rana: You see, it's kind of an experiment.

Feku: It's just an effort to know what kind of specimen are women who belong to the civilized society.

Bishnupriya: I am wearing a thick iron bangle. I won't die without killing at least one of you.

Raja: Come on sister, don't be so upset. Come quietly with us and we assure you your safe return to home. We are assuming that responsibility. We have returned Sushma to her home. Believe me, we don't slip up on promises that we make.

Rana: Don't be afraid. We aren't afraid either. We have prior information that you father has gone to attend a function.

Feku: Before the first bird sings, you will find yourself happily spread out on your own bed.

[*Bishnupriya turns to take a close look at the trio. She then takes a deep breath and wraps the tail of her saree around her waist.*]

Bishnupriya: So you want to devour me. My father is a poor man and you find me beautiful. Since you and your ilk decide the fate of today's Bangladesh, you have the right to enjoy me. But, before anything, may I ask a favour of you?

Raja: What would be that?

Bishnupriya: I wouldn't be alive after you consume me. But before I die, I would like to see myself beautiful. Therefore, allow me to wear a nice saree.

Feku: You mean you want to dress up for the occasion?

Bishnupriya: Something like that.

Raja: Let her go. We will wait here. The moment she comes out, we will grab her.

Rana: No. We must hear her final appeal. What do you say, Feku?

Feku: If we don't run out of providence, we will get her. Let the girl go.

[*Bishnupriya smiles and vanishes through the black curtain on the stage. Soon after, noises can be heard which make it clear that Bishnupriya is using the back door to run away.*]

Feku: What the hell is that?

Raja: She's fled.

Rana: I am going to drag her back. There's no way we can let her go.

[*The three of dash to the right-hand exit of the stage and disappear. Disorderly light is cast to turn the stage into a frightful space. Cacophonic and terrorizing music breaks out loudly. Then they drag the girl in and vanish with her behind the black curtain. The entire stage is dark. Only Bishnupriya's screams can be heard, which finally turns into a groan. It is at that point of time, Raicharan run into the stage with a diary in his hand.*]

Raicharan: Hey listen. You boys come out quickly and bring the girl along. Don't be late. The person whose nephew I was masquerading as, that real-life Inspector General of Police is here. I have never met him before. I am not bothered about what would happen to the three of you when he comes, but one thing is for sure – I will be dead.

[*Carrying an unconscious Bishnupriya, the three boys enter the stage through the curtain. Bishnupriya is in a state of forced undress.*]

Raicharan: What was the need for womanizing? You were doing alright for yourselves as long as you were stealing from train wagons, firing guns and hurling bombs. That reporter Sushovan has returned to the village. His newspaper will flash all your misdeeds. I don't care what happens to you once this case hits the headlines, but I will lose everything.

Raja: Don't worry, boss. We are making arrangements to set things right. Rana, to the line.

Rana: Yes, your Highness.

Feku: A can of kerosene has been kept in the slums next-door.

Raja: Stop throwing dialogues now. Be quick.

[*Rana runs out from the right.*]

Feku: In the meantime, let's all have a dance together. Let's do the Green Tarantula dance, the dance of death.

[*They start dancing but Raicharan doesn't join them. Raja holds Raicharan by the hand, drag him, and slap his hard. Then he says—*]

Come friend, dance with us.

[*Rana arrives hastily with a can of kerosene. He douses Bishnupriya with Kerosene and sets her on fire. The entire stage has to be shown in flames created by lights. Then Sushovan dashes in from the right. Raicharan opens his diary and takes out his pen in order to take Bishnupriya's declaration. Kanika enters.*]

Feku: Taking a cue from all that new and polite language we have learnt, I have to say that we are now leaving for a new horizon.

[*The three of them leave the stage.*]

Raicharan: Look here, Sir. We need to close the case somehow. Therefore, I have to record the girl's dying declaration. The entire village has been surrounded by the police.

[*He climbs the steps towards Bishnupriya.*]

Raicharan: My dear, you are dying. The perpetrators of the crime have run away. I am trapped and I am going to lose everything. Would you say who all are responsible for this crime, for this rampant sinning? Who? Who is responsible for this?

[*Sushovan tries to lift Bishnupriya's face in his cradled arms. In sync with the movement of the girl, as her face is being raised, the scene shifts to the screen that shows a big close-up of Bishnupriya and the voice of Raicharan reverberates—*]

Sushovon: Who is responsible, who?

[*The film shot on the screen shows the girl as looking at the audience. Then she spits. This is where the girl is being physically brought down with the use of a trap-door. Sushovan gets up and stands near the edge of the stage. The cyclorama and all other lights go out, except for two spotlights – one amber and the other white—fall on Sushovan from either sides.*]

Sushovan: How long does this nation have to withstand this disorder? It is no longer possible to survive this terrible situation we find ourselves in, today. Those who have come to see this play will return to the safe refuge of their homes have dinner, go to sleep in peace and wake up on the morrow to be at your workplace on time. But this injustice will continue unabated. Isn't there a way to curb this lawlessness? Think about it.

[*A card drops from the fly. On the card is written: For people to live, they need to rise and agitate. Brothers and sisters, rise while you can. Agitate and break all barriers. Otherwise, nothing will happen. The curtain will then drop slowly and the song, 'Moder deshbashi re', can be heard in the background.*]

That Woman

5

Translator's Note

One must remember that the play, *Shei Meye*, was written at a time when the Indian society was in the midst of trying times. What may seem as a cinch today wasn't so during those tempestuous days – from the 50's to the 70's—when political will and development weren't synonyms, and *vox populi* wasn't the mantra for change. While a hopeful race was striving for progress, a weak socio-economic structure was destabilising the very plinth from which change and improvement in quality of life were being sought. It was during these times that the play was written – a time when compassion and accepting the uncommon as part of life weren't too high on the list of human priorities. If Shanti, the protagonist of the piece, were born in the 21st century, this particular play with its many piquant turns might not have been written. For, despite being mentally scarred and hysteric, she would have been an integral part of society where emancipated humans and an advanced medical science were likely to lend her succour. But then, the unheard stories of the world's unfortunate children need to be told, even if they clash with time. That's because the ills that once besotted societies still remain in their residual slumber, waiting to be collectively awakened by false moves. The Bangla script of 'That Woman' has been supple in the use of the literary technique called Stream of Consciousness. There are portions that called for the technique to be pared to help express the purpose of some dialogues. Besides, certain Bangla words in the script required a whole sentence to be explained in English, such as *Ghomta*, *Tip* and *Sindur*. To bring the readers up to speed, only a married Hindu woman wears a *Ghomta*, which is about using the tail of a saree to cover the head as a mark of respect for the elderly.

A married woman from a traditional Hindu home would do so even in front of her husband. Similarly, when a Hindu woman uses *Sindur*, or the vermilion powder, on the centre-parting of her head, she is marking herself as one who is married. The 'Tip', however, is a cosmetic dot between the brows sported by many women in India – married or unmarried. Keeping this constraint in mind, I have retained *Ghomta*, *Sindur* and *Tip* in the translated script. In the same vein, I have retained *Manik* and *Khokon*. Both these words in Bangla are sometimes used affectionately for a child and need not necessarily be names given to children by their parents. In this script, *Manik* and *Khokon* are not names. There are also single-sentence dialogues in Bangla that needed to be broken down in parts to convey the punch the author desired to deliver.

[The curtain goes up—empty stage. Music starts. An overlay of black cloth hangs at the rear of the stage, flanked by two doors at the back. The one to the left is for entering the interiors and the one to the right is to be used for coming from outside. To the left of the stage is a pedestal, like a dais, aligned with steps. The entire pedestal is wrapped in white cloth with a blue border surrounding it at the bottom. In the middle of the stage is an ordinary table with a green cover. On either side of the table are two chairs facing each other. Some papers and records are kept on the table. To the left of the table is a black easel on which a diagram of a psychiatrist is affixed; it is white in colour and drawn in black backdrop... A wooden railing, as high as average human height, is placed to the left of the stage. The railing is not painted; it retains the original colour of the wood it is made of. In the middle of the railing is a door with a bolt and a padlock. The door, taller than the railing, is pale yellow in colour with patches of grime. This indicates that the door is a symbol and would be used for symbolic purposes. Behind the railing is a bed covered with a white sheet. Next to the bed is an ordinary, four-legged stool. During special moments in the course of the play, the railings will cast their shadow all over the stage. Along the black overlay at the rear of the stage is a row of flower pots in careless blossoms of white, off-white and red flowers. A long stick is being kept, leaning on the easel. It looks like the cue used in billiards. There is a predominance of dramatic white light on the entire stage. Amber and steel-blue lights

are to be used only when the actors are near the bed. In the scenes depicting hallucination, there will be a clash of kaleidoscopic lights on the stage. When the lead actress appears in dream sequences, the stage will see a preponderance of the colour sky-blue. Lights will be used only for those sections of the stage where performance is taking place. During the course of play, the section or sections of the stage not in use will be in complete darkness. On one hand, these stage arrangements can co-exist; again on the other hand four patients can be shown wearing striped inmate clothes, fetching props, as and when required, from the greenrooms to the stage. A large international logo for mental and behavioural disorder, painted in black on a piece of white sheet of paper is stuck to the top-left corner of the black cloth at the rear of the stage. Shanti, a housewife from a struggling village-family, walks coyly into the stage. She is wearing a simple white saree with a red border. On her forehead is a big red dot of Sindur. She is also sporting a liberal dash of Sindur on the centre-parting on her head. She is wearing a nose ring. Her countenance reflects impression of rusticity. As she looks here and there, she notices the audience and she straight walks up to the top of the pedestal in the left hand side of the stage. Then she gave a gentle smile draws ghomta across her face and greets the audience with a namaskar.]

Shanti: I can see that you all are waiting for me here. You won't have to wait anymore. I'm going to tell you everything today. Maybe, someone somewhere will benefit from what I say. Maybe, my parable, someday, would make society think twice before shunning people like us. Maybe, it would not reinvite disease. Perhaps, women like me wouldn't be looked at with sleepless eyes anymore; perhaps people would not doubt our innocence of pouring our heart out and I hope simple, spontaneous stories of women like me would not undergo the scrutiny of suspicion. But is there really anyone who would accept us back when we return? I have much to say, but am strapped for time. The germ of this disease was silently growing deep inside, waiting suddenly to break surface one day. You have no idea of the distance I have travelled; of the many obstacles I have crossed, to be able to speak to you with composure in place. Since this would take time, I would cut the long story short. Once there was a girl called Shanti—[*She steps off the pedestal to pace at the edge of the stage.*] I am not adept at organizing my words and structuring my sentences. After all, I am from village. Oh yes, I used to love skies, rivers and water as well as flowers. You know, white flowers, and white Lotuses, Nyctantheses, Tubarosas and Jasmines. There used to be so many of them. I can't remember all the names now. I used to like anything that which is white as much as I liked the colour sky blue. There used to be so many other flowers without names that I liked. I can't remember all at this moment. But then, something happened. I am losing cue here. Everything is getting jumbled up. I am getting confused. Wait a minute, let me call the doctor. He would be able to tell you the story succinctly and with clarity. Hey doctor, doctor, where are you?

Doctor: [*His voice in the background.*] Shanti, I am busy working.

Shanti: So many people are waiting. Could you please come over here for a while?

[*The doctor enters.*]

Shanti: See, there are so many of them.

Doctor: That's true. But it seems you are after me and would not let me work. How many times do you expect me to tell the same old story? Ask them to leave, please. Besides, your story is not of sadness. Instead, it is about harsh reality. Why do you think these people would love to hear about the brutal truth?

Shanti: [*Excitedly.*] Of course they would love to hear the story. They must get to know what I have to say.

Doctor: These people want a play. Really, life is so devoid of drama—

Shanti: No, they don't need drama. They want to know and comprehend what has happened to me and why, and what happened after that.

Doctor: Oh Shanti! [*Shakes his head.*] Ok, I give up. What can I do more, go inside now while I prepare them with a preamble.

Shanti: In that case, shall I go and put on the make-up with dark circles around my eyes, like I did the first time?

Doctor: Do whatever you have to, but leave now.

Shanti: You know Doctor, you hustle me a lot.

[*Shanti exits the stage. The doctor, clutching his hands behind his back, climbs the pedestal and looks straight in the audience's eye.*]

Doctor: Shanti will leave today. She is bidding you goodbye after three months and eight days. Shanti is a docile girl, who lives near Barasat. Perhaps, you would not like her story; you may feel tired as well. But, if you listen, you might just be able to pluck something meaningful out of it. You see, we treat cases of mental disorder here. I am a psychiatrist as well as a social worker here. Generally such responsibilities are divided among different sets of people. Due to scarcity of time, Responsibilities I would play all the roles tonight. Shanti is my patient. [*Doctor steps off the pedestal to pick up the stick that was leaning on the easel. He would now use the stick to point out areas when he would be speaking next.*] Alright, before I start the story, let me explain the lay-out of this place. The pedestal I was standing upon a few minutes ago would be the place from where I would make comments as and when I am required to do so. Let's now divide the space behind this area with an imaginary diagram. For example, on the other side would be the patient's cabin with a door and a bed. Now draw a straight line in the front of the table, chairs and the bed that are behind me. Beyond that line is my chamber from where I inspect patients. The flower pots at the rear indicate the presence of a garden patients are taken out to for a stroll. As a matter of fact, I have to leave everything to your imagination and sympathy. Please do remember—that Shanti is a good girl. She had arrived here three months and eight days ago on a Thursday. The day was May the first and the year, 1969. I still remember the day. Shanti, however, is not extra-ordinary but there is an element of melancholy about her that may make you feel that she is different—Here she comes.

Shanti: [*Screaming from the wings.*] Where are you taking me, where? Let me go. You are conspiring to kill me. How ruthless could you get?

[Doctor quickly sits down on a chair. Shanti is being dragged by her husband, a nurse and a female attendant towards the doctor's chamber. Her hair is open and flowing like a meteor's tail, her eyes full of fear and her saree hanging loosely from her body. As she reaches the doctor's chamber, Shanti crashes face-first to the floor. She raises her face to touch her forehead where she apparently hurt herself. She wipes her hand across her forehead to see that her palm has been reddened by Sindur -- the vermilion powder a Hindu woman wears at the bottom of the mid-parting on the head, as a signal of her being married. Shanti cries out.]

Shanti: Blood! Blood! See, they are killing me. I am bleeding from the head.

Husband: No, Shanti. That's not blood. It's the sindur that's coming off.

Shanti: [*Raises her face.*] Sindur is used by married women. Tell me, when did I ever get married?

Husband: But Shanti, didn't you...

Shanti: What's all this? Why am I wearing bangles?

Husband: That's the iron bangle around your wrist. It marks you as a woman who is married.

Shanti: Marriage! Sindur! This is all a conspiracy! They want to mislead and kill me. To hell with your iron ring! Take this, take this!

[She throws the iron bangle on the floor, bangs it repeatedly and breaks it. She then rubs the mark of sindur off her forehead.]

[The doctor walks up slowly to Shanti and softly places an arm on her shoulders. Shanti looks at him.]

Doctor: Come and sit on this chair.

Shanti: Who are you?

Doctor: A friend.

Shanti: A friend? But you seem to be new to my village. Have you arrived here recently?

Doctor: Yes

Shanti: Alright then. Where should I sit? Here?

Doctor: Yes.

[*As she turns around to sit, Shanti notices her husband and the nurse. She is visibly frightened.*]

Shanti: [*Addressing the doctor.*] Please send off that man and that woman. They are plotting to kill me. Did you think that I wouldn't be able to lay bare your conspiracy? [*Says to the husband.*] I know, you want me away so that the two of you can have a happy life together. Isn't that true? Please turn them out now, or else I will run away.

Doctor: Sister, please take the gentleman with you and wait outside. The nurse, the husband and the attendant exit the stage. Shanti heaves a sigh of relief and sits down.

Shanti: Ah, what a relief!! You are a nice man. I have begun to like you. You know, they keep beating me up. I hope you are not going to mete out the same treatment to me.

Doctor: No, never. We are friends.

Shanti: In that case, would you always be by my side?

Doctor: Yes. [*looks at the piece of paper.*] You are Sreemati Shantimoyee Dasi, right?

Shanti: Yes.

Doctor: Do you know why you have been brought here?

Shanti: Why wouldn't I? This is our home, but—

Doctor: But?

Shanti: What's all this stuff you have gathered around in this place? How come you call it a hospital?

Doctor: Any idea what a hospital does?

Shanti: No.

Doctor: Alright. What's the day today?

Shanti: Perhaps, Sunday.

Doctor: Are you sure it's not a Thursday?

Shanti: Had it been a Thursday, there would have been arrangements made for Lakshmi Puja. But I see no signs of any such arrangements having been made.

Doctor: What's the date today?

Shanti: Is this a court of law? Why are you continuously asking me questions? I don't remember anything. I have forgotten everything, even myself. By the way doctor—

Doctor: How do you know that I am a doctor?

Shanti: He whispered to my ear.

Doctor: Who is he?

Shanti: My Manik, doctor. He is my Khokonshona, my small, cute child.

Doctor: Oh! I see. What else did he say to you?

Shanti: He tells me a lot of things. He says: Mother—

[*Shanti is almost in tears.*]

Doctor: Where is he now?

Shanti: [*Excitedly.*] He has been snatched away from me.

Doctor: Who did that?

Shanti: Who else but that goddamned, diseased, man!

Doctor: When was Manik taken?

Shanti: Ummm, let me remember. That was probably a long time ago. No, not really. That was not too long ago. Manik was just one-and-half month old and he was taken away from my cradled arms.

Doctor: What else does Manik whisper to you?

Shanti: He says, kill that father before he kills you.

Doctor: Does he say these things clearly to you?

Shanti: Absolutely clearly. It is Khokon who makes me aware of my surroundings.

Doctor: Khokon is not with you anymore. How does he talk to you then?

Shanti: How could you be so naïve? He speaks to me from the radio. He speaks only to me.

Doctor: Is there anyone else who speaks to you as well?

Shanti: You bet! All over the neighbourhood, Khyantadi would talk, [*starts counting on her fingertips.*] so would Maya auntie and then Anjali. There are many more of them. They all say that I have lost my mental balance. They don't believe a word of what I say. They only push me away. I know that they are in league with my husband, like that woman in the white saree. All of them want me out of their way so that they can take slices off my husband. Each one of them is my enemy. I don't have any friend except you.

Doctor: Do they also whisper to you from the radio?

Shanti: What kind of a person are you? Don't you realize that they have no clue to what a radio is? The radio is only for Khokon and me. You know, when I would breastfeed Khokon, he would draw in short bursts. His red infant hands used to be rolled up like soft woollen balls. He hadn't grown any teeth. He was just an infant. Sometimes, he would suddenly bite me with his tender gum. I still hold that feeling in my bosom. Would you take me to Khokon, please?

Doctor: But why?

Shanti: I used to have a dream from my childhood. That dream would leave me in complete disarray and I would not feel like talking to anyone. Let me tell you about that dream. I used to see a house painted in light-blue. The forecourt of the house was full with white flowers beyond which lay an unending green pasture with saffron-coloured slopes. I also used to see Khokon and the sky dotted with flitting white clouds. Only Khokon and I would be there in that place where the narrow Anjana river curved away from beyond the rows of the tall palm trees. That picture-frame frozen in my heart still keeps me confused. Oh! Why am I hurting so much inside, Doctor?

Doctor: You'll be alright. Sister!

Shanti: Who are you calling?

Doctor: I am calling your friend. Another friend like me. She would take you to your bedroom where you would find some rest.

[*The nurse enters. Seeing her, Shanti get up from her chair, frightened and startled.*]

Nurse: Yes, Doctor?

Doctor: Take her to cabin number 5. Where's her husband?

Nurse: He is waiting outside.

Doctor: Send him in, and take this lady along with you.

[*Shanti runs to the left of the stage.*]

Shanti: You, too, Doctor. You, too, have joined my enemies? You are leaving me at the mercy of this witch?

[*The nurse tries to grab Shanti but Shanti grapples and pushes her away with extra-ordinary force.*]

Nurse: Kamla, Kamla, come and help me.

[*The attendant enters. Shanti is being flanked and held from either side by the nurse and the attendant. They start to take her away. Shanti begins to curse the doctor.*]

Shanti: You will burn in hell, doctor, you will burn in hell! Your family and your progeny will be wiped out. You will die a painful death. You are a deadly, venomous snake. With your seemingly comforting words, you are actually enticing me to tell you everything. [*She laughs out in squeals.*] Thank God, I haven't yet told you the main story. You would never get to know about it. If I had, you would have summarily dismissed me and sent me to the gallows.

Doctor: Sister, send her husband in.

Nurse: Yes Sir.

[*They drag Shanti away. Before being taken away, Shanti was clutching onto a table. In the process, the papers lying on the table fell off, cluttering the floor. Doctor begins to collect the papers and rearrange them on the table. Looking morose, the husband enters. The doctor looks at him and asks him to take a seat.*]

Doctor: Sit here, please. [*A little frightened, the husband sits down slowly. The doctor opens a register.*] Are you Nakurchandra Das? You stay at Shimuldaha near Barasat?

Husband: Yes Sir.

Doctor: Who else you have in your family other than your wife?

Husband: I have nobody else.

Doctor: How come?

Husband: Absolutely nobody. Like me, she had only her mother. We have been married for two years.

A little after we got married, my mother-in-law passed away. She had no blood-relations left after her death. Then, suddenly, over the past few months – Oh, I am at the end of my wits! Doctor, Shanti is the only one I can call family. I have nobody else but her.

[*He begins to cry.*]

Doctor: Please regain your composure. Unless you tell me the whole story, how would I be able to bring her under treatment?

Husband: I am going to lose my job now. I am an ordinary clerk. On the one hand, I cannot leave Shanti home alone in her present state. On the other, how can I manage home and work simultaneously? Some neighbours used to come once in a while to look after her while I used to be away at work. But I can't expect them to do it everyday. Why would they continue to take upon themselves the burden of someone else? On top of it, she gets so violent at times that it becomes impossible to bring her under control.

Doctor: She can't stand the sight of you.

Husband: I know. I am the one she is the most scornful of. No matter what, it's me who has to take care of her because I can't afford a maid or an attendant. If the situation doesn't improve, I will lose my job. I had to battle many odds to find a place for her in this hospital. Please help me Doctor. I beg you. You are my only salvation.

[*He kneels to wrap his arms around the doctor's feet, as if he is seeking mercy.*]

Doctor: Come on now, get up. If you break down, no doctor in the world would be able to help you. Control your emotions and answer my questions.

[*Husband Regains his composure and returns to his seat. The doctor walks away slowly, unseen by the husband, and reaches the top of the pedestal. The husband keeps looking at the chair, vacated by the doctor, as if he is not aware of the doctor's presence on the pedestal.*]

Doctor: [*Addressing the audience.*] This is how Shanti arrived here. At present, I am not just a physician but a psychiatric as well. That's the reason why my calling is to travel into the deepest recesses of the human mind to extract the pain trapped within. But more than that, I endeavour to be a social-scientist and a social worker. This is the story of the forgotten, the dismissed. The inhumanity of treating such unfortunate people as refuse and leaving them to rot in segregation is a malaise. Society ostracizes such people and offers them only disdain. They are never accepted back as fellow-human beings. Whatever the little chances of recovery these people have are blighted by the sin of untouchability because inhumanity only deepens the woes of those ruthlessly shunned. My quest is for returning these people to normal life and help shape their dreams. Let's start with Shanti's husband.

[*The doctor returns to his seat. The husband was sitting with his head bowed. Seeing the doctor, he looks up.*]

Doctor: What really happened? You should start from the very beginning. One must not keep any information from a doctor.

[*The husband tries to control himself but couldn't hold back the tears. He covers his face with his hands.*]

Husband: Doctor!

Doctor: [*Admonishing.*] Sit straight and look up. Don't expect me to treat you like a patient. Just keep answering my questions.

[*The husband controls himself.*]

Husband: Ok, ask.

Doctor: How long have you been married?

Husband: According to the Roman calendar, it would be two years on the eighth of this month. As per the Bangla calendar, it would be 25th of Baisakh, first month of Bangla calendar.

Doctor: Did you know your wife from before?

Husband: No. They used to live in Birbhum. Her mother knew someone. As a matter of fact, I own some pieces of land and am a clerk at Harenbabu's shop. So...

Doctor: ...you were deemed a decent and a landed man whom they could give their daughter's hand to.

Husband: Yes, sort of.

Doctor: Have you ever noticed any abnormalities in your wife before?

Husband: No. But I came to know later that her only sister took her own life when she was fourteen or fifteen. I was told that this sister of hers used to appear somewhat lost in something or the other. All she did was to engage in worshipping Goddess Kali and Goddess Lakshmi. As for Shanti, she often used to talk about a house painted light-blue, especially after our son was born. She always appeared caught in her own thoughts. Neither could I figure out what was going on in her mind, nor did I try too hard. After a tiring day at work, I would only want some rest. But yes, Shanti was very docile and the neighbours loved her.

Doctor: Then?

Husband: Khokon came into our lives after that. Carrying Khokon in her lap, she used to sing songs. These were songs she herself had written.

[*Silence prevails on the stage as both the doctor and the husband stop speaking. The light above them dims to complete darkness, through which a very sharp ray of light leads Shanti into the stage. She is singing in a manner as if she is putting her son to sleep with a lullaby.*]

[*Song.*]

Sweet boy, lovely boy
Cry no more
Sleep fairy is on her way
Let's open the door
Sleep well my little one
She is on the way
Cry no more and close your eyes
Wake up when it's day

[*Shanti leaves the stage, singing. The light then begins to brighten on the Doctor and the husband again.*]

Doctor: What happened next?

Husband: Khokon fell ill. He started suffering from acute convulsion. He became too sick and too weak. At first, we tried some herbal medicines but they did not work on him. Later, we had to call a doctor from Barasat, but Khokon's condition did not turn around. Then [*becomes tearful but controls himself quickly.*] Khokon died. But Shanti would not let Khokon go. He was only one-and-half month old. She kept holding Khokon in her cradled arms for three consecutive days before I had to use force to take him away. When I returned home after cremating Khokon, Shanti looked at me with fear visible in her eyes. Since then, it is embedded in her mind that I am responsible for Khokon's disappearance. Doctor, my life has become unbearable now. I, too, had dreams like anyone else. But all my aspirations have been washed away.

Doctor: Alright. You may leave now. I must let you know that this hospital doesn't allow relatives to meet patients during the first seven days. Considering her violent reactions towards you, you must not be here until we want you to. If we feel that the time is right for you to see her, only then shall you come. By the way, I hope you have brought things for her daily needs?

Husband: Yes.

Doctor: Very well. You may go now.

[*The nurse enters.*]

Husband: Sister, please give her these medicines. [*He hands over the prescription.*] Please also take her out on evening rounds in the garden. She may say to you what she may not say to us because you are a woman, too. But make sure that she is not excited or agitated. [*Speaks to the doctor.*]—Doctor, would she be cured?

Doctor: What are you still doing here? Didn't I ask you to leave?

Husband: But...

Doctor: No ifs and buts. You must go now and leave the rest to us.

[*Looking sullen, the husband leaves.*]

Doctor: This case is quite common.

Nurse: Yes, very ordinary case.

Doctor: But you know, such cases really get me going. I don't know why. These patients/ patients like Shanti are more important.

Sister: Sir, the patient is suddenly showing signs of excitement. Delusion is high. It is becoming difficult to keep her restricted to her cabin. She is screaming at the top of her voice.

[*The doctor stands up.*]

Doctor: Sterilise the needle and bring it to me, now!

[*The audience can hear a sharp cry from Shanti. The doctor and the nurse leave the stage. Shanti appears on the pedestal.*]

Shanti: [*To the audience.*] Let me tell you what was happening to me while these people were busy discussing. I do not watch movies but things began to reel off one after the other, as if it was a movie. That woman in white clothes and some others pushed me into a small room that has iron bars. There was an ominous noise when they locked the bolt to the door. I could sense a strike of lightning passing through my head. I felt like a prisoner. I rushed to the door and started shaking it. But none of them turned back. Suddenly, I saw my Khokon come out of the padlock. Initially, he appeared obscure but slowly I could see him clearly. He slipped through the door smiling and stood next to me. I was so surprised to see him walk and slip through the door, for he is an infant. How could he manage to do that? Then I remembered he used to talk to me from the radio. I have never heard him speak before. Why didn't it strike me as odd? Anyway, Khokon can perform miracles. He was standing next to me and smiling. Suddenly, I saw snakes coil up his body, slithering and hissing. The iron bars on the door also turned into serpents. The padlock began shaking to metamorphose into a statue of Goddess Kali. I could see Kali push her malevolent red tongue out and raise her hatchet. My eyes full with tears, I began to wonder why Kali would want to kill my Khokon! I placed myself as a shield in front of Khokon and screamed at her. I told her, Mother Goddess, if you are a mother, you should know that I was born in the same time as you. I am a mother, too. Beware! She began to laugh out. The snakes on the iron bars started moving their forked tongues. Red, blue, green, yellow and black apparitions began circling the walls of room before exiting. I ran towards the snakes and held them in my fist. Goddess Kali said: 'Chant the mother hymn.' But how could I? I told her that I didn't know the hymn. I am an illiterate woman. Nobody ever taught me anything. She ordered me to come close. She asked me to come near her and as I went near her, she said: 'I will whisper the hymn to you for good'. With a full voice, she whispered into my ears:

'Om Swaha, Om hring, Om Kling, Om Kring; chant this mantra for hundred and eight times'. I thought, if by chanting this mantra Khokon is spared, so be it. I kept chanting the mantra and banging my head on the wall.

[*Shanti runs into the cabin and starts banging her head on the wall. *Please note: Her dash to the cabin must be accompanied by music*. The doctor and the nurse enter the stage. Shanti is still banging her head on the wall. Her looks change the moment she spots them. A devilish smile breaks out on her face.*]

Shanti: So you think you have won by imprisoning me? I haven't yet told you the real; secret.. I have killed him.

Doctor: Who have you killed? Khokon?

Shanti: How could you even imagine that? What rubbish! I killed that man, the one who had snatched Khokon from me, and the one who had kept Khokon hidden from me. I am not supposed to wear a colourful Saree anymore. Give me a plain and white of saree like the one that you are wearing! I had once played the game of marriage with that man. [*Shanti looks at her own saree and is frightened.*] O my God! The border of my saree has turned into a snake. It is climbing my body. [*She bangs the door with her fists loudly.*] Open the door, Doctor. Please open the door. This room will throttle me to death. Outside this room are the skies, the white flowers and Khokon. Waiting for me outside are my sweet little home and my small family. Oh, not again! What's this? Now the snake has coiled around my whole body. Is this happening to me because I have killed that man?

Is this happening because I have strangled him to death with my own hands?

[*Shanti attempts to strangulate herself with her hands.*]

[*The doctor opens the door and enters, followed by the nurse and the attendant.*]

Shanti: [*Laughs out impishly.*] That man has run away. You imbecile! Do as you wish. I care a damn about what I have done. If need be, I will do it again. But sister, the border of the saree has become a snake. It's coiling around me and changing colours. It has a pale yellow body with white eyes. Give me your white saree while I tear up mine.

[*Shanti tries to tear up her saree. The nurse and the attendant use force to make Shanti lie down on the bed, with her face towards the audience. The doctor picks up the syringe to give Shanti a shot. The attendant stands to shield the part of Shanti's body where the injection would be administered. With her eyes gaping, Shanti looks at the hypodermic syringe.*]

Shanti: Are you going to drive that long needle into my body? It was so painful the last time when they gave me a shot for TBC or something. Now it's your turn to inflict that pain, right? Is this a punishment? Are you punishing me for telling the truth? Am I being punished for killing him? Aah!

[*The doctor administers the injection. Shanti cries out in pain. Once Shanti stops being hysteric and becomes quiet, the doctor hands over the syringe and the accessories to the nurse and returns to the pedestal. The nurse and the attendant leave as the doctor begins to speak.*]

Doctor: [*To the audience.*] Like this, Shanti was in the grip of delirium over three days and three nights. While in delirium, the number of times Shanti's son visited her is countless. We also lost count of the number of times she killed her husband or spoke of her dreams about a house painted light-blue. She was sleepless, too. But she finally got sleep to wake up 24 hours later. As she woke up, I called the nurse.

[*The doctor leaves the pedestal and returns to his chamber. Shanti wakes up and sits on her bed, slowly, as if she is tired. The nurse walks up to the doctor.*]

Doctor: What's the latest on the patient in cabin number five?

Nurse: She is taking her food and medicines properly. She is no longer hysteric and is not even hallucinating. But she appears very sad. Besides, she has lost weight and become weak.

Doctor: Please call her.

Nurse: I have asked the attendant to bring her here.

[*The attendant walks Shanti slowly out of her cabin and towards the doctor's table.*]

Doctor: Sister, now it's your turn. Take her to the garden and try to make her talk. See if we can find something more about her life. Hello Shanti, how are you now?

Shanti: The head is heavy and my limbs have become sloth.

Doctor: Don't worry. You will be alright after you walk in the open. Are you getting to hear the sound of radio anymore? Or, are you watching movies?

Shanti. No. I only feel sleepy and sluggish. What medicine did you give me?

Doctor: The medicine I have given you is meant to induce sleep. Sleep is your best medicine now. I hope you are eating well.

Shanti: Yes, I am.

Doctor: Do you want to eat something special?

Shanti: Something that cools my head, probably.

Doctor: No problem. Sister, please add a curd-based soft drink to her diet.

Sister: Alright, Sir.

Doctor: Shanti, Sister will take you to the garden now. Go with her. I have to go out on some work now. I hope you don't see the Sister as your enemy anymore.

Shanti: [*Embarrassed.*] No.

Doctor: Very well. I will leave now.

[*The doctor picks up his bag and walks away. The nurse gesticulates to the attendant to leave. After the attendant leaves, the nurse holds Shanti by the hand and goes behind the flower pots. *Please note, the nurse and Shanti will walk around the stage while they talk but all important conversation will take place near the flower pots.**]

Shanti: What's your name?

Nurse: Suchitra.

Shanti: [*Plucks a white flower from a flower pot. The nurse is noticing her. Shanti raiser her face and says.*] A white flower.

Nurse: White is really so soothing and nice, isn't it?

Shanti: White and sky-blue.

Nurse: Your house is painted white and sky-blue.

Shanti: Not yet, but it would be.

Nurse: Where would you build your house?

Shanti: It would come up next to my maternal uncle's place at Bhubandanga in Bolpur. I went to his place once when I was a child. Close to his place flows the river Anjana. I fell for that place. It had rows of palm trees, reddish slopes and one narrow river.

Nurse: When would that house come up?

Shanti: Once Khokon returns.

[*The nurse stops in his tracks for a moment and then resumes her walk.*]

Nurse: Do you know why you are here?

Shanti: Yes.

Nurse: What do you think has happened to you?

Shanti: I am no longer mentally stable.

Nurse: Do you realize that?

Shanti: Yes, I do, from time to time.

Nurse: It's been quite a few days that you are here. It's true that you don't keep mum these days. But don't you wish to be cured completely?

Shanti: Of course, I do. But they keep me away saying I am a lunatic. The way they look at me, it seems as if my eyes are going to devour them.

Nurse: Why care about what they think of you?

Shanti: Why shouldn't I? There is a whisper campaign against me. The moment I get close to them, they stop. The kids in the neighbourhood throw stones at me. They make passes at me. They call me lunatic. I don't understand why all of them have teamed up against me. They don't understand that I am a human being and I, too, want to lead a normal life.

Nurse: Ok. By the way, do you realize that your husband is still alive and that you haven't killed him?

Shanti: Yes, I know.

Nurse: Then?

Shanti: At times I feel it would have been better had I killed him. After all, he is...

Nurse: ...but he didn't do anything to Khokon. Khokon was suffering from a disease and... and... he died.

[*Shanti tries to seal the mouth of the nurse with her hand in an obvious attempt to prevent her from speaking any further on that topic.*]

Shanti: [*Screaming.*] You terrible witch! I am definitely going to kill you today. You are using that same old lie again to drive me mad. You are also a part of that conspiracy. I know you want to have a good time with my husband. Alright, I gift him to you, but if you say one more word about Khokon, you will face terrible consequences. I warn you. You get my point? I am going to kill you if you say one more word about him. Kill you! Kill you! Kill you!

[*In blinding rage, Shanti is set to physically harm the nurse. Hearing the nurse's screams for help, the attendant comes running. Both of them forcibly drag Shanti away but her whimper of protests continues. They exit the stage. The doctor arrives and keeps his bag on the table. He stands atop the pedestal and uses a handkerchief to wipe the beads of sweat off his forehead.*]

Doctor: [*Addressing the audience.*] When I heard about the incident after I returned to the hospital, I made arrangements for new medicines. Shanti was not against being treated. Her mind was always drawn towards the open air and the green pasture. She was mentally quite stable as long as nobody mentioned anything about Khokon. She later set her mind on knitting, especially socks and sweaters for children. But problems erupted the day we had called her husband over to the hospital.

[*The doctor got off the pedestal and took his seat. Shanti and the nurse present themselves in front of the doctor.*]

Doctor: Sit down. [*Shanti takes a seat.*] It's been some days you are here. How are you feeling now?

Shanti: Much better. But doctor, when would you release me from here? The head is no longer heavy and much of the weakness is gone. I have begun to like work. Besides, I feel great when I walk in the garden.

Doctor: Very well. Somebody is coming to meet you today.

[*Shanti, joyful and excited to hear the news.*]

Shanti: Who? Who's coming to meet me?

Doctor: Yes, someone is coming today.

Shanti: Really? Is he coming here? How could he stay away from me for such a long time?

[*Tears roll down her cheeks.*]

Doctor: Please don't cry. He will be here anytime soon.

Shanti: How big has he grown? How does he look these days? What about his health?

Nurse: [*Signals to the doctor.*] Sir—

Doctor: Yes, I know. She needs to be jarred out of her thoughts.

[*The attendant enters.*]

Attendant: Mr. Nakur Das has come.

[*A startled Shanti stares at the attendant. Her eyes portray shock and disbelief. Nakur Das enters. There has been no change in his countenance or appearance.*]

Doctor: Come Nakur. Take Shanti along with you to the garden.

[*In one swift movement, Shanti reaches one corner of the stage, from where she tries to run away. But the nurse and the attendant hold her back.*]

Shanti: Leave me alone. Let me go. He has come here to kill me. Don't you have compassion? Have mercy on me. Let me go. Oh God! Take this murderer away. Take him away.

Doctor: Sister, take her to the cabin please.

[*The nurse and the attendant use force to take Shanti away to her cabin. Nakur covers his face and starts crying.*]

Doctor: This disease is not easy to be cured of. It's not like a play or a novel where miracles happen overnight.

Nakur: But it has been almost three months. My home looks so barren, like an endless desert.

Doctor: I don't think the day is far for her to be fully cured. Her condition has improved a lot. It is possible that you are not being able to notice the improvement. She is much better and normal now except in terms of one issue. Shanti is in better health. She has also gained weight.

[*During the course of this conversation, the nurse and the attendant make Shanti lie down on her bed in the cabin. Thereafter, the nurse comes out and stands in front of the doctor.*]

Doctor: Well Nakur, you have to leave now. We will call you again.

Nakur: Here are some fruits and clothes for her.

Doctor: Leave them here. Sister, take those things from him.

[*Quietly, with folded hands, Nakur bows and leaves.*]

Doctor: [*With a worried look on his face.*] Sister, let me see the bed ticket. [*The doctor starts scribbling as the nurse lifts it for him to read.*] Give her eight ECTs and two shots of insulin a week. Keep a strict watch on her after the first ECT.

[*The nurse writes down the prescription and the doctor walks up slowly to the top of the pedestal.*]

Doctor: [*Addressing the audience.*] ECT is the abbreviation of Electric Convulsion Therapy. It is about a wave of electric shocks run through the head to help untie the knots inside the brain. There are times when the brain gets entangled in knots. We could have used injections, too, but that process is expensive and often painful. I consider the use of ECT to be the right move at this point of time. However, I would like to show you what happened during and after the last ECT because you would not like to watch the many repeats of this process.

[*The doctor turns around and steps off the pedestal. He reappears along with the nurse, the female attendant and three other attendants. Carrying the ECT equipment, all of them enter the cabin. Shanti sits up on her bed.*]

Shanti: What are these? Oh, that pain again! All of you suspect me of still being mentally unstable. Don't you? Please doctor, I beg of you. I am alright now. Don't punish me anymore. Please spare me the pain. I promise not to be insolent again. I will do whatever you want me to do. Oh Doctor, how cruel could you be?

[*The nurse places a pipe inside her mouth and straps the headgear on. The female attendant and the others pin Shanti down on the bed. The doctor switches the machine on. Convulsion begins. Shanti collapses on the bed, groaning. Darkness descends on the stage. Music and Shanti's screams begin to reverberate. Then complete silence prevails. Thereafter, from the depths of the darkness, can be heard the conversation between Shanti and the doctor.*]

Doctor: How do you feel, Shanti?

Shanti: I feel light. Breathing is... umm...

Doctor: ...laboured?

Shanti: No. It's a feeling of being unhurried, a sense of relief rather. I wish to sleep now.

Doctor: Go to sleep.

[*The audience can hear Shanti sing melodiously—Sweet boy, lovely boy, cry no more.*]

Doctor: [*His voice rises from depths of the darkness.*] An island suddenly rises in the middle of the river through the silt that gathered in layers for ages. The faint light of the dawn can be seen at the end of the dark hours. The long treatment has slowly shown signs of success and seems not too far. After many days, I have called Nakur over to the hospital today.

[*The lights reappear on the stage. Nakur and the doctor could be seen sitting next to each other.*]

Doctor: Have you readied yourself?

Nakur: Yes, but...

Doctor: Leave the rest to me. Take her home. Your real test lies ahead. She has to blend with the normal societal life. It is you who have to shield her from ridicule and scorn that surround her. That, incidentally, is the most onerous task in our country.

Nakur: But she hates me.

[*Shanti arrives with the nurse. Nakur leaves his seat and stands up. Nakur and Shanti lock eyes. Nakur appears tense. Shanti suddenly pulls a 'ghomta' across her head.*]

Doctor: Shanti, you are going home today. Your husband is here to take you home.

[*No response from Shanti.*]

Doctor: Why aren't you speaking? Come, sit here.

[*Shanti doesn't utter a word. Instead, she touches the feet of Nakur first and then, of the doctor, as a mark of respect for elders. Surprised, Nakur pulls away and Shanti steps closer to the doctor.*]

Doctor: What's this? Shanti, why are you crying?

Shanti: How do I present myself in front of him? He is like my God and the kinds of names I have called him…

Doctor: Do you remember all that?

Shanti: Yes. I remember everything. I am melting in embarrassment.

Doctor: No Shanti, you were not the one who said all those bad things about him. It was the disease that was speaking. You were unwell because you have the soft mind of a mother. It was a mother that was crying, far removed as she was from rationality. I hope you realize now that Khokon is gone forever.

[*Shanti nods her head in agreement.*]

Doctor: Don't cry, Shanti. Your Khokon will come back in a new avatar. Yes, we all feel sad when love is shorn of its fruits. But the tree that bears fruit doesn't die. It would blossom again. Go home, Shanti, go home. Rise to your calling now.

Shanti: Are you releasing me?

Nurse: Yes. You are completely cured. It's time for you to shake off the ridicule and mistrust of the people and be at the palm grove on the banks of Anjana to build a garden of white flowers and a house painted light-blue. Another Khokon will come. Build him a home.

[*Shanti walks away from everyone and stands atop the pedestal.*]

Shanti: This is my story. No matter the pain, there is cure for every suffering. I used to think that these people were punishing me for no reason. But today, I realize that they always wished me well. They have done me a good turn. I will now return to the great sweep of humanity. Before I begin that journey, I will say adieu to as many people as I can. Sister Suchitra, could you please put some sindur powder on my head? [*Smilingly, Suchitra, the nurse, does that.*] Please don't mind. I am still a little girl.

[*Shanti holds Nakur by one hand, picks up her luggage by the other, and exits the stage with quick steps. The nurse smiles. And the doctor reaches the top of the pedestal again.*]

Doctor: Even though the story ends here, we have to keep waiting for those who have been rejected by society. We must wait for those destroyed by poverty and for those who are never counted as human beings. We wait only for the dismissed. [*The nurse leaves the stage.*] People are continuing to hurt. Weakened by waves of pain, we think of death. But new life tears open the camouflage of death to launch a fresh beginning. Every birth is like that. Shanti has left for her home today. But, much as I want the chapter closed, Shanti may return one day suffering from the same mental disorder. So what? Tuberculosis can be cured but it can strike back. Even if it strikes back, it can be weeded out once again and, probably, forever. What Shanti was suffering from is like tuberculosis. If not in one attempt, mental disorder could be cured with repeated and sustained treatment over a certain period of time. To be cured, all that they need are compassion, kindness, affection, cooperation and an ability on our part to consider them to be as human as we are. There is no reason why we should keep them at a distance. Unfortunately, that environment has not come into being yet. True treatment is all about love and care that deeply troubled people like Shanti deserve. Would they get it? This is my last incisive question. I need answers. When do I get them? When?

[*The doctor thrusts both his arms into the air, and the nurse walks in rapidly.*]

Nurse: Sir, we have a new patient.

[*A married woman, accompanied by a man, collapses on the floor.*]

New woman: [*Raises her face.*] Where have you brought me? Is this a prison?

[*Everybody on the stage looks quietly at her. The curtain drops. A song plays.*]

---

*The music of the song used in the Bangla play was scored by the Late Pandit Ravi Shankar.